Imperial Women in Byzantium 1025–1204

D1571242

WOMEN AND MEN IN HISTORY

This series, published for students, scholars and interested general readers, will tackle themes in gender history from the early medieval period through to the present day. Gender issues are now an integral part of all history courses and yet many traditional texts do not reflect this change. Much exciting work is now being done to redress the gender imbalances of the past, and we hope that these books will make their own substantial contribution to that process. This is an open-ended series, which means that many new titles can be included. We hope that these will both synthesise and shape future developments in gender studies.

The General Editors of the series are *Patricia Skinner* (University of Southampton) for the medieval period; *Pamela Sharpe* (University of Bristol) for the early modern period; and *Penny Summerfield* (University of Lancaster) for the modern period. *Margaret Walsh* (University of Nottingham) was the Founding Editor of the series.

Published books:

Imperial Women in Byzantium 1025–1204: Power, Patronage and Ideology
Barbara Hill

Masculinity in Medieval Europe
D.M. Hadley (ed.)

Gender and Society in Renaissance Italy
Judith C. Brown and Robert C. Davis (eds)

Gender, Church and State in Early Modern Germany: Essays by Merry E. Wiesner
Merry E. Wiesner

Manhood in Early Modern England: Honour, Sex and Marriage
Elizabeth W. Foyster

Disorderly Women in Eighteenth-Century London: Prostitution in the Metropolis 1730–1830
Tony Henderson

Gender, Power and the Unitarians in England, 1760–1860
Ruth Watts

Women and Work in Russia, 1880–1930: A Study in Continuity through Change
Jane McDermid and Anna Hillyar

The Family Story: Blood, Contract and Intimacy, 1830–1960
Leonore Davidoff, Megan Doolittle, Janet Fink and Katherine Holden

More than Munitions: Women, Work and the Engineering Industries 1900–1950
Clare Wightman

Imperial Women in Byzantium 1025–1204:
Power, Patronage and Ideology

BARBARA HILL

Longman

Pearson Education Limited
Edinburgh Gate,
Harlow, Essex CM20 2JE, United Kingdom
and Associated Companies throughout the world

Published in the United States of America by Pearson Education Inc., New York

© Pearson Education Limited 1999

First published 1999 by Pearson Education Limited

ISBN 0 582 30353 2 CSD
ISBN 0 582 30352 4 PPR

Visit us on the World Wide Web site at
http://www.awl-he.com

British Library Cataloguing in Publication Data

A catalogue record for this book is available from the British Library

Library of Congress Cataloging-in-Publication Data

Hill, Barbara.
Imperial women in Byzantium, 1025–1204: power, patronage,
and ideology / Barbara Hill.
p.   cm. – (Women and men in history)
Includes bibliographical references and index.
ISBN 0–582–30353–2 (csd). – ISBN 0–582–30352–4 (ppr)
1. Empresses – Byzantine Empire – History. 2. Byzantine Empire
– History – 1025–1081. 3. Byzantine Empire – History – 1081–1453.
4. Leadership in women – Byzantine Empire – History. I. Title.
II. Series.
DF591.3.H56   1999
949.5′02′0922 – dc21
98–52955
CIP

Set by 35 in 10/12pt Baskerville
Printed in Singapore

Contents

List of Maps, Figures and Family Trees

Maps

Figures

Family Trees

List of abbreviations

AHR	American Historical Review
B	Byzantion
BF	Byzantinische Forschungen
BMGS	Byzantine and Modern Greek Studies
BS	Byzantinoslavica
BS/EB	Byzantine Studies/Études byzantines
BSHAR	Bulletin de la Section Historique, Académie Roumaine
BZ	Byzantinische Zeitschrift
DOP	Dumbarton Oaks Papers
IRAIK	Izvestija Russkago Archeoliceskago Instituta v Konstanti-nople
JÖB	Jahrbuch der Österreichischen Byzantinistik
JRS	Journal of Roman Studies
JThS	Journal of Theological Studies
NE	Neos Ellenika
OCA	Orientalia Christiana Analecta
P&P	Past & Present
REB	Revue des études byzantines
TM	Travaux et mémoires
TRHS	Transactions of the Royal Historical Society
VV	Vizantijskij Vremennik

Glossary

Words defined in the Glossary are asterisked on their first appearance in the book.

affines:	persons related by marriage
augousta:	title of crowned empress
basileia:	power holding
basilikos logos:	set speeches in honour of an emperor (pl. *basilikoi logoi*)
basilissa basilis:	empress (pl. *basilissai*)
beneficia:	grants and rewards which can be bestowed
chrysobull:	decree issued by the emperor
despoina:	mistress of the house, also used for empresses
despotes:	a title for the emperor, but one which focuses on his practical duties rather than imperial majesty
diataxis:	decree
didaskalos:	teacher
eisiterioi:	verses of welcome
filiation:	a system which hands property from father to son
gambroi:	plural of *gambros* – a relative
habitus:	thought-world
imperium:	emperorship
kaisarissa:	wife of a Caesar
kouropalatissa [*kouropalates*]:	wife of kouropalate
lemma:	heading of a poem or speech stating its dedication (pl. *lemmata*)
magistrisse:	wife of *magistros*
morning gift:	gift given to bride on morning after wedding – often a percentage of dowry
oikos:	household in the largest sense

philanthropia:	generosity to those poorer than oneself
phronema:	highmindedness
pittakion:	decree
porphyrogennitos:	born in purple chamber reserved for wife of emperor
potestas:	power
primogeniture:	system of inheritance by eldest son
propemptic talk:	speech of advice
prostaxis:	decree
protosebastos:	son of first son in Komnenian system of titles
sebastokrator:	son or brother of the emperor
sebastokratorissa:	wife of a *sebastokrator*
spiritual kinship:	creation of godparents
theatron:	literary circle (pl. *theatra*)
typikon:	foundation charter of a monastery (pl. *typika*)

Author's acknowledgements

This book started life as my doctoral thesis, completed for the Queen's University of Belfast in 1994. Special thanks go of course to my supervisor, Margaret Mullett, who introduced me to Byzantium in the first place and remained an inspiration and example throughout. To Liz James must go much of the credit for getting this book published, since she mentioned the thesis to my academic editor, Patricia Skinner. Patricia's academic excellence and generous support facilitated the transition from thesis to book. The Longman team of Hilary Shaw, Terka Bagley and Verina Pettigrew deserve many thanks for their patience and expertise. Finally, as always, thanks to my husband Ross who proof-read the manuscript and helped greatly in the preparation and production of the index.

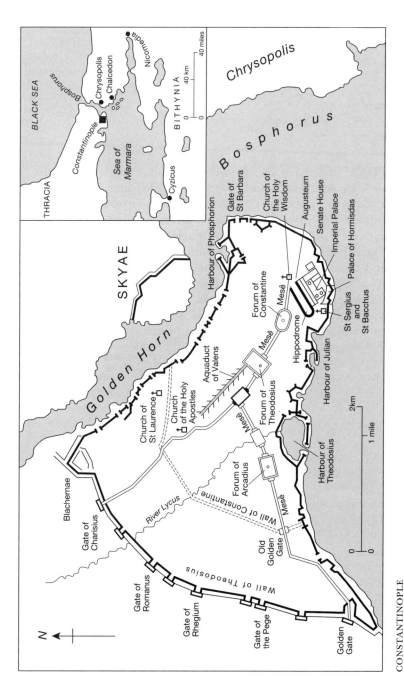

CONSTANTINOPLE

Source: A. Bridge, *Theodora* (Chicago, 1993), opposite p. 1.

xii

CHAPTER ONE

Introduction

The study of women is currently fashionable during this second women's movement of the twentieth century. Byzantine women have not been neglected in the upsurge of interest in the lives of women in general. And yet, despite increased interest over the last twenty years, the investigation and knowledge of women still have a long way to go before they are on a level with many other areas of Byzantine culture and history. The relatively recent *Oxford Dictionary of Byzantium* does not have an entry on 'empress'. For information on this person, readers are directed to the entry on 'emperor'.[1] Even primary evidence can be misrepresented, and perhaps therefore misread; this fact is demonstrated by the usual characterisation of the mosaic in the south gallery of Hagia Sophia as 'the Constantine panel', despite the fact that Constantine was clearly not the original donor of the panel and was only emperor in any case by his marriage to the reigning empress, Zoe the Macedonian, who is also represented in the panel. This should be described as the Zoe panel.[2] The error is further compounded by the inclusion of the panel in the very accessible *Byzantium* by R. Loverance. On page 44 the photograph of the panel excludes Zoe altogether, only showing Christ and Constantine. Loverance does have the grace to include Zoe in the caption, but the photograph is more likely to be remembered and few casual readers will read the caption. The bitter extreme of exclusion of women is that scholarly attempts are made to remove

---

1. *The Oxford Dictionary of Byzantium*, A. Kazhdan (ed.), 3 vols (New York and Oxford, 1991).
2. See B. Hill, L. James and D.C. Smythe, 'Zoe and the rhythm method of imperial renewal', in P. Magdalino (ed.), *New Constantines: the Rhythm of Imperial Renewal in Byzantium, 4th–13th Centuries* (Aldershot, 1994), pp. 215–29.

1

their visibility in cases where they have been visible. For example, J. Howard-Johnston would like to turn the *Alexiad* of Anna Komnene into the *Alexiad* of Nikephoros Bryennios, edited by Anna Komnene, on the ludicrous, not to say unproved and chauvinistic, grounds that women cannot write about battles.[3] Howard-Johnston is not doing anything new: denying authorship to women is a time-honoured tradition the absurdity and bias of which have been convincingly laid bare by Joanna Russ.[4]

It is no longer necessary to make excuses for or to justify studying women: most scholars accept that such work is axiomatic for the full understanding of social life, and that ignoring over half the human race results in a distorted picture of human life. Even histories of the most male-dominated areas of Byzantine life like military usurpations are no longer complete without the consideration of the role of women within them.[5] Women appear as actors on every stage.

Before it is assumed that men and women are now equally represented as subjects in history-writing, a historiographical note of caution should be sounded. There are more articles written every year about women in Byzantium, and a chronological survey shows immediately the vast difference between this decade and the 1940s for example, but the authors have also changed. In the 1940s three very eminent men wrote about Byzantine women: in the 1980s male writers were heavily outnumbered by women. Has the study of Byzantine women become a specialised subject, only undertaken by women, ignored by Byzantinists as a whole? Has it been marginalised? The good general histories of the decade, like Angold's *The Byzantine Empire 1025–1204* and the works deliberately engaging with culture, like Kazhdan and Constable's *People and Power in Byzantium*, and Kazhdan and Epstein's *Change in Byzantine Culture*, do mention women, usually in the context of the family, but there are few specific articles written by men. In the 1980s the only man interested in women was one of those who was writing in the 1940s, namely Steven Runciman. Of course, there is an alternative view of the preponderance of women writers over men writers, which is that women have taken charge in this area of research. The fact

---

3. J. Howard-Johnston, 'Anna Komnene and the Alexiad', in M.E. Mullett and D.C. Smythe (eds), *Alexios I Komnenos* (Belfast, 1996), pp. 260–301.

4. J. Russ, *How to Suppress Women's Writing* (Austin, 1983). The flat denial of agency to the woman is the first option she discusses.

5. J-P. Cheynet, *Pouvoir et contestations à Byzance (963–1210)* (Paris, 1990), includes a consideration of the legitimising role of women between 1028–1081.

that much women's history is written by female historians has not been lost on feminists, some of whom are now keen to include interested men in their discussions, and see such combinations as the way forward.[6]

The women in this study can be divided into two groups. The first group consists of two sovereign empresses, Zoe and Theodora, the last heirs of the long-standing Macedonian dynasty. The second group is composed of the women who were powerful because they were related to emperors. Most of them belong to the Komnenian dynasty which seized power in 1081, establishing an unbroken rule until the capture of the city in 1204 by the soldiers of the Fourth Crusade. These women were all imperial in the context of the Komnenoi, but not all were empresses. They were mothers, wives, sisters, sisters-in-law and daughters of emperors. Such a definition of their status is not a concession to traditional history which always defines women in relation to men. In any autocracy men and women are defined in relation to the autocrat, and Byzantium was no different. Since all the men around the emperor were defined in terms of their relation to him, it is permissible in the historical context of the Komnenian era to do the same with the women. This is not a gender difference; it is a political system. The women's relation with the emperor was one of the most important things about them and about their society at this particular time. Some were wives and some were widows. The effect of differing marital status in Byzantine society and ideology will likewise become clear.

Secondary sources

Studies on women vary widely, from attempts to elucidate the role of women in society, through studies on one aspect of women's life, to detailed work on one woman. Paul Adams was the first to feel the fascination of Byzantine women, writing in 1893 a book on *Princesses byzantines*, which included Eirene Doukaina and Anna Komnene. However, modern scholarship can be said to have started with Charles Diehl, whose charming but uncritical biographies of Byzantine women, *Figures byzantines*, performed the function of

---

6. On the effects of the 1970s on history writing and the new breed of feminist men, see A. Farge, 'Methods and effects of women's history', in M. Perrot (ed.), *Writing Women's History* (French ed. 1984, tr. F. Pleasant, Oxford, 1992), pp. 10–24.

pulling together all that the sources had to say about each into one place. They are still a good place to start learning the 'facts' about the women he chose. The tradition was carried on by Bernard Leib, who after translating the *Alexiad* found so much material that he proceeded to write many articles about Alexios's reign, incorporating the women around him: indeed, given such source material he could hardly have done otherwise. His 'La role des femmes dans la révolution des Comnènes à Byzance' is the most relevant to the present study. He too gathers the source material into one place, but there is no attempt to criticise the source or to analyse Byzantine society. Steven Runciman is the last great follower of this tradition. His work is very gallant, but in the course of five articles specifically on Byzantine women he does not go far beyond narration. His interest is consistent: in a book on the emperor Romanos Lekapenos he includes a chapter on his empress Zoe Karbonopsina, which is the only detailed treatment of this crucial and much maligned character. His article on the fall of Anna Dalassene is an attempt to penetrate the silence of the sources and analyse the events on other grounds: it is not his fault that the state of our knowledge has progressed, leaving his work out of date. A slightly different approach is taken by Grosdidier de Matons in 'La femme dans l'empire byzantin'. Although he has only the same source material at his disposal, he avoids a narrative account, and attempts to present a thematic description of the life of women. He includes the highly interesting and generally neglected subjects of dangers of childbirth and the superstitious rites in which women took part in order to ensure either conception or contraception, the birth of a son, or an abortion.

Thematic studies of single aspects of women's life do exist. The first treatment of women and law was that of Georgina Buckler: her work on Anna Komnene still stands as the only full-scale study of this woman in English. The best and most exhaustive study of the law as it applies to women is by Beaucamp, which has so far not been bettered. Bensammar's study of the titles of the empress and their significance is the only such study relating to women, in strong contrast to the numerous articles on the titulature of the emperor. In 1985 *Women and Monasticism* was published, addressing such aspects of Byzantine women's monastic experience as choices in becoming a nun, the ideology and the reality contrasted, and the values that nuns were supposed to hold. A second volume, on *Women and Byzantine Monasticism*, was published in 1991, including articles on founders of monasteries, imperial women and the monastic life, and equality in monasticism. Patlagean's work on transvestite nuns, including an essay in this volume, has illuminated the monastic choices open to women in the middle period, and the consequences of choosing them. This study is invaluable not only for its subject matter, but for its pointers towards the type of further research which needs to be done. Alice-Mary Talbot has explored the education available in monasteries of the later period.[7]

Much of the evidence for women in monastic life relates to imperial or aristocratic women, who had both the money or property to endow monasteries and the education to write about their aims. On a smaller scale, these same women paid for artistic decoration in churches or for icons even if they still lived in the secular world. The question of Byzantine devotion to icons was a contested point then and still merits discussions today. Women's devotion to certain images above others and their relationship to the Virgin Mary have been discussed by Robin Cormack and Judith Herrin.

Other important articles on the lives of Byzantine women cannot be categorised into strict themes, but each add information which is crucial. Speeches or artefacts can be used to explore the role of women: Robert Browning's article on the funeral oration of Anna Komnene is one example,[8] Ioli Kalavrezou-Maxeiner's discussion of the place of the empress Eudokia from an ivory from the mid-eleventh century is another.[9] Some work has been done on the question of women and power. For instance, Averil Cameron has shown that the fifth-century empress Sophia was the power behind her sick husband, and Margaret Mullett has revealed the changing political role of the ex-empress Maria of Alania. Steven Runciman has chronicled the career of the famous empress Eirene the Athenian in the eighth century and has also written more widespread articles attempting to define the role of aristocratic women in general and the empress in particular. For the later period, Alice-Mary Talbot has examined the role of the empress regent Theodora Palaeologina in all areas of her life.[10]

7. A-M. Talbot, 'Blue-stocking nuns: intellectual life in the convents of late Byzantium', *Okeanos: Essays presented to Ihor Ševčenko* (Cambridge, Mass., 1984), pp. 604–18.

8. R. Browning, 'An unpublished funeral oration on Anna Comnena', *Proceedings of the Cambridge Philosophical Society*, 188 (ns 8) (Cambridge, 1962), pp. 1–12.

9. I. Kalavrezou-Maxeiner, 'Eudocia Makrembolitissa and the Romanos ivory', *DOP* 31 (1977), pp. 305–28.

10. A-M. Talbot, 'Empress Theodora Palaiologina, wife of Michael VIII', *DOP* 46 (1992), pp. 295–304.

Recent scholarship

Since the 1980s analytical overview studies have been published by Laiou[11] and Herrin,[12] which are arguably the most accessible and useful secondary sources for women in Byzantium. These two are contiguous with the great explosion of interest in ancient and medieval women at the beginning of the 1980s. They take different approaches: Laiou analyses clearly demarcated areas while Herrin chooses three avenues which are less clear-cut. They concur in the usefulness of law as evidence and in the importance they attach to property and its management, as well as in the explicit aim of differentiating reality and ideals. Laiou ignores the church but explores attitudes to women. Herrin investigates Christian beliefs and their effect, but is concerned to illuminate practical reality rather than an ideal. Laiou is interested in aristocratic and imperial women because of their importance for property management and transference and sees the emergence of aristocratic women as a class into society and politics. Herrin would prefer to concentrate on women other than imperial or aristocratic, but eventually has to come to terms with their role since the property evidence leads that way. Herrin in particular notices the increased freedom and privileged position of widows. Despite their differing approaches, both Laiou and Herrin conclude that in Byzantium women were subordinate to men, being subject to limitations which affected all women from the aristocrat to the peasant, despite some loosening of attitudes in the eleventh and twelfth centuries. Most recently, Laiou has published a detailed treatment of marriage, love and relationship in Byzantium in the eleventh to thirteenth centuries.[13] This book not only explores the development of civil and canon law in relation to impediments to marriage, and the economic consequences of marriage alliances for the succession and management of property, but also discusses the emotional side of marriage, love and desire. From a thorough examination of all cases of disputed marriages, Laiou shows that the aristocracy and the emperor were highly concerned to control the organisation of marriage, an activity which placed them in direct conflict with the church, which was

11. A. Laiou, 'The role of women in Byzantine society', *JÖB* 31/1 (1981), pp. 233–60.
12. J. Herrin, 'In search of Byzantine women: three avenues of approach', in Averil Cameron and A. Kuhrt (eds), *Images of Women in Antiquity* (London, 1983), pp. 167–89.
13. A. Laiou, *Mariage, amour et parenté à Byzance aux XIe – XIIIe siècles* (Paris, 1992).

equally determined to exercise ultimate jurisdiction. A certain gap between law and practice is exposed, spawning the numerous court cases dealing with the dissolution of unions as the aristocracy sought to manipulate marriage alliances for their own social, political and economic advancement. Laiou demonstrates the circular nature of the problem: the aristocracy found their matrimonial strategies influenced by legal impediments to marriage, but in their attempts to carry out their plans through the legal process they contributed to the development of these impediments.

Keith Holum's *Theodosian Empresses* was also published in the 1980s, and deals with the mother, wives and sister of the fourth-century emperor Theodosios II. Despite Holum's stated aim that he is writing about female **basileia*, the imperial dominion of women, the title ties these women down firmly in their place around a man. The book proceeds on a narrative basis from the beginning of the period to the end. Although it does make available the evidence on the women of the fourth century with some critical analysis of sources, it does not start from the point of view of the women, nor are they the focus of investigation throughout.

The most interesting discussion of attitudes to women in the eleventh and twelfth centuries is found in an article by Catia Galatariotou on the ideas of a twelfth-century Byzantine monk, Neophytos the Recluse, titled 'Holy women and witches: aspects of Byzantine concepts of gender'.[14] As the title suggests, this article uses feminist and anthropological theory explicitly. Neophytos was a monk on the island of Cyprus and his individual concepts cannot be taken as a general comment on the attitudes of all Byzantine males or even all monks, but they do demonstrate one extreme view of the evil in women. To Neophytos, all women were created in the image of Eve, a temptress by nature who would lead men away from God and from righteousness. Woman was universally bad. Galatariotou's discussion is convincing and points to the richness of the material on women. Other males in other parts of the empire, notably the court, had different views, or at least did not express themselves as stridently as Neophytos.

Lastly, the work of Lynda Garland on imperial women and sexual morality in the eleventh and twelfth centuries explores the difference between ideology and reality for women in Byzantium. Her 'Life and ideology of Byzantine women' attempts to illuminate the

14. C. Galatariotou, 'Holy women and witches: aspects of Byzantine concepts of gender', *BMGS* 9 (1984/5), pp. 55–94.

reality of women's lives behind the ideology in Byzantium, using the ideology to highlight the reality by contrasting what the sources claim is correct and what we see happening in them. Garland sees ideology contributing to the freedom of women by covering them with a protective veil which allowed them to do very much what they wanted. She concludes that imperial women in Byzantium could be 'in their own right the obvious and unchallenged embodiment of Byzantine imperialism',[15] with a range of power options which included ruling from behind the scenes and motherhood. I disagree with this conclusion on grounds which will appear throughout this book. Briefly, Garland conflates sovereign empresses with consorts in her judgement of what imperial women could do and tends towards a narrative account without much theoretical analysis. As a literary scholar, she also tends to judge historical sources as literature first and foremost, failing to seek the historical reasons for the opinions advanced by Byzantine historians. Notwithstanding these criticisms, Garland pulls together many sources and presents arguments to stimulate discussion.

Sources

The original source material for the eleventh and twelfth centuries is rich. There are many histories written by contemporaries which have been edited and in some cases translated into English. The most accessible is Michael Psellos's *Chronographia*, published in translation as *Fourteen Byzantine Rulers*, written by a jurist and a courtier in the eleventh century about his own times. Much of it is taken from his own personal experience, and he knew many of the rulers he describes personally. The same is true of John Skylitzes, who was a jurist during the reign of Alexios I Komnenos. The third historian of the eleventh century is Michael Attaleiates, also a jurist, who was active during the reign of Nikephoros Botaneiates. Several members of the Komnenos family wrote history also: most famously Anna Komnene in the *Alexiad*, but also her husband, the Caesar Nikephoros Bryennios, who wrote at the request of his mother-in-law, Eirene Doukaina. Anna Komnene's history is the only book written by a woman throughout the history of Byzantium. It has of course been used extensively by historians searching for historical

15. L. Garland, 'The life and ideology of Byzantine women: a further note on conventions of behaviour and social reality as reflected in eleventh- and twelfth-century historical sources', *B* 58 (1988), pp. 361–93, p. 393.

women, for women authors and for the views of an imperial woman about her life and society. This book is no exception to that rule.

In the twelfth century the history of John and Manuel Komnenos was written by John Kinnamos and Niketas Choniates. Kinnamos was of the court, but Choniates was writing after the fall of Constantinople to the Fourth Crusade and must be taken with a pinch of salt, since he was, by his own admission, searching for the faults in the rulers which had led to the worst disaster in Byzantine history to date. The bishop Eustathios of Thessalonike set down his thoughts after the fall of Thessalonike in 1180, describing with contemporary knowledge the state of affairs at court. He is important for his account of the regency of Maria of Antioch. Another author is John Zonaras, whose chronicle of the world uses Psellos, Attaleiates and Skylitzes for the events of the eleventh century. Zonaras was in a position to know the events of the twelfth century at first hand, since he was an official at court before becoming a monk.

Some care must be taken when reading these histories. Attaleiates clearly was writing as an admirer of Nikephoros Botaneiates, Psellos was a Doukas supporter, Bryennios was married to a Komnene, Zonaras was in monastic retirement during the reign of Manuel Komnenos and Choniates was searching for the explanation of 1204. All were educated and all were using literary rules in the construction of their work. All were also the products of their society, both reflecting and reproducing what they considered normal and correct.

Other primary sources are legal compilations and monastic documents, including lists of attendants at church synods. Byzantine law was based on the *Institutes* of Justinian, but new laws were passed by successive emperors which were collected into various compilations by jurists eager to impose order on a vast body of law, some of which was contradictory. There are also collections of case law, like the *Peira*, used by Georgina Buckler. Byzantium had a system of church law as well as imperial law: some of these laws have been collected by V. Grumel into a volume entitled *Regestes des actes du Patriarchate de Constantinople*. The synodal lists show who was considered an indispensable part of policy-making and who accompanied the emperor at such functions. These are all-male lists. There is also a rich body of monastic acts of emperors, granting property to various monasteries, and many **typika*, or rules drawn up for monasteries and nunneries by founders, which often give detailed descriptions of the founder's family. These allow insight into one of the most popular eleventh-century activities, founding a monastery, often for retirement purposes. They equally usefully plot patterns of property management and show property in the hands of women. These *typika* will be used extensively in Chapter 6. Other original source materials are coins featuring Komnenian women and seals belonging to them, as well as pictures and objects which depict them or were possibly commissioned by them. These objects also reveal patterns of patronage and the image of herself which the imperial woman wished to present.

Another form of communication which reveals patterns of friendship, or at least acquaintance, is letters. Although an art form in Byzantium, replete with rules and conventions, letters can reveal how a correspondent dealt with the situations facing him. Unfortunately women's letter collections are fewer in number and less often published than those of emperors or bishops. Imperial women in particular must have received letters and one or two from the large letter collections of Michael Psellos and Theophylact of Ochrid are addressed to empresses. The *sebastokratorissa* Eirene wrote and received letters from the monk Iakobos. Several substantial letter collections survive: those of Theophylact of Ochrid, who had contacts at court, and Michael Italikos, who knew several imperial ladies well. Not only letters were conventional in Byzantium. Since Byzantine culture was formal and ceremonial there were many opportunities for delivering speeches and orations at court. The recommended layout for orations was presented by Menander Rhetor in the fourth century. Many of these orations survive precisely because they were often delivered in praise of imperial or rich people by well-known figures whose work was admired and therefore preserved. Theophylact of Ochrid and Michael Italikos gave speeches at court in honour of imperial women. Other famous orations are those of John the Oxite, who criticised the imperial system under Alexios Komnenos, and of Theodore Prodromos, the most prolific speech-writer for occasions such as birthdays, weddings and funerals. A long funeral oration survives for Bertha-Eirene from the pen of the bishop Basil of Ochrid, and an equally long one for Anna Komnene by Tornikes. These same imperial people also received laudatory poetry on various occasions which again reveals contacts among those who lived at court. These speeches and poems are particularly useful for discovering the ideology of the period.

Feminism, sex and gender

This book takes a feminist approach to imperial women. Feminism and feminist are difficult to define and should not be narrowly

defined.[16] The whole point about feminist criticism is that men
have defined meanings and values, excluding anything that is outside their immediate experience.[17] To be true to feminist aims,
feminists should always endeavour not to exclude, which implies a
wide-ranging definition of what feminism is and does.[18] *The Dictionary
of Feminist Theory* attempts to explain various aspects of feminism.
Feminism 'incorporates both a doctrine of equal rights for women
. . . and an ideology of social transformation aiming to create a
world for women beyond simple social equality.' The root belief of
feminism is 'that women suffer injustice because of [their] sex'. It
is not necessary that all feminists should agree on the causes, or
agents, of female oppression. Marxist feminists see the sexual division
of labour as a root cause: sexuality is seen by other feminists as the
primary social sphere of male power. Feminism is interdisciplinary
by its very nature. Scholars in all disciplines can be feminists and
use feminism in their work. Anthropology has sprinted ahead, closely
followed by sociology, but history, literary studies, psychology, art
history and social work are all following.[19]

Feminist anthropology provided the starting point of feminist
theory which is that sex and gender are two different things.
Margaret Mead was the pioneer who demonstrated from cross-
cultural examples that sexual division of labour is not the same in
all societies, therefore does not have a biological basis, and therefore is *not* 'natural'. Gender is a cultural construction which can be
deconstructed in order to understand and analyse a society, which
is the theoretical aim of feminism, or changed, which is feminism's
political goal. In other words, sex is the biological differences between
women and men; gender is what society does with these differences,
building them into a social system. In Oakley's catch-phrase, sex is
biological, gender is cultural. The relationship between the two is

16. For the difficulties of defining feminism and a discussion on whether it is viable
or useful see R. Delmar, 'What is feminism?', in A. Oakley and J. Mitchell (eds),
What is Feminism? (Oxford, 1980), pp. 8–33; D. Spender, *Women of Ideas* (London,
1982), p. 8, n.2.

17. Spender, *Women of Ideas*, p. 8, 'feminism refers to the alternative meanings put
forward by feminists.'

18. See G. Lerner in 'Politics and culture in women's history: a symposium',
J. Walkowitz *et al.* (eds), *Feminist Studies* 6 (1980) pp. 49–54, esp. p. 49, 'Feminism
means a) a doctrine advocating social and political rights of women equal to those
of men; b) an organised movement for the attainment of those rights; c) the assertion of the claims of women as a group and d) belief in the necessity of large-scale
social change to increase the power of women.'

19. To the extent that books are now being published about the effect of feminism on academic disciplines, e.g. K. Campbell (ed.), *Critical Feminism: Argument in the
Disciplines* (Oxford, 1992).

of crucial interest for feminists because what are actually gender rules are presented and justified as sex rules, in other words, natural, unchangeable, right. Elizabeth Fox-Genovese in her seminal 'Placing women's history in history' summarises the relationship as follows: 'Feminist scholarship has correctly insisted upon the social construction of gender. It is now widely accepted that all societies promote identities and roles taken to be appropriate to the genders and, normally, present those identities and roles as natural emanations of sexual difference.'[20] Feminists perceive that women are oppressed by gender systems, which always value male attributes and activities as superior. Mead saw and understood that in society it was not the actual activity performed by a person, but the sex of the performer, which determined whether the activity would be valued or not. This held even when the same activities were performed by both sexes. Whatever was done by men, whether it was childminding or hunting, was valued in the society and whatever was done by women, whether hunting or childminding, was not. In some societies, when both sexes performed the same activities, only men derived honour from such performance. In Rosaldo's words, 'But what is most striking and surprising is the fact that male, as opposed to female, activities are always recognised as predominantly important, and cultural systems give authority and value to the roles and activities of men'.[21] The same tendency is perceived today by feminists confronted, even if more subtly, by the prevailing prestige systems[22] in twentieth-century western culture.

Simone de Beauvoir coined the phrase 'the second sex'. Understanding her society and how it worked enabled her to feel free of its constraints.[23] Ever since, feminists have been trying to discover if women are the second sex and explore why. De Beauvoir also was the first to enunciate the notion of women as 'other' in the view of society, with men as the 'norm', the universal, the human,

20. A. Oakley, *Sex, Gender and Society* (London, 1972); E. Fox-Genovese, 'Placing women's history in history' *New Left Review*, 133 (1982), pp. 5–29, p. 14.

21. M. Rosaldo, 'Women, culture and society: a theoretical overview', in M. Rosaldo and L. Lamphere (eds), *Women, Culture and Society* (Stanford, 1974), pp. 17–42, p. 19.

22. S. Ortner and H. Whitehead, 'Introduction: accounting for sexual meanings', in S. Ortner and H. Whitehead (eds), *Sexual Meanings: The Cultural Construction of Gender and Sexuality* (Cambridge, 1981), pp. 1–27, p. 13 'Prestige – or 'social honor' or 'social value' – assumes slightly different qualities and falls in different quantities on different persons and groups within any society.'

23. S. de Beauvoir, *The Second Sex* (New York, 1953): see D. Spender, *Women of Ideas* (London, 1982) on de Beauvoir.

the standard against which women were tested and found lacking. She understood such a system as a cultural construct, with no basis in nature, and further, she demonstrated one of the ways in which it was constructed. This is through the control of knowledge. What women know comes through men and in that knowledge men are portrayed positively and women negatively. This point is taken up by anthropologists Rosaldo and Lamphere in *Women, Culture and Society*, a volume of essays challenging traditional anthropology and traditional assumptions by taking the woman's perspective. At the very beginning Rosaldo and Lamphere remind us that a first step in fighting inequities is recognising that 'in learning to be women in our own society, we have accepted, and even internalised, what is all too often a derogatory and constraining image of ourselves'.[24] The prospects of escaping this image are a matter of debate among feminists. Spender, while admiring de Beauvoir's ability to feel free once she had understood her constraints, thinks it is more likely that feminists will agree with Mary Daly's point of view that while feminists struggle to escape the mindset of patriarchy, it still exerts a firm hold over our consciousness.[25] Consciousness is an important concept in feminism. Becoming conscious of women's unfavourable place in society is the first step, consciousness-raising is the method employed to achieve it.[26]

Let it not be thought that only gender is in need of definition and study. 'Sex' is not a straightforward, biological entity either, at least not when it leads the parade to determine the roles of men and women in society. Here gender is masquerading as sex, natural, biological and unalterable. Anthropology has again led the field in exploring sexual meanings. *Sexual Meanings: The Cultural Construction of Gender and Sexuality*, edited by Ortner and Whitehead, sets out to question the assumption that scholars know what women and men are, the 'bias that often underlies studies of both sex roles and male dominance'.[27] Although few anthropologists today use an explicit model of biological determinism, by neglect of the subject or by referring to biologically-grounded psychological theory, the naturalistic bias has dominated anthropology. Not only anthropologists are interested in sex. The historian Thomas Laqueur, searching for the history of female sexual gratification, found himself writing a book about the body and its meanings throughout history. He discovered

24. Rosaldo and Lamphere, 'Introduction', *Women, Culture and Society*, p. 1.
25. Spender, *Women of Ideas*, p. 715.
26. Delmar, 'What is feminism?', p. 12.
27. Ortner and Whitehead, 'Introduction: accounting for sexual meanings', p. 1.

not only that the body, a 'natural' form if ever there was one, had changed in its occupiers' perceptions over time, but that attempting to use the body as any sort of determinant was fruitless. In sum 'the more the body was pressed into service as the foundation for sex, the less solid the boundaries became.'[28] An insistence on regarding sex as merely biology has other consequences: it prevents researchers from understanding how sex works in society.[29]

It is no easier to define 'feminist' than feminism. A remark by Rebecca West expresses the difficulty. She said 'I myself have never been able to find out precisely what feminism is. I only know that people call me a feminist whenever I express sentiments that differentiate me from a doormat.'[30] Dale Spender feels obliged to 'give some indication' of her use of the term and explains herself as follows: 'a feminist is a woman who does not accept man's socially sanctioned view of herself'.[31] Feminists have many differing affinities, of race, class, and sexual preference, so a single definition can never be complete. *The Dictionary of Feminist Theory* defines a feminist as a woman who recognises herself, and is recognised by others, as a feminist. At the most basic level of definition, 'all feminists share a commitment to, and enjoyment of, a woman-centred perspective.'[32]

Women in Byzantium: an introduction

Byzantium has a reputation for misogyny and is often dubbed a patriarchal state. Certainly there were misogynists in Byzantium and they were in a position to be heard at the time and to leave behind evidence of their opinions. As members of the educated clergy or literate ascetics, they were respected for their holiness by their contemporaries and their writings were collected and copied for the benefit of the next generation. They survive for historians to study because they were important in their own time. But the prevalence of unflattering opinions or prescriptive denouncements on women signals several things. As in the case of all frequently voiced material,

28. T. Laqueur, *Making Sex* (London, 1990), p. ix. For a fuller analysis of the body as more than biology, see C. Shilling, *The Body in Social Theory* (London, 1993).

29. J. Revel, 'Masculine and feminine: The historiographical use of sexual roles', in Perrot, *Writing Women's History*, pp. 90–105.

30. R. West, *The Clarion*, 14 November 1913, quoted in A. Humm, *The Dictionary of Feminist Theory* (London, 1989), pp. 75–6 and C. Kramarie and P. Treichler (eds), *A Feminist Dictionary* (London, 1985), sv. 'feminist', p. 160.

31. D. Spender, *Women of Ideas*, p. 8.

32. *Dictionary of Feminist Theory*, sv. feminist, p. 76.

whether it is a law or a sermon, its very frequency often betrays that its demands are not being obeyed. It has been said that the perennial problem of a patriarchal society is that women are absolutely crucial to its continuance but they must never be allowed to realise their importance or act on it. Byzantium recognised the importance of women in economic terms and in terms of their function as child-bearers, particularly in law.

Divorce by consent was permitted until the sixth century. There-after there was a list of reasons for which divorce was allowed: adultery, impotence, madness, and treason. The church saw mar-riage as a union of two people intended by God to last until the death of one of the parties. The consequences of this development for women can be argued two ways. In one way, easy divorce dis-advantaged women because their husbands could legally dispose of them in favour of a younger or prettier woman; alternatively, they themselves could also escape an unhappy marriage more easily. On the other hand, the church, while insisting that the union was indis-soluble, also advocated choice in marriage, a novel development for a culture which had not previously consulted a woman's prefer-ences. However, the list of possible reasons for divorce was more comprehensive for men, including in some ages a wife displeasing her husband by staying out of the house for too long. Another new development was the licence allowed by the church if one of the parties wished to enter the monastic life. Either a husband or a wife could divorce their spouse to take holy vows: sometimes a virtuous couple separated to live in different monasteries after their children were grown up.

A woman's rights over her dowry, the property a woman took from her family to a marriage, were vigorously defended. Because so much property was tied up in marriage, property disputes are one of the most common areas in which to see the law applied to women. The dowry belonged to the wife, although her husband could administer it. If he allowed it to diminish, the wife could administer it herself. The wife also had the full ownership and use of the nuptial gift from her husband, which was given at marriage and which was set at a percentage of the dowry. Of course both dowry and nuptial gift were intended to benefit the children of the marriage ultimately, and should the wife die before her husband, the children were next in line to inherit it before their father. When the man of the family died, his widow was the natural guard-ian of their children and the estate. As head of the family, she had all the responsibilities of a man and the legal authority to carry them out. On her shoulders rested estate administration, and the education, dowering and marriage of the children. This included the administration of the empire if the widow was an empress. Widowhood was the most powerful position that a woman could hold as far as legal rights went. On remarriage, the widow normally lost all control over her first family, and of the property of the family, except for her nuptial gift.

Remarriage was therefore a disabling option for women. This was not the only restriction on their activity. The emperor Leo VI (886–912) had forbidden women to appear as witnesses or to give testimony in court. He felt that it violated the natural order of things. Despite this law, many women did appear on their own behalf, especially well-born or rich women. There were other strange assumptions enshrined in the law which do not shine a favourable light on the morals of Byzantine men or the expected intelligence of Byzantine women. For example, women were unpunished in many cases because they could not be expected to understand the law or to know the difference between right and wrong, since they were women. The only crimes for which a woman was normally convicted were murder and adultery.

Byzantine women were not cloistered and they were not subject to constricting dress codes. But it was not usual to see many women on the streets, and it was usual for them to wear a veil. Often a contemporary historian will make a point of describing women in the streets or tearing their veils to emphasise how shocking an event was. The eleventh-century mumblings of the old general Kekaumenos about the wisdom of keeping your womenfolk from meeting strange men in your own house and the dangers that could result show that normally women were at large in their own homes. Although the empress had 'women's quarters' in the palace these were only curtained off from the main receiving rooms and men were certainly allowed into them. There was a separate room, covered in purple, in which the empress spent her last days of pregnancy and gave birth. This gave rise to the epithet 'purple-born' or *porphyrogennitos which designated the legitimate children of the emperor. In these quarters in her last days of pregnancy she probably sewed clothes for the forthcoming child. Clothes-making was one of the most important activities of women of all social levels, although it was by no means their only commercial activity. Documents survive revealing women's activities in retail trade, group exploitation of mines, production and sale of food, and investment in long-distance trade. The aristocratic widows mentioned above often managed the fortune of the family directly, not only the day-to-day running of the estate. This commercial activity necessitated contact with the world of men to an extent which seems at odds with the dominant ideology of female submission propounded by the early church fathers of Byzantium.

The ideology of the eleventh century with regard to women will be discussed in Chapters 3 and 7. Although Byzantines themselves were resistant to change or to admitting change, the attitudes towards women in the eleventh and twelfth centuries would have been unrecognisable to a Roman, with his conception of women as a possession inside their father or husband's *potestas* or absolute power. The fourth-century church fathers, whose writings were the basis for so much of Byzantine culture, were of the opinion that women were the offspring primarily of Eve and would lead a man astray either intentionally or by their nature alone. The fourth-century preacher John Chrysostom in particular regarded women as 'a necessary evil' and the ascetic saints of the desert who fled from the temptation of their lusts characterised women as the enemy. The most praiseworthy state for a woman in the early centuries of the empire until the seventh century was virginal. This was not an easy position to maintain given the need for marriages to transmit property, build alliances and perpetuate the population. Some girls fled to monasteries, disguising themselves as men, others retired to the desert to become ascetics and lose their feminine traits with their sins. From the seventh century there was a change in ideology and the married, fertile woman was seen as sanctified. This sanctity was easier to achieve and opened great vistas of influence to women.

The empress had a privileged position in Byzantium. She was crowned on her marriage to the emperor and after that was re-garded as a transmitter of imperial legitimacy. She took part in the ceremonies and rituals already mentioned, dressed in her own elabor-ate robes and attended by her own women. She had a table at banquets with her own manager. In the event of the emperor's death it was customary from the earliest centuries of the empire to appeal to the empress to choose or marry the successor. Although Byzantium was not a hereditary society it still appreciated some link between ruling families. The marriage of the former empress to the new emperor achieved this link in the most economical way. The actual choice of the new emperor might also be on the initiative of the empress, depending on her personality and the particular situ-ation of the empire at the time. Many empresses were regents for their underage sons, most notably Eirene the Athenian in the eighth century and Theodora in the ninth. However, the political power of the women of the eleventh century and their eclipse in the twelfth is not merely a function of individual competence or a lack thereof but also a phenomenon which requires explanation.

Towards a feminist history of Byzantium

As a feminist I enjoy, and am committed to, a 'woman-centred perspective' and therefore my overall aim in this book is to recover Byzantine women from the vacuum into which traditional history has thrust them. Women are invisible in historical accounts, by and large, because scholars of so-called mainstream history tend to disbelieve that women can be important to the correct understanding of their subject.[33] Part of my task therefore is to make Byzantine women visible. Recovery of women is a basic feminist goal, albeit a limited one. Mere recovery is insufficient, although in the face of the invisibility of women in history any inclusion of them is welcomed.[34] The invisibility of women is a problem that women have to contend with: it is equally a problem for history as a discipline. Besides the serious accusation that historians have been guilty of ignoring over half of their subject matter, the human race, the implication of such a practice is that the record itself is distorted and inaccurate. At best, the result is partial and one-sided, one that the actors themselves would not recognise were they to read it. At worst, in the words of one anthropologist 'by ignoring women as social actors the social sciences have seriously impaired their understanding of total social reality'.[35] The anthropologists' reaction has been strong: history must not lag behind.

So how do we put the women back in? There is concern that the pendulum will swing the other way and that only women will be considered as social actors, the very practice for which feminists criticise traditionalists.[36] One solution is to treat gender as a category

33. See the recent volume making the same point, J. Kleinberg (ed.), *Retrieving Women's History* (Oxford, 1992).

34. One work of recovery, albeit flawed, is B. Anderson and J. Zinsser, *A History of Their Own* (Harmondsworth, 1988).

35. L. Dube, 'Introduction', in L. Dube, E. Leacock and S. Ardener (eds), *Visibility and Power* (Oxford, 1986), p. xi.

36. Spender, 'I know that I am the product of a particular group in a particular culture and that I am being critical of another group that has presumed to treat its particular and limited experience as the whole. I would not wish to make the same mistake as those of whom I am critical. I do not assume that my experience of the world is all that there is.' *Women of Ideas*, p. 18.

of historical analysis.[37] In anthropologist Michelle Rosaldo's words 'what we know is constrained by the interpretative frameworks which . . . limit our thinking. What we can know is determined by the kinds of questions we learn to ask.'[38] The questions must engage with gender if we are ever to relate the experiences of women and men into one reality which will at least make an attempt accurately to describe a world in which both sexes live together. On the other hand, it must be realised that gender is not always the dominant identity factor, and its intersections with other factors such as race or class must be investigated.[39]

Gender is perhaps especially relevant to Byzantium as a society in which race and class were not present in the same way in which they are now. Other identity factors in Byzantium were religion and *taxis*, the system of order in society which was felt to be a reflection of the divine order.[40] The usefulness of gender as a category of analysis has recently been challenged by post-modern theory,[41] but the prevailing opinion is that feminists must not abandon it until it no longer functions as a category of discrimination.[42] Scholarship since the late 1980s has inevitably become more sophisticated under the influence of time, further study and criticism. Once the mere separation of sex and gender was enough: now it is necessary to use the insights of theories such as deconstruction to a certain extent to refine the tool. Jane Flax calls for more deconstruction of the meanings attached to biology, sex, gender and nature, for a more self-critical use of these terms. Such deconstruction is neither complete nor easy, but must be carried out to retain the usefulness of gender as a category.[43]

The results of treating gender as a category to analyse Byzantine society on a large scale would be revolutionary. The present study

37. Fox-Genovese, 'Placing women's history in history', pp. 14–15; J. Scott, 'Gender: a useful category of historical analysis', *AHR* 91 (1986), pp. 1053–75.
38. M. Rosaldo, 'The use and abuse of anthropology: reflections on feminism and cross cultural understanding', *Signs* 5 (1980), pp. 389–417, p. 390.
39. R. Perry, 'Review of Chodorow, Flax, and Yaeger', *Signs* 16.3 (1991), p. 600; cf. A. Laiou, 'Addendum to the report on the role of women in Byzantine society', *JÖB* 32/1 (1982), pp. 198–204.
40. For a consideration of how the Byzantines defined 'others', see D. Smythe, *Perceptions of the Outsider* (unpublished PhD thesis, St Andrews, 1993).
41. S. Bordo, 'Feminism, postmodernism, and gender-scepticism', in L. Nicholson (ed.), *Feminism/Postmodernism* (New York, 1990), pp. 133–56.
42. Perry, 'Review', p. 603.
43. J. Flax, 'Postmodernism and gender relations in feminist theory', *Signs* 12 (1987), pp. 621–43. On feminism and deconstruction see M. Poovey, 'Feminism and deconstruction', *Feminist Studies* 14.1 (1988), pp. 51–65.

has a rather more limited focus. In so far as the evidence allows, it is in line with Fox-Genovese's insistence that 'historians must accept the gender identities and roles that different societies assign to males and females are historical facts that require historical analysis'.[44] The group of women included is coherent in several important ways. They are all imperial. They are all visible in the sources, appearing in the contemporary histories of Michael Attaleiates, Michael Psellos, John Kinnamos, John Zonaras and Niketas Choniates. They have never before been examined in detail as a group at the top of the social ladder, with specific privileges such as money and education. There is no attempt to claim that their experience was a common or representative one, for it is very clear that it was not, even perhaps among imperial women. However, there is sufficient evidence to attempt a detailed analysis for a specific historical period, which is what is needed to make possible an understanding of how the Byzantine sex/gender system operated.

These general considerations are integral to this book and form the foundation principles on which it is based. Other analytical models might have been chosen. One divides the social world which encompasses both women and men into two spheres, one public, the other private. At first sight this alternative is tempting to a Byzantinist because Byzantium, quite falsely, has a reputation for secluding its women. It might appear that by interpreting the evidence along public/private lines two purposes could be served, showing what place imperial women did hold in relation to emperors and disproving the popular notion of seclusion. The theoretical groundwork was done by Rosaldo who used the dichotomy in 1973 as the 'basis of a structural framework necessary to identify and explore the place of male and female in psychological, cultural, social and economic aspects of human life'.[45] But by 1980 Rosaldo was thinking again. The public/private dichotomy now appeared to be too universal, too structural, capable of making sense in rough terms of the place of women in society, but of no use when it came to explaining why. The model 'based on the opposition of the two spheres assumes – where it should rather help illuminate and explain – too much about how gender really works.'[46] On other grounds the model is untenable because of the clear interconnectedness of the two spheres in what could be characterised as

44. Fox-Genovese, 'Women's history in history', p. 14.
45. Rosaldo, 'Theoretical overview', pp. 17–42.
46. Rosaldo, 'Use and abuse', p. 399.

the most private of areas: sexuality and procreation. The state has often seen the public good as depending on control of these private areas and has interfered accordingly. A model which relates the spheres of women and men is more useful.

A second alternative was a division of the sexes into 'natural' or cultural categories, best articulated by Sherry Ortner.[47] This approach is burdened by the same disadvantages as public/private, to which it corresponds. It is too universal, too structural, assumes the meanings of nature and culture to be already defined and separates the two rather than attempting to integrate them. It can perhaps describe what a researcher would see on the ground, but carries no explanatory power.[48] So-called 'natural' differences are immediately suspect and open to investigation.

The third possible alternative was an analysis of women and men according to whether they exercised power or authority. This has been a fruitful model of analysis, since it is clear that women every-where have influence, or power, but that, at the same time, this power is not the same, nor as visible, as male power.[49] The first step is one of definition. Neither power nor authority are absolute truths, and discussions on women or men's power, or the amount, the exercise, or the lack, often achieve nothing because the terms have not been defined. Feminist anthropologists have used Weber's defini-tions as a starting point for understanding of power and authority. Louise Lamphere,[50] for example, as an 'alternative perspective' to the family or marriage practices, neither of which actually concen-trates on women, examines the distribution of power and authority in the family, and women's relationship to their allocation. By necessity she explores the difference between power and authority. Power was defined by Weber as 'the probability that one actor within a social relationship will be in a position to carry out his own will, despite resistance, regardless of the basis on which this probability rests'.[51] Therefore it can be used to describe the result of a wide

47. S. Ortner, 'Is female to male as nature is to culture?', in Rosaldo and Lamphere, *Women, Culture and Society*, pp. 67–88.

48. For a criticism of Ortner and a comparison of her work to that of Bachofen, see K. Sacks, *Sisters and Wives: The Future and Past of Sexual Equality* (Westport, 1979), ch. 1, pp. 57–61; for the limitations of the nature/culture division, see Dube, 'Intro-duction', p. xvi.

49. E. Leacock, 'Women, power and authority', in Dube, Leacock and Ardener, *Visibility and Power*, pp. 107–35.

50. L. Lamphere, 'Strategies, co-operation and conflict among women in domestic groups', in Rosaldo and Lamphere, *Women, Culture and Society*, pp. 97–112.

51. M. Weber, *The Theory of Social and Economic Organisation* (New York, 1947), p. 152; quoted in Lamphere, 'Domestic groups', p. 99.

range of methods, many of which are open to women. Authority is the name given to power which rests on legitimacy, and is exercised within a hierarchy of roles. It is much more circumscribed and precise. It is the general understanding that female power has usually existed in a framework of male authority, and that the balance of power in society lies with men. Many sources of power have been located, among them consciousness, language and sexuality.

However, the question is complex, and particularly so when applied to a historical society. There are many analyses of power but most refer to modern, capitalist, industrialised societies, and are of little help to Byzantinists. There are studies of modern Greece, which are of considerably more help, especially the excellent volume edited by Jill Dubisch, *Gender and Power in Rural Greece*.[52] In her introduction, Dubisch highlights some of the complexities of gender and its analysis, not least of which is the inevitable cultural bias of the observer. Even a feminist, alert to androcentric models, may miss the tell-tale signs of women's power because it is not what she is expecting to see, or because the informants, both men and women, play it down. Dubisch believes that a search for spheres of women's power may be of more use than an attempt to differentiate between the related concepts of power and influence. The best way forward is to assume that women have goals, which they work to reach, often in culturally acceptable ways, such as fulfilling the expectations of the ideal female, sometimes by tactics like nagging or quarrels.[53] The important question for Dubisch is not whether women have power, for she assumes that they do, but in what spheres it is exercised.

Power is always social, always exercised over someone else, and it is merely our androcentric bias which propels us to search for and value political or material power rather than, or above, power in the domestic sphere. This tendency survives despite most people's opinion that the family is more important than the marketplace, demonstrating the strength of the male world-view. The roots of power, ideological and material, may reinforce one another, or they may diverge, leaving the observer unsure of what the 'real' status of women is. Determining how a woman's status should be calculated, let alone what it is, is a central problem for historians. This is so because there is no single criterion which can be applied, like political power or economic success or overt decision-making for men, which results in a satisfactory answer. Women's status is

52. J. Dubisch (ed.), *Gender and Power in Rural Greece* (Princeton, 1986).
53. J. Collier, 'Women in politics', in Rosaldo and Lamphere, *Women, Culture and Society*, pp. 89–96.

hard to grasp, a slippery concept, because society is predicated on and around men and male values. Men are the positive members: women are the Other. It is easier to say what women are not or have not, than what they are or have. Ideology and social reality may relate to each other in startling ways or a society may have a conflicting mixture of ideologies, which some anthropologists have claimed is true of Greece.[54] Women may obtain their social and their personal identities from different sources, and ideology may not be talking about gender roles at all, but about wider issues like social ideals.[55]

All these angles can provide fascinating and important approaches to women in Byzantium, making us aware of the complexities in trying to understand ideology and gender in a society, and attempt to make every allowance for the belittling or criticism of women's influence where it is visible. Leacock's method speaks to the same concerns. In order to assess power and authority in a given society, it is necessary to survey all the important decisions to be made in that society and to ascertain, as far as possible, how they are made. She is aware of our tendency to search for 'politics' in the sphere which is familiar to us and warns that the stereotyped lump which is 'domestic' to us varies in significance from society to society; it may be the most important decision-making forum in another society.[56]

On the other hand, it must not of course be assumed that women do not have authority: any historical search must pose the question and answer it. But the distinction power/authority may not even be particularly helpful as a tool of analysis for most of this study, when the intense family atmosphere of the administration entailed a blurring of the divide between power and authority. Searching for spheres of power is perhaps more helpful, but only if women's spheres are constantly related to those of men, for it seems that the two were interrelated in highly complicated ways under the Komnenian system.

Therefore this book examines the evidence for imperial women, asking constantly how much power they were able to exercise in what spheres. Sometimes they will have authority, sometimes it will be by way of influence that they achieve their goals. But their goals will be a matter of investigation and it will be assumed that they did have goals and an interest in achieving them. These women did not

54. M. Herzfeld, 'Within and without: the category of "female" in the ethnography of modern Greece', in Dubisch, *Gender and Power*, pp. 215–33.

55. Dubisch, 'Introduction', *Gender and Power*, pp. 3–41.

56. Leacock, 'Women, power and authority', in Dube, Leacock and Ardener, *Visibility and Power*, p. 110.

sit on the sidelines of their society, uninterested in anything except their domestic circumstances. This disclaimer in itself is problematic: their domestic circumstances occasionally were the very centre of social issues, not the sidelines at all.

A related question concerns patriarchy, which is a concept that has 'plagued all attempts to describe the persistence of male dominance over women and children'.[57] It was first used in an overtly feminist sense to mean a system which oppresses women. Thus used 'patriarchy' neatly encapsulates the standard feminist definition of 'a system of social order in which power and the means of acquiring and perpetuating it (economic, political, ideological) have been assumed by the male sex'[58] into one word.[59] This has obvious advantages: feminists understand the point of other feminists' analyses without tedious explanations. For polemical use it has few rivals. But history is not polemic, and 'patriarchy' as a tool of historical analysis has a great disadvantage: it is ahistorical. Feminists proclaim that male authority is universal, radical feminists accuse all societies everywhere at all times of oppressing women under the cloak of patriarchy.[60] Twentieth-century western society is characterised as patriarchal, with all its choices for women. How then can the same word be used profitably to describe past societies in which most modern choices were not open to women? If patriarchy merely shifts its ground, what is the point in talking about it at all? Feminists have expressed concern over this point already. Patriarchy 'is treated at a level of abstraction that obfuscates rather than reveals the intimate inner workings of culturally and historically distinct arrangements between the genders.'[61] Another disadvantage of this ahistoricity is that patriarchy implies a structure which is fixed and neither provides any notion of how women may act to transform their situation, nor any sense of how women have managed to achieve a better position for themselves in the past. Using the word also allows the biological determinists to enter the debate, for one

57. Fox-Genovese, 'Women's history in history', p. 22.

58. Galatariotou, 'Holy women and witches', p. 56.

59. Another more detailed definition of patriarchy defines it as men's control over women's sexuality and fertility. S. Rowbotham, 'The trouble with "patriarchy"', in R. Samuel (ed.), *People's History and Socialist Theory* (London, 1981), pp. 363–9.

60. Chief among these is medievalist Judith Bennett in her articles ' "History that stands still": women's work in the European past', *Feminist Studies* 14 (1987); 'Feminism and history', *Gender and History* 1 (1989); 'Women's history: a study in continuity and change', *Women's History Review* 2 (1993).

61. D. Kandiyoti, 'Bargaining with patriarchy', in J. Lorber and S. Farrell (eds), *The Social Construction of Gender* (London, 1991), pp. 104–18, p. 104.

way of explaining the universalism of patriarchy is to appeal to innate, unchangeable, sexual differences. And what about the attitude of women themselves to men and other women, for it has been noticed that women sometimes fight against changes that outsiders understand as liberating? Deniz Kandiyoti discusses the problem of women's acceptance of their prescribed roles, and hostility to change, which is sometimes understood as a 'false consciousness' on the part of women. She makes the sapient point that women see themselves losing the benefits they have suffered to gain, without any empowering alternative or consequent compensation.[62] 'Patriarchy' has no room for such subtleties. It is clear that what is needed is an approach which can 'encompass both conflict and complementary association between the sexes'.[63]

To conclude that Byzantine women were the victims of patriarchy says nothing at all. On a cursory glance, Byzantium undoubtedly seems to be patriarchal, but there were important differences with the contemporary west and with the Islamic east which deserve to be highlighted: the whole of the world in the eleventh and twelfth centuries surely should not be tarred with the same broad patriarchal brush. Male dominance may be universal (although this is open to debate) but the specific form it takes is not.[64] An examination of Byzantium's particular form of patriarchy will advance historians' knowledge of it, but it will still mean nothing in comparative terms because it is not sufficiently subtle.

Deniz Kandiyoti has shown that in order to make sense of women's attitudes to their society the view from the ground must always be taken into account. Unfortunately this view is the most elusive area of evidence about imperial women between 1025 and 1204. Few women in any historical society have left evidence of their impressions of what it felt like to be a woman, and Byzantium is no different. Only Anna Komnene's *Alexiad* with all its attendant problems gives a clue to the experience of being an imperial woman in the eleventh and twelfth centuries. Unlike modern anthropologists who can ask women how they understand their society and what

62. Kandiyoti, 'Bargaining with patriarchy', p. 111.
63. Rowbotham, 'Trouble', p. 366.
64. Fox-Genovese, 'Women's history in history', p. 15; R.W. Connell, *Gender and Power: Society, the Person and Sexual Politics* (Oxford, 1987), p. 58 'It is possible to combine a clear recognition of the exploitation and subordination of women, and the fundamental character of the social changes needed to correct it, with an equally strong recognition of the specific ways in which subordination is embedded in different cultures, the different forms it takes and the different strategies therefore required.'

they feel about men, the historian is handicapped in this area. So although this book is committed to a woman-centred approach which assumes that women had goals which they pursued, actually finding the goals is difficult.

If one method of determining women's power is to survey the range of important decisions of the time and assess women's part in them, then a consideration of women's involvement in the most significant areas of Komnenian theory and activity should reveal the extent of their power. Influence is not in question. It is accepted that all women have influence over the people they are close to, but influence by its private and unrecorded nature cannot be quantified. The criterion for this book is visibility. Women who appear in official documents or are credited in the sources with independent action will be viewed as more powerful than those who are not. This is an arbitrary division, but it is the only way to make sense of the evidence of women's lives which, as we are all aware, is far from complete. The women included in Anna Komnene's *Alexiad* are obviously privileged, and the accidents of survival may have distorted the picture because of the loss of personal seals or letters belonging to these imperial women which could have shown the part they played in the court and how they were regarded by the men around them.

The question of power is approached from four angles, chosen because they were of great importance to the society of the time. These four areas are the titles by means of which people of the imperial court were arranged into a hierarchy; the kinship system, which was the basis of that nomenclature; patronage, which was the way to get on in life; and ideology, which is at the base of every society's rules for living.

Titulature defines the range of women included in this book; only those included among the **basilissai* appear. The titles of imperial women, even of the empress, are neglected in comparison to the wealth of scholarly interest in the titles of the emperor. To my knowledge only one full-length article is devoted to the empress.[65] Empresses' titles may not reveal as much as those of the emperor, since they are essentially derivative, but I suspect that this is not the reason they have been ignored. In particular, the study of the coronation ceremony and the granting of the title of **augousta* to the empress will help in determining how automatic this grant was and on what basis it was awarded. Titulature also sets the scene in which these imperial women moved, in a court where titles were the basis of prestige. This section demonstrates that Alexios Komnenos's system privileged the male on the basis of sex, which was his way of instituting patriarchy, and asks whether a woman derived any power from her title alone. It also includes a case study of Anna Dalassene, who was given a title by Alexios to express her authority. Since a seal of Anna's and a document issued by her survive, the historian can perhaps discover how she saw herself.

The second area is kinship, a key phenomenon of this period which was first highlighted by Stiernon and who has been followed by Lemerle, Macrides and Magdalino[66] among others. An anthropological analysis of Byzantium shows how its kinship structures affected women. Traditional anthropologists have always found room for women in their analyses of kinship and marriage systems. Indeed, these are usually the only areas where women have been included. Feminist anthropologists have not abandoned interest in kinship for this reason, but have looked again with fresh insights gained from their view that gender is a cultural construction. This has enabled them to assess the part that kin systems play in the cultural construction of gender. Most analyses of kin systems concentrate on so-called simple societies, so their use for Byzantium, a very complex society, is limited. Nevertheless, they can be used as a starting place and for comparison. This is one area where women can be seen pursuing their own goals by means of the manipulation of marriage alliances, and it therefore deserves a full treatment.

The third area is patronage. All of the women under consideration are credited as personal or literary patrons by Byzantinists, which makes it especially important to consider their activities in this field. Patronage was the basis of life in Byzantium in the absence of any system of impersonal promotion, where all authority emanated from the emperor. No works so far have grouped these women together as a coherent whole to highlight the connections or differences between them, and this approach is long overdue. There is a wealth of theory, both anthropological and sociological, which declares that patronage is a kind of power. Therefore, although there are no explicit goals stated by these women who were all patrons, it is important to gauge what part they played in extending patronage.

66. P. Lemerle, *Cinq études sur le XIe siècle byzantin* (Paris, 1977), pp. 294–9. R. Macrides, 'The Byzantine godfather', *BMGS* 11 (1987), pp. 139–62; 'Kinship by arrangement', *DOP* 44 (1990), pp. 109–18. P. Magdalino, *The Empire of Manuel Komnenos, 1143–1180* (Cambridge, 1993).

Finally, a consideration of ideology. From examining areas of women's experience, the analysis moves to the underlying understanding of the world to deconstruct the ideal imperial woman as she appears in Byzantine thought and to show the roles that women could play. This chapter draws heavily on feminist theory, which contends that there is a cultural construct of expectations built up around women in society, which can be deconstructed because it is not natural. Much has been written on the ideal emperor, from at least the third century AD by Menander Rhetor, to Kazhdan and Epstein in the twentieth, but there is little on the ideal empress. This is not due to lack of contemporary source material, but to lack of scholarly interest. Ideology is concerned not with what a woman does or is, but with what she ought to do and be. Discovering what power the Byzantine imperial woman was supposed to exercise is one step forward. No society is a monolith: discovering if the women themselves agreed with the ideal is another step forward. Reality and ideology are related in complicated ways, and actual behaviour is usually more varied than the ideal stereotype allows: discovering what real power ideology conferred on imperial women between 1080 and 1180 is the last step this chapter takes.

Before embarking on these lines of research, it is worth pausing briefly to introduce the social and political history of the empire, and to introduce briefly the women on whom this study focuses.

Byzantium: an introduction

The Byzantine empire, as a political entity, exists only in modern textbooks.[67] The inhabitants of the empire which stretched from the Adriatic Straits in the west to the Tigres and Euphrates Rivers in the east called themselves Romans and referred to their city, Constantinople, as the New Rome. Development is not a term found in Byzantine thought: the emphasis there is on continuity and tradition. But to believe that the empire saw no development is to fall into a trap of the empire's own making. The changes apparent in the eleventh and twelfth centuries are the subject of this book.

There are two popular and useful ways of characterising the empire. One is that it was a blend of Greek culture, Roman law and Christianity. The other is that it stood on two pillars, the church

67. M. Angold, *The Byzantine Empire, 1025–1204. A Political History* (2nd ed., London, 1997).

and the imperial power. The former encapsulates the mix of the three most basic components of any civilisation. The rich literature of the Greeks, encompassing philosophy, language, rhetoric, poetry, myth and medicine comprised the educational curriculum of Byzantium. The continual copying of manuscripts in Byzantine monasteries and courts ensured their survival. Roman law was and continued to be the basis for Byzantine law, codified and added to by several emperors. In Byzantium, the emperor made the laws or gave judgements which were then compiled. The laws were influenced by Christianity to a certain extent, as was the culture of the empire. Christianity became the official religion of the empire in 378. There were also several branches of Christianity to which one could adhere. The growth of heresies necessitated the gathering of oecumenical councils and facilitated both the creation of church law and the participation of the emperor. Such heresies as Arianism, Nestorianism and Monophysitism were more than religious debates alone and in the context of the empire carried political connotations.

This leads to the second characterisation of the empire – that it stood on the two pillars of the church and the imperial power. Because the emperors became involved in church disputes very early in the history both of Byzantium and Christianity the two grew together into a normally mutually supporting relationship. The balance of power varied from age to age since in the absolutist regime of the empire the personality of the emperor was crucial. Given a strong head of the church, or patriarch, and a weak or young emperor, the church could grow rich and privileged. Ever since the creation of a body of church, or canon, law, there was a constant battle for control of justice. Patriarchs could be removed from office by the emperor, or the office could be left vacant if the emperor wished. Generally however, the emperor preferred to either gain the support of the patriarch or appoint someone favourable to himself. Byzantine history is full of patriarchs who defied or criticised emperors, often achieving their own aims by making them the price of their resignation. In many other situations, the patriarchs were left in control of the city or of offspring by the emperor. Constantine X in the eleventh century made his empress swear an oath to the patriarch that she would not marry again as a safeguard for his young sons for whom she was regent.

Both the imperial court and the church were run by a hierarchical bureaucracy. Byzantine government is often regarded as an example of tortuous complexity, but it was very sophisticated for its time and it worked. For the administrative machinery of the empire the best evidence survives for the ninth and tenth centuries, although certain changes to it can be detailed for later periods. During these centuries there were eighteen ranks of titles, which did not imply any office but did confer prestige and reward. The three highest were Caesar, *nobilissimos* and *curopalate*. The only rank granted to women in their own right was that of the *zoste patrika*, the belted patrician. Then there were many offices, all of which conferred a rank and a salary. Although there were instances of nepotism, these offices and titles were open to any talented male, for Byzantium was not a classed society. The lists of officials for the ninth and tenth centuries gives a total of sixty officials, all reporting to the emperor as their superior. They were all personally appointed by him and could be dismissed at his will. The military officials tended to be more important, and better paid, but the same official could move from a civil post to a military one if the emperor wished. The church had its own hierarchy through which one could rise to become patriarch. For the imperial throne itself, the best avenue of approach was via the military, since a successful general won vast support. The frontiers of the empire were so wide and the enemies so numerous that military success was highly feted. There was a set of virtues and qualities which the ideal emperor was supposed to display, explained best by the fourth-century orator Menander Rhetor. Although good birth was included in the list, Menander's advice was to ignore the topic if nothing good could be said. The pre-eminence of military victory in Byzantine thought was made manifest as a stumbling block for women in the eleventh century who sought to hold imperial power.

The ideal imperial virtues given voice by Menander Rhetor form part of a speech of praise to the emperor. Court life was regulated by ritual of which speeches formed a large part. Not only were *encomia*, or laudatory speeches, given in front of the emperor, but also wedding speeches, funeral speeches, and epitaphs. There was a schedule of religious festivals when processions took place around the city and also ceremonies of promotion to office or games at the Hippodrome which punctuated the life of the court. In all processions, banquets or ceremonies the order of rank was rigidly adhered to, led by the imperial couple, followed by the Caesar, *nobilissimos* and *curopalate*. All these titles and offices were allocated insignia denoting their rank. The emperor wore a bright purple-red colour exclusive to himself and he wrote in purple ink. Other colours near to purple were designated to those ranks nearest the emperor. The importance of these rules becomes clear when one considers the personal nature of absolute rule in which access to the emperor is paramount.

The eleventh century is characterised in textbooks as a century of crisis. Begun brilliantly by one of the most spectacular of soldier emperors, Basil II, the empire proceeded thereafter to lose vast tracts of territory during the century in both east and west and to spend a vast amount of money which had been accumulated by the tight-fisted Basil. Coincidentally, this is also the century in which women are most conspicuous in the Byzantine histories of the time and where this study of imperial women commences. Three empresses' names appear as sole rulers. Many theories have been advanced to explain the 'crisis'; the over-expansion by Basil II, the growth of the great families and the 'aristocratic principle' which undermined the edifice of the state, infighting between civil and military cliques which ignored the real problems, or the appearance of individualism. Recent scholarship has suggested that in economic and monetary terms the empire was healthy. However, there is no doubt that there was a crisis of leadership which encouraged a great outlay of money to buy support and which tended to focus the eyes of leaders on their own survival rather than the good of the empire.

Basil II died in 1025, having made no real provision for the succession. His brother Constantine became emperor in his old age, having never had any share in or experience of ruling an empire. Extravagant to a fault, he began the spending of the vast treasury that Basil had built up. He died in 1028, also having made minimal provision for the empire's future. He was succeeded by his second daughter Zoe and her husband Romanos Argyros. Zoe was around fifty years old at the time and Romanos was even older. Between 1028 and 1050 Zoe ruled as empress with two husbands, an adopted son and her sister Theodora, who ruled for one year, 1056, until she too died. Zoe's life was spent mainly in the palace, apart from one stint in a monastery through the jealousy of her adopted son. She was famous for generosity, her devotion to the church and the making of perfumes.

Zoe's sister Theodora spent most of her life in a monastery. Banished there by either Zoe or her second husband, she became empress briefly during a riot in 1042 and then in her own right after the death of Zoe and Zoe's third husband in 1056. Theodora was taller and more practical than Zoe and was famous mainly for her parsimony and her refusal to marry on her accession.

Zoe and Theodora were the last of the house of Macedonia, a dynasty which had been ruling since 867, when Basil I took the

throne. Although this dynasty ruled for so long, there was no hereditary principle in operation in Byzantium, which still subscribed in
theory to the Roman ideal of the best man. When the Macedonian
house was gone, there was a great scramble among all the possible
claimants to the throne. Although between 1025 and 1056 there
had been no spectacular victories for the empire, after the end of
the Macedonian house there was no clear legitimacy either and the
pace of change of emperors increased with all the instability which
that implied in an absolutist regime.

An old civil servant was raised to the throne on Theodora's death
to give the potential claimants a breathing space, but on his death
the next year, the first of the 'family names' which were to become
such a feature of the last centuries of the empire succeeded in gaining the throne. Isaac Komnenos was a general who had experience
on the battlefield but he did not have the political *savoir-faire* to
survive more than two years on the throne. In 1059 he was forced
to resign as the end result of a contretemps with his patriarch the
year before. He abdicated the throne, assumed the habit of a monk,
and died soon after. His former friend and eventual rival Constantine
Doukas became emperor. He was married to Keroularios's niece,
Eudokia Makrembolitissa, who would later be regent for their young
sons when Constantine died in 1067. She was very well educated:
some of her letters have survived, but she demonstrated the difficulties of reigning alone which assailed every woman in power. She
needed a general to fight the empire's enemies who were closing
in on the empire, sensing the internal uncertainty. Breaking the
oath she had sworn to Constantine not to marry again, she elevated
the general Romanos Diogenes to the throne. His military record
is besmirched by the defeat at Mantzikurt against the Turks in
1071; this defeat is cited as one of the worst military disasters in
the history of the empire. Brought about partly by treachery by the
empress's in-laws, it was exacerbated by lack of command after the
first not very decisive battle. The Turks were able to ravage some of
the heartland of the empire and advance far into Byzantine territory
due more to lack of any opposition than a military victory. Romanos
was captured and although he struck a deal with the sultan and was
on his way back to the capital, he found that the same internal
enemies had deposed him and elevated Eudokia and Constantine's
young son to the throne. Eudokia, meanwhile, was betrayed by her
brother-in-law and forced to flee to a monastery, after being threatened
with violence by the soldiers. She never regained the throne but
remained a powerful influence for the next twenty years.

The young Michael Doukas ruled for seven years but did not have the force of personality to pull the empire together. He was deposed in his turn in 1078 by Nikephoros Botaneiates, a general who had fought his way from Antioch. But Nikephoros was an old man too and did not have the support to secure his own throne. In 1081 he was overthrown by Alexios I Komnenos who had much military experience and success and a unified family behind him. Due to the marriage policies of his mother, Anna Dalassene, every powerful family was joined to the Komnenos family and therefore had every reason to support his candidature. Central to the history of these years were four women: Maria of Alania, Anna Dalassene, Maria of Bulgaria and Eirene Doukaina.

Maria of Alania was the daughter of Bagrat of Georgia, and married Michael Doukas after he became emperor, around 1073. From this marriage resulted Constantine Doukas, born in 1074. After the usurpation of Nikephoros Botaneiates, Maria and Constantine retired to the monastery of Petrion. Apparently on the advice of the Caesar John Doukas, Maria married the usurper, thereby committing adultery in the strictest sense of the term, and becoming *basilissa* once again. The young Komnenos brothers, Isaac and Alexios, won her favour; Isaac was married to her niece or cousin, and Alexios was adopted by her. After the succession of Alexios, rumours in the city credited her with being the reason for the delay in the coronation of Eirene Doukaina, and that Alexios wished to marry her. Her political career after this crisis is more obscure and has been best illuminated by Mullett. She retired with honour, looked after the young Anna Komnene when she was betrothed to Constantine, and is last heard of on her country estate, harbouring conspirators against the reigning emperor.

Anna Dalassene's family was illustrious, and one of them, Constantine, had been deemed worthy of marriage with Zoe the Macedonian in 1028 by virtue of his family and his wealth. Born around 1025, Anna married John Komnenos between the years 1040 and 1045, producing eight children: five boys and three girls. During his illness in 1059, Isaac Komnenos supposedly offered the throne to his brother, who refused, much to the chagrin of Anna. After the death of John Komnenos in 1067, Anna was head of the family. A skilled player of the political game, and an enemy of the Doukas family, she ensured her family's survival and eventual victory in 1081. After Alexios's accession, she was regent while he spent most of his time on the frontiers. She was fond of monks and monasticism, founded the monastery of Pantepoptes, and retired there in obscure circumstances at an unknown date. The date of her death is likewise unknown.

Maria of Bulgaria, the mother of Eirene Doukaina, is little known. Daughter of Trojan, granddaughter of Samuel, she married Andronikos Doukas around 1066, bearing him five children: two sons and three daughters, of which the first was Eirene. She is most often referred to by the female form of her husband's title, *protovestiaria*. Bryennios accords her the crucial role in the marriage of Alexios Komnenos and Eirene: she told the Caesar it was time the family had a protector, chose Alexios as the one, and worked hard to bring it about. She had influence over George Palaiologos, another son-in-law, and was so beautiful that all men were concerned about her.

Eirene Doukaina is one of the better known Byzantine women. Daughter of Andronikos Doukas and Maria of Bulgaria, she was married to Alexios Komnenos in 1078 at the age of fifteen, and bore him seven children: four daughters and three sons. Her career is described in the *Alexiad* by her dutiful daughter, by Zonaras in a neutral fashion, and unkindly by Choniates. At first her husband ignored her, but later he came to love and depend on her, and her influence grew accordingly. She was educated, adventurous enough to accompany Alexios on campaign, and pious, founding the convent of Kecharitomene, to which she retired on the death of Alexios, and in which she enjoyed her literary pursuits. Her ambitions on the death of Alexios are ambiguous: she may have planned to set Anna on the throne rather than John. The date of her death is disputed, favoured dates being 1133 or 1138.

Alexios succeeded in halting the ruinous course of instability upon which the empire was foundering. He ruled until 1118 and handed on his throne to his son, having reconquered much of Asia Minor, re-established control in the Balkans, stabilised the currency, reformed the church, and changed the style and substance of government. Much of what we know of these years is contained in Anna Komnene's *Alexiad*. Anna Komnene is probably the best-known Byzantine woman, due to this biography of her father, which is the only work in the whole of the *Corpus Scriptorum Historiae Byzantinae* written by a woman. Betrothed in her youth to Constantine Doukas, she married Nikephoros Bryennios after Constantine's death and bore at least four children: two sons and two daughters. Well educated, as she herself informs us, and ambitious, she may have attempted to claim the throne on the death of her father. She retired to Kecharitomene when her brother was emperor, where she shared in the literary interests of her mother. She died around 1148, bemoaning the long years spent in retirement and the miseries that had befallen her.

Alexios's son, John II Komnenos, held on to all that his father had gained and managed to attach more of the ancient holdings in Asia Minor to his crown. Little is known of his wife, Eirene of Hungary, who took the Byzantine name of Eirene on her arrival in Byzantium, except that she had reddish hair and was involved in the founding of the monastery of Pantokrator. She died before the completion of the monastery in 1136, having borne eight children: four sons and four daughters. Even the date of John and Eirene's marriage is unknown, being some time before the death of Alexios. Theodore Prodromos recorded her death. John was on campaign in Cilicia in the far east of Asia Minor when he died unexpectedly in 1143. His youngest son Manuel became emperor despite the existence of an older brother and reigned until he died in 1180. He reformed the church again, took part in religious controversies, and favoured westerners at court. Manuel married twice. His first wife was Bertha of Sulzbach, the relative of Conrad of Germany, but she took the Byzantine name of Eirene on her marriage in 1146. For ease of identification, she will be referred to as Bertha-Eirene. The chroniclers are unkind about her appearance, and Manuel took his time about marrying her: she had arrived in Constantinople in 1142. She appears to have made an attempt to fit into the cultured society into which she was plunged. Tzetzes wrote several works for her, as did Prodromos. Her part in politics is obscure, but she seems to have had influence with Conrad, and her philanthropy was widespread. She died in 1159/60, having borne two daughters, one of whom died before she was six. She was buried in the Pantokrator monastery. Basil of Ochrid wrote a funeral oration for her. After Bertha-Eirene's death, Manuel married Maria of Antioch, the daughter of Raymond of Antioch, in 1161. She bore him the desired son, and was regent after Manuel's death. She was drowned on the orders of Andronikos Komnenos who had come to power on the back of Byzantine disapproval of Maria and her lover, Alexios the *protosebastos*. She may have commissioned the *eisiterioi* for Agnes of France, and a manuscript portrait of her survives, but otherwise little is known of her life and activities.

Manuel's son Alexios was murdered in 1183 by his uncle Andronikos, who was later lynched by an angry Constantinopolitan mob in 1185. Eirene the *sebastokratorissa*, the wife of Andronikos Komnenos, has left behind the most evidence of literary interests of these imperial women. Her political involvement is also of interest: she was exiled from court twice for obscure reasons. Byzantine authors who wrote for her include Theodore Prodromos, Constantine Manasses, and John Tzetzes. She had a rich correspondence with the monk Iakobos, who was possibly her spiritual father. She died perhaps in 1155, although the date is speculative.

After Andronikos was murdered the throne went to a cousin, Isaac Angelos, who ruled for ten years until 1195. Isaac was usurped and blinded by his elder brother Alexios in 1195. Alexios Angelos was a weak emperor and his wife Euphrosyne made all the decisions in a visible enough manner to be strongly criticised for it. Alexios was convinced by a group of courtiers than Euphrosyne had been unfaithful to him and exiled her to a monastery. She was soon back at court, but Alexios himself was usurped by his brother. Euphrosyne's personal qualities were a talent for communication, for picking good ministers, and for cutting the dead wood out of an organisation. Alexios was politically unsure and was deposed in 1203 by Isaac and his son. However, the civil rivalry allowed the Latin forces to assume a position of great importance as the warring brothers sought outside support, and in 1204 the Latins marched into the city to establish a Latin empire. The dynasty established by Alexios Komnenos allowed the empire to survive and while there was a mature emperor to keep control of various divisive elements the system worked. That system produced problems of its own, but it did usher in a period of stability in which the civilisation of the empire could develop. One area in which development took place was the position of women. The following chapters will investigate that development and the background to the power exercised by these women.

CHAPTER TWO

The role of women in eleventh-century politics

Introduction

The eleventh century is one of the most fertile grounds for examining the role of women in politics in Byzantium. It is also the century long regarded as a crisis in the history of Byzantium, when instability led to political collapse and the loss of vast tracts of the empire's former possessions. The juxtaposition of these two facts inevitably raises questions about the role of women in Byzantine politics. Although recent scholarship has revised the traditional view of economic and financial collapse, the political instability is undeniable. The loss of territory is a fact which cannot be disregarded. Basil II ruled for forty-nine years and Alexios Komnenos for thirty-seven. In contrast, in the fifty-six years between the death of Basil II and the accession of Alexios I Komnenos twelve emperors were crowned and subsequently lost the throne or died. Such a period of uncertainty demands an explanation and various scholars have approached the crisis from political, economic and ideological points of view.

One explanation by George Ostrogorsky, in his monumental *A History of the Byzantine State,* posits a struggle between civil nobility based in Constantinople and military nobility based in the provinces.[1] This is too simplistic a divide, since with the incursions of the Turks into Anatolia those families whose landed wealth might have been in that region fled to their city homes, the Komnenoi among them. The amount of land owned ceased to be of vital importance, replaced by influence exerted in the city. In any case, most of the prominent families were represented in the military ranks and in the civil government.

1. G. Ostrogorsky, *A History of the Byzantine State* (Oxford, 1968).

An attractive explanation is presented by Michael Angold in his history of the empire between 1025 and 1204.[2] He turns the reputation of the revered Basil II on its head to show how Basil's legacy was beyond the control of other less talented emperors. Basil was a good soldier and a determined campaigner who spent most of his reign on the frontiers. He put the empire on a military footing backed up by the necessary financial policies. He rejuvenated laws which prevented the rich buying up peasant property and made them liable for tax arrears in their districts. A hoard of treasure was built up by the tight-fisted emperor, providing him with a vast fund for paying armies. Basil succeeded in accumulating so much treasure that he was able to repeal the tax on the poor for the last two years of his reign, enabling them to stay on their plots of land. Basil's understanding of the economic wealth of the empire was traditional: in his view the maintenance of the peasant farmer was essential. Undeniably legitimate and safe from the powerful families because he had confiscated their fortunes, Basil established a method of ruling which was individual and unrepeatable.

After his death, chaos ensued because the following emperors were obliged to spend the treasure Basil had amassed in securing support for their reigns. Lacking Basil's personal asceticism, they also indulged their whims, encouraged by the seemingly bottomless treasury. At the same time that effective generalship was removed from the Byzantine empire, outside enemies were working through their internal difficulties, unharassed by any Byzantine armies. Basil had had years to perfect his style: his successors had to react to events without his experience. Financial problems soon surfaced making effective military action increasingly difficult. Bad decisions on the part of subsequent emperors resulted in wasting of what money was available. Even reforming emperors like Constantine Monomachos were unable to carry out their programmes for lack of money. Their plans upset established interests at court who had to be bought off, depriving the emperors of the money they needed to effect the reforms. Once the last of the Macedonian house, the empress Theodora, was dead in 1056, and with her the last shreds of legitimacy, the most powerful families at court were at leisure to fight over the empire. The state of the empire declined until Alexios Komnenos took control with a new style of government which depended on a network of support rather than the traditional image of the isolated emperor.

2. M. Angold, *The Byzantine Empire, 1025–1204. A Political History* (2nd ed., London, 1997).

Angold has also drawn attention to the challenge to imperial authority presented by the church in the eleventh century. Normally emperors prevailed over patriarchs, but Michael Keroularios (1043–1058), one of the most strong-willed of Byzantine patriarchs, defeated two emperors. In 1054, the emperor Constantine Monomachos was making overtures to the papacy. Keroularios was suspicious of the direction he was taking and used his popular support among the people of Constantinople to force the emperor to end his support for the papal legates in the city at the time. Monomachos had to comply. Isaac Komnenos also fell foul of Keroularios in 1057. The issue which provoked the breach between emperor and patriarch is not clearly explained by any source but it was probably Isaac's revival of anti-monastic legislation, which Keroularios saw as a challenge to his own authority. Isaac exiled him from the capital on a trumped-up charge but Keroularios died before he could be tried. His death ensured his status as a martyr, from whose grave miracles might be sought. Isaac himself was forced to resign soon afterwards. A sustained claim for the authority of the church over the emperor, which included the right to chastise emperors for their conduct, lessened the absolute status of the emperorship. Keroularios's career demonstrates another development of the eleventh century which was also a challenge to imperial authority: the role of the mob of Constantinople. Keroularios was powerful because he could count on the support of the mob. Subsequent emperors were obliged to pander to the mob's demands. Only Alexios Komnenos managed to reduce its influence to nothing.

Angold's second edition includes a summary of all the work done on the period since his first edition was published. This is extremely useful since it melds the many individual theories into coherent arguments.

Kazhdan and Constable's *People and Power in Byzantium*[3] relates the role of economics and the newly powerful families to explain the instability of the middle years. The provinces were enjoying a period of economic expansion during the eleventh century, which the authors see as connected with the interests of the noble families. There was an alliance between the newly prosperous towns and the families whose land was in those areas. The turbulence resulted from a struggle between the new towns and nobles and the old imperial power for control over trade. Although this theory is valuable because it moves away from the traditional view of decline in

3. A. Kazhdan and G. Constable, *People and Power in Byzantium: An Introduction to Modern Byzantine Studies* (Washington, 1982).

all areas during the century, economics cannot explain everything, such as the increasing presence of Turks all over Anatolia and the lack of direction from the top in Constantinople.

This lack of direction was very clear. This is the traditional view, and although the years between 1025 and 1056 can be reinterpreted to show that the Macedonian empresses Zoe and Theodora provided a vital stability and continuity, after Theodora died in 1056 that imperial link was gone. In the twenty-five years between 1056 and 1081 six emperors reigned, indicating the instability which has given a name to the whole century. During this time, the enemies of the empire invaded large tracts of it, sensing the lack of uniformity at the top which handicapped effective action away from Constantinople. The army and navy were allowed to decay to save money, resulting in the incursions of invaders over areas of the empire crucial for tax collection, making the government poorer than before. Isaac Komnenos attempted military recovery by stiff economic retrenchment. This was unpopular, so after his abdication in 1059 his successor Constantine Doukas concentrated on law and justice in the capital, saving money by running down the army. The Turks began their gradual conquest of Anatolia, causing great dissatisfaction since the size of the empire was a source of pride. When Constantine died in 1067, his empress married a general to turn back the tide of Turks. His failure was due to internal treachery as much as lack of military resources and the Turks completed their occupation of modern-day Turkey, drawn in as allies by both sides in a series of civil wars which lasted until 1081.

Not only the Turks benefited from the need for support felt by successive emperors. In the city itself, promotions were made with increasing frequency, grants of state lands and revenues were given at a greater rate. The government had to debase the coinage to pay its increased wages in a situation where the amount of revenue had decreased due to loss of taxes from conquered lands and loss of revenues from state lands granted to supporters. In 1080 the number of benefits to which people of the street were entitled had grown so much that they did not bother to collect them all. In a situation where the traditional honours and rewards had become meaningless, a new approach was essential. This was provided by Alexios Komnenos in 1081.

From the point of view of the imperial women who inherited the throne or were left as guardians of it during the minority of the emperor, it was a matter of retaining control while legitimising a general to fight invading enemies. As the situation on the frontiers worsened, the importance of military success for imperial ideology increased. Since Byzantine ideology did not permit a woman to lead armies, it was necessary to provide a man with the authority to command Byzantine forces. It was therefore in these years that the role of women as legitimisers of imperial power was most clearly seen. Between 1028 and 1081 six out of ten emperors ruled because they were married to an imperial woman who was recognised as the carrier of imperial majesty. Imperial legitimisation was not the only visible role that women played. Zoe and Theodora ruled as sovereign empresses and the successful coup of 1081 was founded on the alliances arranged by a series of mothers who had political insight and ambition. The eleventh century therefore provides the most fertile ground for examining the political roles that women could play.

The primary source material for the eleventh century is particularly rich, but it is necessary to beware of taking the historians at face value since they were not following the same rule of presenting some kind of objective truth which is in force for twentieth-century historians. The most entertaining and most accessible account is that of Michael Psellos, who lived most of his life at court, held several positions there over the course of his life and was an extremely influential character. His influence affects those of us who read his work, for his claim to personal knowledge is compelling. He gave advice to the empresses Theodora and Eudokia Makrembolitissa, was influential in the development of education under the emperor Constantine Monomachos and reached the pinnacle of his influence when he was created tutor to the young Michael Doukas. Some of his importance may be self-created, but his official posts are not in question. Much of the characters of the empresses Zoe, Theodora and Eudokia are his creation, for he described them in much more detail than any other historian.

Older works have at times taken Psellos's character studies as fact and have interpreted other historical evidence in the light of his pronouncements. This is a doubtful policy because his narrative was coloured at all times by his own prospects of survival in every twist of change. Psellos was an educated man, given an education by the determination of his mother, who encouraged him emotionally and worked hard to provide the material resources for his education. Psellos wrote a moving funeral oration for her and also one for his daughter who died while still an infant. Therefore, he had a connected family life and relationships with women; that with his mother in particular may have been complicated. Through the breadth of his reputation his work influenced other writers of history and traces of Psellos can be detected in the narratives of Nikephoros Bryennios, Anna Komnene, and Niketas Choniates. His shadow looms large over any interpretation of the eleventh century and its actors.

Other authors whose work is invaluable because it is equally contemporary are John Skylitzes and Michael Attaleiates. Skylitzes was a jurist during the reign of Alexios Komnenos. He is very concerned with the legality of some of the events of the eleventh century and this angle tends to be his interest, as Psellos's was his own prospects. His history is much more to the point than Psellos's, which tends to digress into discussions on education and philosophy. Another jurist, Michael Attaleiates, wrote a history which had as its culmination the reign of Nikephoros Botaneiates, who was Attaleiates's hero. He is therefore dismissive of the emperor Michael VII whom Nikephoros usurped and most of his detail is concerned with that reign.

Zoe

The most recent work on the role of Zoe as a powerful woman in her own right and the effect that her imperial lineage had on the unfolding of history in the eleventh century is 'Zoe: the rhythm method of imperial renewal'.[4] This article presents Zoe as the arbiter of events as opposed to the helpmeet of her husbands from a consideration of the visual representations in Skylitzes and Psellos's detailed accounts.

Zoe is one of the most visible of Byzantine women to the modern historian. Indeed, her reputation casts nearly as long a shadow over the study of women in Byzantium as that of her soldier uncle does over the general history of the empire. Immortalised in mosaic in the south gallery of Hagia Sophia, Zoe's history appears in the pages of every account written by eleventh-century historians. She is famous beyond the bounds of Byzantine scholarship for her multiple marriages. These deserve attention because they all represented political choices about the destiny of the empire. However, if Zoe is regarded merely as a legitimiser of emperors, important though

---

4. B. Hill, L. James and D.C. Smythe, 'Zoe: the rhythm method of imperial renewal', in P. Magdalino (ed.), *New Constantines: The Rhythm of Imperial Renewal in Byzantium 4th–13th Centuries* (Aldershot, 1994), pp. 215–29.

that function is, insights into the nature of women's rule will be lost. Zoe's relationship to other powerful women is also of interest, for instance with her own sister and with her sisters-in-law. The personal nature of emperorship is demonstrated in Zoe's life, both in the significance of her personal tastes for the destiny of the empire and in the dread that she inspired in others. Hers was a many faceted character: she was a scientist, immersed in her experiments, but also a generous patron to the church and courtiers. The double edged sword of public opinion was a factor in Zoe's life. The popular mob played a significant role during Zoe's reign and contemporary scholarly judgements, like those of Psellos and Skylitzes, rated her as at once the rightful empress and unsuited for the job. The scholars were responding to an increasing notion that there could be hereditary succession and that Zoe's Macedonian lineage qualified her as the proper successor, an opinion which was voiced more and more fervently as the treatment meted out to her by the men in her life deteriorated. Most of the evidence for the political part that Zoe played comes from Psellos, followed by Skylitzes. It is therefore a major task to attempt to separate what Psellos wrote from what might have actually happened. His own development of opinion is of crucial value for determining how Zoe's role was perceived by the courtiers of the time, for Psellos possessed the gifts of sharp eyes and an eloquent tongue. I shall therefore relate the events of Zoe's life as Psellos and Skylitzes portrayed them, and afterwards analyse what can be said about her role by a modern observer.

Zoe lived her entire life in the palace, maybe as the leading woman of the court since her uncle Basil II had no wife, her own mother was dead, and her elder sister Eudokia had been dedicated to the church after an attack of smallpox disfigured her face. She was educated in accordance with her rank, an education which would not have included lessons on strategy or military technicalities. She was therefore already at a disadvantage in comparison with the men around her who would mostly have military experience if not academic instruction.

The sources say most about Zoe's relationships with men, particularly those she raised to be emperor. In 1028 Zoe was merely the link of legitimation between the end of one reign and the start of the next. Her father, Constantine VIII, did not consider Zoe as a possible sole heir of the empire, although she was a mature woman at the time, not a young girl. It was only twenty-eight years later that a woman could become sole ruler without a spouse, when Theodora came to the throne. The decades of Zoe's visibility and the joint rule of 1042 changed the perceptions of the time to that extent. In 1028 Romanos and Zoe were crowned together, with the depictions of the time showing Romanos as the central character in the imperial garb and Zoe in 'woman's dress'.[5] Her job was to help perpetuate the new dynasty which her husband hoped to found. In his opinion, the house of Macedon was defunct. Both Zoe and Romanos were old for childbearing, and despite the use of the medical practices of the time and recourse to magic, no child was born. Romanos gave up at that point and concentrated on military glory, ignoring Zoe and restricting her access to the treasure chambers. This was tantamount to cutting her off from any powerful role, since the distribution of money or treasure was essential to create support groups. Zoe resented both the diminution of Romanos's attentions towards her and her restricted role. Although Psellos mentions no details, it is clear that Zoe was distrusted by Romanos's advisors, especially his sister Pulcheria, and that her actions were being deliberately curtailed.

Having spent her whole life in the palace, among courtly society, and with a reputation of generosity, Zoe was in a prime position to usurp Romanos had she been given the chance. Her value as the receptacle of power was recognised by others around the court. A prominent eunuch, John, who had been trusted by Basil II, saw an opportunity to advance his own family through Zoe's good graces. He introduced her to his younger brother Michael, with whom Zoe fell in love. Disgruntled by the lack of marital relations with Romanos, she soon entered into a physical relationship with Michael, showering him with all the honours that powerful people normally accorded to their paramours. However, in line with the hopes of the eunuch John, Zoe soon began to talk of higher honours for Michael and even seated him on the throne and dressed him up in imperial regalia. The decline of Romanos from this date on is a matter of conjecture but the chroniclers of the time either state that Zoe was poisoning him or present the story in such a way as to imply it. Romanos lost his appetite, began to waste away and was eventually drowned in his bath either by Michael's friends or on Zoe's orders. He had ruled for six years, from 1028 to 1034.

We cannot of course know what Zoe actually felt. Psellos's interest in the progression of the affair and his detailed narrative of it are part of his own enjoyment of gossip, amply demonstrated in the

<hr/>

5. Hill, James and Smythe, 'Zoe: rhythm method', p. 218.

rest of the book. Skylitzes, who was always much more interested in legal matters surrounding the marriages of the empress, did not give any details but he too was convinced that Zoe had committed adultery with Michael. While it is not necessary to take on board a view of Zoe as the sexually insatiable woman that Psellos implies, a sexual affair seems to be undeniable. It is possible to interpret Zoe's actions as a result of her desire for a return to power rather than for a lover. In her present circumstances, cut off from the treasury, she needed to create an alternative power group for herself. At Zoe's age, her sexual favours were hardly an inducement to a man younger than herself. Her political favours were unquestionably valuable, but a measure of sexual enjoyment must be attributed to Zoe herself, and not read merely as Psellos's restatement of the stereotype of the frustrated, sexually deprived woman. With regard to the poisoning of Romanos, Zoe's interest and expertise in the preparation of perfumes must not be forgotten. No charge was ever brought, for there was nobody in a position to indict Zoe, but the attitude of all the historians was that Romanos had been disposed of by Zoe. Michael's physical attributes may have been the reason he was chosen to be Zoe's lover, but her determination to grasp the reins of government again cannot be doubted. Skylitzes commented that Zoe now imagined that she had a slave and a servant rather than a man and an emperor, and was already filling the palace with the eunuchs loyal to herself that she had inherited from her father.

Her first priority was to ensure that Michael was crowned emperor. Her power is shown by the fact that a hasty marriage was performed and then a coronation. By law, a widow should wait a year before contracting another marriage, if she was eligible to do so at all. Zoe was married to Michael the very night Romanos died, by the patriarch whose reluctance to perform the ceremony was overcome with a bribe of fifty pounds of gold. Once again, this is the witness of Skylitzes, not Psellos, who did not describe the marriage at all. In pictorial representations of this coronation, Zoe is blessed by the patriarch, while only Michael is dressed in imperial insignia, but the couple are joined underneath a veil, signifying their equal status. This shows that the reign was still considered mainly as that of Michael, legitimised by Zoe.[6] Although Zoe disregarded the advice of counsellors around the court in crowning Michael, he was soon accepted in the face of a *fait accompli*, and indeed was judged one of the better of Byzantine emperors by

6. Hill, James and Smythe, 'Zoe: rhythm method', p. 218.

Psellos. Even Skylitzes considered him as pious and benevolent, except for his crime towards Romanos.

Psellos and Skylitzes had different attitudes towards Zoe's conduct, but their narration of the main facts is consistent. Psellos implied crimes by Zoe but was quick to dismiss them as rumours. Skylitzes gave more details, like the bribing of the patriarch, and named Zoe an adulteress without hesitation. Skylitzes had an independent source, probably ecclesiastical, for he included bad omens and visions in his condemnation of Michael IV's reign, but his opinion of Zoe is his own. He was scandalised by her behaviour and called on both parties to the murder and adultery to penalise themselves, since no one else could, by abstaining from any intercourse with each other.[7] His attitude demonstrated the raw power wielded by Zoe. All that any detractor could do was to call for moral repentance and voluntary penance, for the church did not and no other official could impose it. The patriarch could have made punishment of the adulteress a condition of Michael's coronation, as the patriarch Polyeuktos had done with the empress Theophano in the ninth century, but Zoe's lineage made that unlikely.

Michael was involved in military campaigns to stave off foreign attacks, and had some success, but his health was bad and he suffered from epilepsy. Partly because of his embarrassment over his illness and partly because of his conscience he soon began to avoid Zoe. He went further than Romanos in denying her any liberty whatsoever. Her accessibility to ambitious people of the court which had facilitated his own rise to the throne was not to be repeated. She was kept in her own apartments with a guard on the door to prevent any exit or unapproved visitors. Cut off once more from the treasure source which would have won her support, Zoe bided her time, acting modestly and without complaint. However, the attitude of the historians shows that this was considered inappropriate treatment for the real heir to the throne. Psellos was also unable to deny that, in his opinion, Michael had every reason to be afraid of Zoe once he started to avoid her. In the end, Michael's failing health forced John to develop a further plan to keep the family in power, and, by necessity, it involved Zoe as the legitimate empress. The plan was that Zoe should adopt John and Michael's nephew Michael Kalaphates as her son to be like a slave to her and

7. On Skylitzes's opinion on marriages in the eleventh century, see A. Laiou, 'Imperial marriages and their critics in the eleventh century: the case of Skylitzes' *DOP* 46 (1992), pp. 165–76.

Michael's successor. Zoe had little choice since she was cut off from all possible support, but the brothers also made the proposal attractive by emphasising that Zoe would be the real wielder of power and Michael merely her servant to do her bidding. Possibly Zoe considered that she had a real chance of controlling the young man: in any case her position would be an improvement on the present one. According to Skylitzes, she made every attempt to safeguard her own position, interviewing Michael for three days and insisting that he swear obedience to her on the most terrible oaths. On those conditions, she adopted him and proclaimed him emperor of the Romans.

As always, in attempting to judge the order of events, the historian is at the mercy of the contemporary chronicler and what he chose to record. Surely Zoe did not just accept her relegation to unimportance. Psellos praised her for modesty and submission to her husband's actions, which may imply that he approved of her. In this submission, however, was, in Psellos's opinion, a clever gentleness which made each person believe that they had influence over Zoe. Like the most able orators, Zoe adjusted herself to each condition and enemy so that they were disarmed. This talent was a vital survival technique which puts a different face on Zoe's so-called submission. Zoe already knew John and it is likely that he at least was able to visit her. It is difficult to believe that the woman who certainly played an active part in bringing Michael to the throne did nothing to better her own position. Psellos presents her as left with little choice but to accept John's suggestions. But what his account does show is that Zoe was still considered the real conduit of imperial power. It may not be an accurate representation of the facts that John formulated a plan and then introduced it to Zoe, but it is an indication of her status in the opinion of those who would be power-brokers at court. The words that were put into John's mouth show the general opinion of the time: 'the empire belongs to Zoe by inheritance and the whole nation owes greater allegiance to her because she is a woman and heir to the throne.'[8]

Zoe adopted Michael in the usual ceremony and raised him to the high dignity of Caesar, the usual term for the heir to the throne. When Michael IV died in 1041, Michael was crowned as Michael V and for his first months was respectful to both Zoe and his uncle John. Zoe played an important part in the transfer of power. Due

---

8. Psellos, *Chronographia*, trans. E. Sewter, *Fourteen Byzantine Rulers* (Harmondsworth, 1966), p. 100.

to the instability which a lack of hereditary succession created, the city was in an uproar every time an emperor died. Zoe took control once more and quieted the city by a proclamation to keep the peace, probably delivered from the balcony of the Great Palace from which emperors addressed their subjects. The whole situation revolved around her decision, which was for the coronation of Michael. Once crowned emperor, Michael elevated his favourite uncle Constantine to the dignity of *nobeillissimos* and together they plotted to remove John and leave Michael in sole command. The removal of John was only one stage in the plot. Zoe also had to be removed if Michael was to stand alone. In 1042 Michael had her carried off to a monastery in secret, fulfilling his desire to be rid of his 'mother' for whom he had now conceived a violent hatred. The news leaked out in the city and the population promptly rioted in support of Zoe. The emperor and his uncle Constantine fled for their own safety and Zoe and her sister Theodora, who had been living in a monastery since the reign of Romanos Argyros, were both carried into the city in triumph. For a few months they ruled together once the emperor and his accomplice had been blinded. During the accounts of the revolt, all the historians described Zoe as the rightful heir to the throne and as the one carrying the imperial blood in her veins.

The changing attitude of the historians, and particularly Psellos, to Zoe's role raises the most questions about the developments in Byzantine thought during the long dominance of the Macedonian dynasty. The less opinionated Skylitzes commented that the people shouted that they did not want the cross-trampling Kalaphates but the chief offspring and heir, their mother Zoe. Psellos, who as a contemporary spectator of the events had an unparalleled opportunity for expressing the common view, moved from a position of general belief in Zoe's capacity to transmit legitimacy to an outright belief that she was the sole inheritor of empire and that her dignity as the source of imperial majesty should not be compromised. He started with general statements about Zoe's blood qualifying her as the heir of empire; but after the assault on her person by Michael V he not only declared that Michael's treatment of the real ruler was despicable but put a speech into Zoe's mouth in which she harked back to her illustrious uncle, Basil II, and recalled how he had prepared her for imperial rule. Psellos often proclaimed his beliefs in the form of speeches attributed to his characters. In this example, Zoe recalled Basil's training of her for he recognised that she was like himself, and entreated his protection in her present circumstances.

Psellos finished off his grand defence of Zoe's role with the narration of the punishment of the perpetrators; in his judgement they had received divine retribution for their heinous deeds. It can be seen therefore that an attack on Zoe's imperial dignity was sufficient to push these men from a position of ambivalent support for Zoe to a declaration that she was the real ruler of the empire.

This was the high point in Zoe's career. Acclaimed by all as the legitimate empress and heir of the empire, she was able to rule without the backing of an emperor. Together, Theodora and she carried out all the business of government, which included hearing embassies, giving judgements, and making decisions around the court. The rule of the two sisters was seen as fair and equitable by the historians. Both Psellos and Skylitzes agreed that offices were no longer for sale and that injustice was removed from the courts. Psellos opined that the executive power seemed to have gained an added magnificence in those days, an added prestige. Skylitzes as usual had little more to say concerning the fitness of the sisters for sole rule, but Psellos stated that they did not have the aptitude for government and confused the trifles of the women's quarters with weighty matters of state. Both Psellos and Skylitzes stated that it was the opinion of everyone that an emperor should be chosen. According to Skylitzes, Zoe wished to promote an emperor in concert with everyone else, and everyone was agreed that it was Zoe's job; in Psellos's account Zoe seized power again for herself and then turned to the task of choosing a partner. The bridegroom in this case was Constantine Monomachos and with his marriage he took over the reigns of power. In the depictions of this coronation, Zoe is clearly the imperial figure handing over power to the man. Zoe and Theodora were still very much regarded as imperial even if they no longer took the decisions. A sumptuous piece of jewellery presented to the King of Hungary at the time demonstrated this in pictorial form. All three, Zoe, Theodora and Constantine Monomachos, are dressed in imperial robes with crowns on their heads. The historians of the time were happier with a man in charge: their support for the two imperial sisters was based on the growing concern with family inheritance but its ambiguity revealed their instinctive feelings about the proper holder of power.

Psellos is the main witness for Constantine Monomachos and his chapter on this emperor is longer than any other in the *Chrono-graphia*. Psellos played an influential part during Constantine's reign and has first-hand knowledge at his fingertips. Constantine was his favourite emperor but he was determined to present a balanced view of him and did indeed record unfavourable opinions of some his deeds.

Constantine had known Zoe for many years. They had had a good relationship in the years that Romanos was emperor and Michael IV had exiled him because of his friendship with Zoe. He treated Zoe well at first, entertaining her with shows and games, but as she got older he imported his mistress, Maria Skleraina, into the palace and gave her an imperial title and a position in ceremonies directly behind the two empresses. Psellos criticised him for this unseemly behaviour but Zoe herself seemed to accept the situation and graciously signed the paper dividing honours between the three ladies. Constantine apparently solicited advice from both ladies, but was more ready to accept that of his younger consort. Zoe died in 1050 leaving Constantine to rule until his death in 1055.

Zoe's main function during the years 1028 to 1050 was to ensure the peaceful succession of emperors by marrying or adopting the next candidate. She could do this because she was considered the receptacle of imperial majesty and the heir of the empire. As a sovereign empress with the imperial blood she had much more choice over her spouses than other women, no matter what their degree. She was also free to indulge in extramarital affairs to a certain extent, because her power was great enough to freeze criticism. There is not enough evidence to know what part Zoe took in the decision-making of her husbands or what her own policies would have been. But around the court she was feared, wielding a raw brute power which showed itself in some instances and was implied in the strict precautions taken against her by successive husbands. This power was partly external and partly personal. She was the heir to the throne of her father and uncle and therefore was respected. But personally she was a ruthless woman intent on controlling the rhythms of her world, which she proceeded to do regardless of the disadvantages which accrued to her sex in Byzantium.[9] Unable to lead armies in person, she provided a leader in the form of her husbands. Shut up by them she waited until they made a false step and then triumphed. Loved by the people of the city and accorded respect by the courtiers, she had several trump cards which were invincible. Until Zoe herself gave up the game, she was the main player between 1028 and 1050.

9. Hill, James and Smythe, 'Zoe: rhythm method'.

ZOE AND HER SISTERS

Zoe's relationships with other women reveal some of the tensions attached to imperial rule. Most obviously, Zoe and her sister Theodora did not have a smooth or sympathetic relationship. Theodora spent most of her life in a monastery, banished there by either Zoe or her first husband Romanos. Zoe certainly did not protest her sister's banishment. This early antagonism might be explained by Skylitzes's story that Theodora was the first choice for an imperial marriage, but that she had refused on grounds of kinship between Romanos and the two sisters. This reminds us that Byzantium did not operate on a system of primogeniture. Theodora was younger and therefore more likely to have a child, which may have been the reason for choosing her first. Zoe did not forget that power could be taken from her by her sister and therefore was happy to leave her away from the eyes of the world. Monasteries were favourite places of exile for dangerous and powerful people, but they often proved ineffective. In Theodora's case, she was remembered during the riot of the people against Michael V and carried in triumph to Hagia Sophia, where she was crowned. Once the two sisters were reconciled in some fashion and ruling together, and the situation had been brought under control, Zoe did not hesitate to demote Theodora once more. Her fear of her sister is more easily understood when one remembers that Theodora had been carried in triumph into Hagia Sophia and crowned by public support. It was Theodora who ordered the blinding of Michael V and his uncle Constantine the *nobellissimos*. Theodora had a support group who believed that she should be sole empress because she had been on the side of the people without any ambiguity. Once again, Theodora had been chosen for imperial power and Zoe felt threatened.

Skylitzes related several stories about Zoe's activities which demonstrate her power and her relationship with Theodora. Skylitzes stated that it was Zoe who exiled Theodora to the monastery of Petrion, swooping down on her unexpectedly and having her tonsured before anyone could interfere. The ostensible reason was the number of plots which revolved round Theodora. For instance, Zoe was told by Theophanos of Thessalonike that Constantine Diogenes was plotting with her sister to escape to Illyricum with the knowledge of some bishops. The emperor was in Mesanakta planning his invasion into Syria but Zoe had Constantine examined in the palace of Blachernae by John, who later became the Orphanotrophos, resulting in Constantine's death by being hurled from the walls. The bishops were sent to the emperor, who set them free. Zoe's actions seem more decisive than those of Romanos, perhaps indicating the survival skills that Zoe possessed.

Zoe's relationships with the women who became her sisters by marriage is described in less detail, but it is obvious from the snippets which appear that Zoe was feared by them. Romanos's sister Pulcheria advised him to beware of Zoe. There was obviously no solidarity among women as a sex at the court at this time. The realities of power were divisive and Zoe tended to stand alone. During the months leading up to the promotion of Michael IV, when Pulcheria begged her brother to take care and see what was happening in front of him, there was a factional war with Zoe on one side and Romanos's supporters on the other. Ultimately Zoe was the victor, for Pulcheria died along with another friend. One more friend was banished from the palace at the 'express wish of the emperor'. The rest of the faction held their tongues, no doubt cowed by the two deaths. There is no accusation in the sources that Zoe engineered these deaths, but the banishment must have been at her instigation. Having neutralised all opposition, Zoe continued her affair with Michael openly.

Yet when Zoe was older, she accepted the imposition of Skleraina to the imperial dignity although she had every reason to resent it. Constantine's chamber was between that of Zoe and Skleraina, comprising a *ménage à trois* which it is hard to believe Zoe would have accepted in her younger years. The explanation of the historians that Zoe's age was the reason is a plausible one. She was in her seventies at that time.

ZOE AS EMPEROR

Although there is little evidence to suggest what policies Zoe might have followed had she ruled alone, a profile of Zoe as an emperor can be drawn. The most obvious area to examine first is the power she wielded in order to achieve her agenda. Zoe intended to be married; the need for a general could be one reason, her own personal tastes another. The main point is that she was in a position to carry out that desire whether her reasons were political or personal. Her power was irresistible. The curtailment of her activities by the men she enthroned may seem to overshadow her authority, but they are really a confirmation of it. Zoe was too dangerous to be allowed to form alternative groups. The emperor's legitimacy was routed through her and she could bring her protégés down if their treatment of her was perceived as inappropriate for the heir of the Macedonians. An adult male had resources that Zoe could not counter openly, like physical force and a career on the battlefield, and what her story proves over and over again is the real power of an emperor once crowned. However, her strategy of mild acceptance while she waited for the inevitable enabled her to survive a court full of intrigue with a history of murdering emperors through several changes in government.

One man who seems to have had a long association with Zoe through these years was John the eunuch. Chosen by her to carry out the examination of the traitor Diogenes, he was later promoted to the post of Orphanotrophos. He introduced his younger brother to her and later his nephew, both men who achieved power through Zoe. Skylitzes states that Zoe was poisoning Romanos in order to raise the elder Michael to the throne, and that after his death, John and Zoe in concert bribed the patriarch and the clergy to perform the wedding ceremony. John was powerful until his nephew became emperor. Psellos, who perhaps wished to paint the younger Michael in very black colours, stated that Michael exiled John from the court, but Skylitzes, in a position to know as much and with no axe to grind, stated that it was Zoe who exiled him before Michael had succeeded to the throne. The reason is not far to seek given Skylitzes's account of Zoe's imprisonment at John's orders. Having seen what had happened to Romanos, John had no intention of allowing Zoe to set Michael aside when she saw someone more attractive, so he instituted the strict controls over her access to the treasury and to the court. Zoe was part of a plot to poison him, but it was discovered. In the event of her adoption of Michael and her renewed movement about the court, Zoe banished both John and another brother, Constantine. Both of them warned Michael to beware of her; or in Skylitzes's words, Michael had been corrupted by them. Michael tried to banish Zoe, leading to the riot and his own blinding. In Skylitzes's account of the times, Zoe was an active participant in court intrigues, managing to carry out her own desires despite opposition. In every change of emperor, it was Zoe who had either orchestrated it or contributed the essential component: legitimacy.

Zoe lived the life of an emperor in other ways. Where emperors spent their time in devising and leading military campaigns or developing the system of justice, Zoe followed her own interests by experimenting with perfumes and potions in her quarters. Psellos tended to despise this activity, complaining that the rooms were suffocating in summer, but a modern scholar, accustomed to hearing important experiments denigrated when they are performed by women, can perhaps admire Zoe for her interest and expertise in what we would now call science.

Other areas in which emperors traditionally demonstrated their power and their resources were philanthropy and patronage. Unfortunately, no official decrees survive documentating Zoe's patronage, and the most famous representation of her, the mosaic in Hagia Sophia, cannot supply the identity of its donor. Modern analyses of this panel have tended to start from the emperor depicted, but as Hill, James and Smythe point out in 'Zoe: the rhythm method', the emperor whose head is there now is not the one who commissioned the panel, since all the heads have been changed. It is more likely Zoe's panel, especially as the depiction of Christ is a form which Psellos revealed was particularly favoured by Zoe. Psellos provided the general information that Zoe was famous for her generosity to people around the court, a reputation which greatly increased the esteem in which she was held. When her successive husbands and son prevented her from accessing the treasure chambers they were cutting her off from that traditional role in a deliberate attempt to curtail her power. The importance of patronage in an absolute regime should not be underestimated, and will be explored later in Chapter 6. The support of a more powerful person was crucial to success in life. Yet Zoe for all her generosity seemed to distribute money rather than positions at court or titles. The random and careless granting of titles was one of the most damning accusations brought against the emperors of the eleventh century as they sought for support. Zoe did not participate in that cheapening of the court hierarchy upon which the respect of the court was built. In this, she perhaps understood the underpinnings of her society more clearly than the men she raised to rule. Furthermore, she was beyond the need of that kind of support, bolstered by her lineage.

The rights of that lineage were developed by the historians of the time. Both Psellos and Skylitzes stated that Zoe was the heir of the empire by right through her blood. Their support for her legitimacy was absolute. If it reflected a general feeling in the court of the time it was a great weapon for Zoe to use. Her power was strongest when the court and the mob were on her side, such as during Michael's failed attempt to set her aside. But even the support of the voices of the time did not mean that Zoe could rule alone. Both Psellos and Skylitzes were more comfortable with a male emperor, and not just for military reasons, although that must have been a paramount concern. It is obvious from Psellos's account in particular that the notion of a female absolute ruler went against his deepest instincts.[10] The contradiction between his belief that Zoe had the right to rule because of her ancestry and his inherent conviction that the controller of the empire should be a master rather than a mistress showed itself in his judgement on Zoe and Theodora's period of sole rule. After praising the fairness of the rule instituted by the sisters, he then opined that they confused the trifles of the women's quarters with weighty affairs of state and did not have the temperament to rule. In his opinion, the people felt that it was not right that two women should be at the head of the empire. Such ambiguity in the support for imperial women in power handicapped full-scale authority and was no doubt an accurate sample of the opinions of most of the men of the court. Zoe's treatment by the men she attached to herself had to degenerate a long way before anyone would protest. Even a woman bolstered by a great lineage and a growing commitment to legitimate succession could not be secure as an absolute ruler in a society which was accustomed to a man as supreme leader. This notwithstanding, Zoe and Theodora had ruled jointly without a male partner briefly, and Theodora would do so again.

Theodora

Zoe's younger sister Theodora ruled alone for nearly a year between 1055, the death of Constantine Monomachos, and her own death in 1056. Although she was a sovereign empress, very little has been preserved about her regime. Psellos, as usual, records the most about her, but even his account does not give the detail which would allow the modern reader to draw a full picture of what a woman as absolute ruler would be like. Theodora was affected by Zoe's actions for so much of her life that her portrait has to be drawn from snippets let fall in accounts of earlier times. For example, she refused the marriage with Romanos Argyros which would presumably have placed her on the throne in 1028 on grounds of consanguinity. Incidently this is the only reference in the historians' accounts to the swelling controversy over marriage rules which would

10. See B. Hill, 'Imperial women and the ideology of womanhood in the eleventh and twelfth centuries', in L. James (ed.), *Women, Men and Eunuchs: Gender In Byzantium* (London, 1997), pp. 76–99.

create such a problem for the power-hungry families of the later eleventh century. Her reasons for doing so are only a matter of conjecture: whether a sincere distaste for what she considered wrong or merely a distaste for the man in question. She had some contact at some time with Psellos, for he mentioned briefly that he had given her advice. She was obviously considered an important figure round the court for rebellions and plots grew up around her which forced Zoe into preventative action.

Having been suspected of many things during Zoe's reign and banished to a monastery where she would be out of the way of possible conspirators, Theodora finally came into her own. She had been kept in seclusion for so long that it was doubtful whether Zoe's husband Michael and his nephew even knew that she existed. During the riot against Michael V, some of the mob remembered her and marched to her place of exile, persuading her to assume the royal robes, and then carried her in triumph to Hagia Sophia, where she was proclaimed empress. It was Theodora who gave the order that Michael and his uncle and supporter, Constantine, should be dragged out of the church into which they had fled for refuge and blinded. During the period of sole rule, both Zoe and Theodora received ambassadors and gave orders, exercising all the functions of a male emperor. Demoted once again by Zoe, Theodora lived privately except for public ceremonies until Constantine Mono-machos's death.

When her turn came, Theodora proved that she had learnt something from her sister's career and resolutely refused to marry. In many ways, she was analogous to Elizabeth I of England in a later age, forced to survive during an older sister's reign and ready to use her political value as a marriage token to her own advantage. Psellos had to admit that he could see why she did not marry but he expressed the opinion that the rest of the court was surprised. As soon as she was securely in power, Theodora hunted down all those who had opposed her rule, confiscated all their possessions and banished them. She sent out eunuchs into the provinces to fight any there who had opposed her, returning to a certain extent to the policies of her uncle Basil II. In other ways, Theodora returned to his style, appointing eunuchs to all the prominent positions in the government. Since eunuchs were barred from imperial rule by their physical imperfection both Basil and Theodora found them safe servants. Theodora kept all decisions in her own hands during her rule, her chief advisor being a eunuch called Leo, whose statecraft was favourably judged by everyone except Psellos, who was jealous of him. Another way in which Theodora returned to Basil's policies was in her refusal to spend money. When she came to the throne in 1055 she dispensed with the usual gifts of money to the army and courtiers, using the argument that this accession was not her first one but merely a continuance. Psellos obviously considered this bad policy; he would probably have been one of the beneficiaries. This tendency towards a miserly rule displeased the court in general, accustomed by this time to the generosity of Zoe and her successive husbands, and might have caused a problem for Theodora had she reigned for longer.

The paucity of documents preserved from Theodora's reign tell their own story about her short regime. Only three survive, all relating to the monastery of Chios on the island of Cos. This monastery seems to be the only one in which Theodora took an interest or to which she displayed the virtue of philanthropy. These acts granted land and permission to extend the buildings of this monastery. It is interesting that Chios was equally a favourite of Constantine Monomachos. Theodora was never as generous as Zoe in her pious *philanthropia*. Careful with money from a lifetime of restricted access to it, Theodora was no more eager to spread it to the church than to the courtiers.

In common with her father Constantine, Theodora would not appoint a successor until she was on her death bed. Given the tendency that existed in Byzantium to follow a man legitimised by an imperial woman, it was for her own protection that she resolutely refused to name one. An old civil servant was eventually chosen to be the next emperor, but he was obviously a stopgap until a stronger, younger man could succeed.

Although so little evidence remains about Theodora's reign, the snippets that Psellos let fall do show a woman determined to rule in her own way, even if that meant disregarding some of the time-honoured customs of the court.

The double standard of public opinion was still in operation for Theodora. Psellos, for example, although admiring Theodora for her abilities in understanding politics and expressing herself clearly, thought that the situation called for an energetic man. No doubt he thought he himself would have been the obvious advisor for Theodora since she had in earlier times asked his advice about dealing with her private affairs. In the event Theodora chose Leo to help her. Psellos again expresses his contradictory opinions about the fairness of Theodora's government and the inherent feeling of the people that a man should be at the helm. Certainly military affairs would have necessitated some kind of arrangement if Theodora had not died. The use of eunuchs was one solution but the army preferred a complete man as its leader. Theodora, like Zoe, was judged in two contradictory ways by the historians because she was filling two roles, normally mutually exclusive. As a woman, her expected role was as a helper, perhaps even the carrier of majesty, to a man. She was not expected to be an absolute ruler, but she was also the last heir of a dynasty in a time when inheritance was becoming more entrenched in the perceptions of the time. Therein lay the ambivalence which makes the role of powerful women so hard to grasp and analyse. The growth of family feeling which fed the acceptance of inheritance as a concept not only allowed two women to rule as sovereigns but changed the face of the empire, leading to several decades of factional strife and a successful dynasty which was the first to view itself consciously in that way.

Family government in the eleventh century

All scholars agree that one of the most significant developments of the eleventh century was the rise of families who regarded themselves as entities.[11] This trend can be seen during the reigns of the Macedonian princesses, but its origins date to the ninth century. Although the contribution of family politics to the instability of the eleventh century is a matter of dispute, their existence is not in doubt, nor the growth of a family sentiment which is redolent in Psellos's narrative and in that of Choniates. As with so much else in Byzantine culture, the increasing importance attached to the family is connected to changing religious attitudes. From the fourth to the ninth centuries, the most holy or virtuous state was virginity for both men and women. Men devoted themselves to the church, the monasteries, or the desert, becoming ascetics and sometimes gathering a group around them. Women became nuns, renouncing the world with determination in the face of parental opposition, disguising themselves as men or fleeing to the desert where they too sometimes collected a following and achieved a reputation for sanctity. Sexual contact was considered a pollution for both men and women. Emperors reigned alone, trusting their servants and rarely dignifying family members with imperial positions apart from the hope that a son might succeed to the throne. A change in ideology

11. A. Kazhdan and A. Epstein, *Change in Byzantine Culture in the Eleventh and Twelfth Centuries* (Los Angeles, 1985), pp. 74–117.

can be seen in which the avoidance of sex and marriage was no longer necessary and the family with fertile mothers became the most admired and virtuous state. Once the family had an honoured place in religious ideology it was free to develop. However, not only emperors began to emphasise dynastic links; other families too grew in self-confidence. The development of surnames, used regularly, was a symptom of this burgeoning self-identity. The increasing solidarity of kin groups led to a rise in factional strife; the results were clear by the eleventh century.

Until the reign of Basil II the imperial power had not dealt with this phenomenon with aggression, probably slow to recognise its potential. Basil himself had great experience of the damage these families could inflict, for not only had the empire passed to Nikephoras Phocas and then John Tzimiskes during his own minority, creating difficulties for his eventual succession in 976, but the Skleros family revolted against him in 979 and both the Phocas and Skleros families in 987. Basil put these rebellions down with the utmost savagery and proceeded to break the power of the families using the vast legal means at his disposal. One such measure was the ruling on legal marriages promulgated in 997 by the patriarch Sisinnios which introduced new impediments to marriage between the in-laws created by marriage itself. In the course of a careful argument demonstrating how marriage alliances tied into the attainment and exercise of political and social power Laiou linked this controversial and contested document with Basil's determination to prevent a consolidation of power in any hands but his own.[12] After his death the families regained their prominence, leading revolts against the husbands of Zoe. One such revolt was that of Skleros, related to the mistress of Constantine Monomachos. In fact, most of the emperors who reigned in the eleventh century were linked by marriage to the Macedonian dynasty and to each other, demonstrating the strength of the network created by marriage alliance. It is therefore unsurprising that Basil's successors continued the trend of trust in family. Zoe's marriage to Michael and her subsequent adoption of his nephew under the guidance of John the Orphanotrophos is only one example. The role of Romanos Argyros's sister Pulcheria as one of his advisors demonstrates the trust placed in family members of either sex, presaging the increased role for women in such a milieu.

12. A. Laiou, *Mariage, amour et parenté à Byzance aux XIe – XIIIe siècles* (Paris, 1992), p. 25.

The Byzantines had several methods at their disposal for creating family. Actual physical marriage was only one of them, albeit a very important one. Another popular means was *spiritual kinship, the creation of godparents, a tie which carried the same obligations as physical kinship. An even more popular method was adoption. This was not an innovation: it had been widespread for centuries. But it was used with increasing frequency over the eleventh and twelfth centuries, indicating the rising importance attached to the creation of a tie which carried mutual obligations and loyalty with it. Zoe's adoption of Michael V is one example from the early part of the period. Romanos IV Diogenes adopted the powerful Nikephoros Bryennios as his brother and Nikephoros Botaneiates offered adoption as his son to Bryennios during his reign. Botaneiates also tried to adopt Alexios Komnenos to safeguard himself after the revolt of 1081, but Alexios was already the adopted son of Botaneiates's wife, Maria of Alania. Once emperor, Alexios adopted large numbers of noble crusader leaders in an attempt to ensure their loyalty and the return of any former Byzantine possessions they might capture from the Turks during their passage through his territory.

Marriage alliances necessarily increased in significance and number over the period, signalling a change in culture which was completed by the successful Komnenoi to transform the empire. The empire which survived into the fifteenth century was not the empire ruled by the Macedonians, although the roots of the change were present in their time. The use of family names merely highlighted the underlying importance of family and by extension, marriage alliances. Where alliances between families are important, women have a role as partners, although their power of choice over spouses and their significance once married differs from society to society. For most of the eleventh century women of the imperial family were able to enjoy freedom of speech over marriages and often to arrange them because they were seen as acting in the family's interests. This ideology conferred real power and promoted visibility of women in the historical sources since the politics of the eleventh century revolved around the acquisition of imperial power by building support groups.

The concept of building up support groups by marriage alliances has been called the 'dynastic principle' by Michael Angold.[13] In the political situation of the eleventh century, a support group was vital. At the same time, women appear in the sources as mothers and

13. Angold, *Byzantine Empire*, p. 128.

wives, creating alliances and reacting to their husbands' decisions about family matters. When Isaac Komnenos (1057–1059) reached the point of forced resignation because of his clash with Michael Keroularios, discussed earlier, his solution was to enter the monastic life. His wife, Catherine, begged him not to abdicate, recalling to his mind the fate which would befall her and their daughter if they were unprotected in the world. This speech, which is put into the mouth of Catherine by Psellos, may never have been spoken at all, but it is an example of the feelings, and behaviour, that a contemporary courtier felt were appropriate to an imperial woman. Catherine was not disposed to take her demotion with any submission, but failing to move Isaac from his decision to become a monk, she commanded him to nominate a man who would be like a son to her. Psellos may have been more of a leading light in this decision than he cared to admit, but once again, it was considered appropriate behaviour for a wife to advise on political affairs of paramount importance. Catherine's fears reveal another side to Byzantine society. The possibility that she and their daughter might be treated roughly after the withdrawal of protection by her husband does not reflect well on the treatment of women. But it must be remembered that Catherine was a Hungarian and therefore removed from her network of relatives, who would have protected her. The current preoccupation with family may have yielded more advantages for women than for men, given the need for protection which is a constant of most societies even today.

The speech Psellos gave to Catherine was reused for Anna Dalassene in the account of Nikephoros Bryennios. Anna would be one of the most powerful women ever to control the Byzantine empire after the coup of 1081, but in 1059 she was the wife of John Komnenos, and the sister-in-law of Isaac. According to Bryennios, Isaac offered John the throne and he refused it. Anna then made the speech about her fears for herself and their children if the imperial throne went to another who would mistreat them. Bryennios, married to Anna's granddaughter, was writing the history after 1100; some literary borrowing is therefore likely. The ambition of Anna Dalassene is not in question. A proud member of a family prominent since the beginning of the century, her very successful groundwork ensured her son's succession to the throne in 1081. Dalassene was the family name of Anna's mother, not her father, reflecting both which blood line Anna preferred to call her own and the fluidity of the family naming system, where the children were at leisure to choose whichever they pleased. The prominence of the family is shown by the fact that one of the family had been the first candidate chosen to marry Zoe by Constantine VIII in 1028, but was finally passed over because he was already married.

Constantine Doukas was the man who finally inherited the throne from Isaac Komnenos. The Doukas family was the equal of the Komnenos family in brilliance, wealth and background. They either traced or invented a lineage for themselves which went back to the ninth century. Constantine's first wife was a Dalassene, but on her death he had married the niece of the patriarch Michael Keroularios, Eudokia Makrembolitissa. This may have been the main reason for the choice of Constantine as successor and it also gave him an advantage in establishing control, since the treatment meted out to Keroularios by Isaac was one of the factors in the latter's resignation. This transfer of power from the Komnenos family to the Doukai may have been the reason for Anna Dalassene's hatred of the latter, which manifested itself later in a series of pitched battles with John Doukas, the brother of Constantine. Constantine died after eight years in power, leaving Eudokia as regent for their young son Michael Doukas.

Eudokia Makrembolitissa

Eudokia Makrembolitissa is one of the most intriguing women of this period. Seemingly so successful as regent and mother, the question is why she married Romanos Diogenes, an action which alienated most of those who might have supported her. After Romanos was defeated in battle, Eudokia's position was far from secure and she was exiled to a monastery in an attempt to curtail her political activities. That this solution failed is demonstrated by the fact that even Alexios Komnenos treated her in a manner befitting an empress after his accession in 1081 and provided for her daughter by marrying her to his own younger brother Adrian. What made Eudokia still worthy of cultivation in 1081, when in 1067 she had been rushed off in disgrace by her husband's brother?

Eudokia was an educated and intelligent woman who understood her times. Psellos had a spiritual relationship with her father and he knew her well and admired her so long as she followed his advice. He was also tutor to the young Michael Doukas, the oldest son of Constantine and Eudokia. He described Eudokia as moderate, not extravagant, punctilious in learning her duties, and authoritative. He was not surprised at this for he judged her a very clever woman.

Skylitzes judged Eudokia as most competent in administering public affairs and as most moderate (high praise) and accustomed to dealing with men and raising children. Constantine followed tradition in creating her regent for their sons on his death, but aware, like any person of the eleventh century, of how majesty was embodied in the empress, he tried to safeguard his children's inheritance by making her promise that she would not marry again. The members of the court had also been made to swear that they would accept no one else as emperor except Michael, who had been crowned co-emperor before his father's death. Constantine's brother, the Caesar John, was on hand to advise Eudokia when needed and to fight her battles. Constantine had left a legacy of military problems, being more concerned during his reign with legal administration than military action. By 1067 the Turks had plundered Armenia and Iberia, and the Uzes had crossed the Danube and ravaged as far south as Greece.

Eudokia was left with a situation that she could not resolve in person. She could not lead armies on the battlefield, and Byzantium needed to show some strength to prevent a collapse. Since appointing generals to fight battles on her behalf was dangerous because of the immense potential value of military victory, Eudokia had to provide a general she could either trust or control. One possible solution was to marry someone. Therefore, Eudokia's first task was to release herself from the oath she had sworn to Constantine in front of the patriarch, John Xiphilinos. Xiphilinos was an educated and unworldly man but he had a weak spot in his love for his nephew. By implying that if she were free she would wed this nephew, Eudokia secured her freedom. Once free, she had the choice of two generals, Nikephoros Botaneiates and Romanos Diogenes. Botaneiates was in Antioch, while Diogenes was in Constantinople on trial for treason, but Eudokia saved him. She succeeded in marrying him, keeping the deed secret from her sons until it was done, moving quietly at night, presenting the city with a *fait accompli.*

The contemporary historians are divided on her motives for choosing Diogenes. Psellos's opinion was that no woman had ever set such an example of wisdom or lived a life comparable to hers up to that point. After that he defended her by insisting that she retained her moderation, not giving way to pleasure, and that her wise tower was shaken by many worries, one of them being the need to protect her sons. Others concentrated on the need for a good general to rescue the empire, but all of them implied or stated, even if only by defending her against accusations, that Eudokia fell in love with his handsome looks and disregarded the good of the empire. It should be remembered that second marriages were considered wrong if there were already children of the first marriage because of the possibility of creating more heirs to share the property. In this case, all the informants were jurists, in an excellent position to know and honour the law, and the property in question was the empire. Their views could have been unfavourable on these grounds alone. It is reasonable to interpret Eudokia's actions as an attempt to protect the empire for her sons and provide the more aggressive military strategy that the empire needed. Nearly all of the historians state that Eudokia thought that, having rescued Romanos from punishment, she could control him after raising him to be emperor. A piece of contemporary evidence which confirms this suggestion is a coin minted after Romanos's accession. On this coin, Eudokia and Romanos are presented as equals, but Eudokia is designated by the title *basilissa*, while Romanos is only *despotes. The title of *basilissa* had been used most recently in coinage by the joint sovereigns Zoe and Theodora and before that by the most powerful regent and sole ruler Eirene the Athenian. Eudokia's intentions are clear: she was to be regarded as the senior ruler and Romanos as her helper. Coinage by its function as a means of exchange in the empire was the most widespread of all possible propaganda and by its official nature as set by the government was to be considered as imperial policy.

Her plans went awry, however. Pregnant almost immediately, she was forced into the background as Romanos gained confidence in himself. He refused to listen to her and even insulted her. His behaviour was criticised by Psellos as rash and arrogant, one of the worst character assessments a Byzantine could make. He also suspected the Caesar John, but was unable to find a good reason for exiling him. His suspicions were proved correct at the battle of Mantzikert in 1071, one of the worst military disasters in Byzantine history. The son of the Caesar prevented his troops from fighting, depriving Romanos of a huge section of the army. After the first skirmish ended with the Byzantine army retreating, Andronikos provoked a rout. Romanos was captured by the sultan. Although he concluded a truce and was making his way back to the capital, the Caesar John took the initiative and deposed him *in absentia*. The Senate was divided on whether Eudokia and Michael should rule jointly, but the Caesar managed to ensure the accession of Michael alone. Eudokia was in league with Romanos, because despite his treatment of her she was still in a stronger position with him as emperor than with her brother-in-law ruling as Michael's advisor.

John threatened her with violence and, losing her nerve, she fled from the palace to exile at the monastery of Petrion.

Michael then ruled until he was deposed in 1078 by the general Nikephoros Botaneiates. Although Eudokia was in exile, she remained an influence on politics, particularly in the succession of Nikephoros Botaneiates. He had been one of her choices for marriage, and he remained keen to marry her once he had become emperor. Marriage negotiations were carried on by letter between Botaneiates and Eudokia, either for her own hand in marriage or that of her daughter Zoe. Eudokia nearly succeeded in returning to power as a consort for the third time. However, the legal difficulties of a third marriage, even more thorny than those for a second marriage, made it impossible for her, particularly once she had been reminded of them by a very pious monk, who persuaded her not to accept the offer. Although Botaneiates failed to marry Eudokia, and she remained in the monastery, he nevertheless showered money and gifts on her and treated her like an empress. The historian Michael Attaleiates, who was an admirer of Botaneiates, commended him for his kind treatment of her, contrasting it favourably with the treatment meted out to Eudokia by her real son, Michael VII Doukas.

Eudokia was at least an acquaintance, if not a friend, of Anna Dalassene. The short reign of Michael Doukas saw the disgrace of the Doukas family and its loss of imperial power for ever. All its enemies leagued together to undermine the family's hold on power and Eudokia was one of those enemies. Anna Dalassene was another, since she resented the ascendancy of the family over that of Komnenos. Eudokia and Anna worked together in 1071 to restore Romanos Diogenes to power against the schemes of John Doukas. Eudokia was already in exile and Anna was tried for treason and sentenced to loss of property, which was merely an acquittal of sorts. None of her property was ever actually seized because Michael Doukas fell under the influence of a eunuch called Nikephoritzes. He engineered the disgrace of the Caesar John Doukas and promoted the Komnenoi to prominent military positions. Nikephoritzes did not survive his master's fall, but the alliance between Eudokia and Anna Dalassene seems to have continued, for when Alexios Komnenos came to the throne, he was careful to load wealth and honours on Eudokia and to marry her daughter inside his own family. Despite her exile, Eudokia and her daughter had the legitimacy that any usurper would need to stake a successful claim for the empire. Under those circumstances Eudokia remained a force to be reckoned with while she lived, since her association with Romanos

Diogenes and Nikephoros Botaneiates from her monastery had made it only too clear that that place of exile was more like a retreat than a seclusion. Eudokia's political value and her evident willingness to use it necessitated gaining her support long after her own particular spell as empress was ended.

Eudokia's justification for holding power was different from that of Zoe and Theodora and exemplifies another strand of Byzantine ideology. Zoe and Theodora were imperial in their own right, because of their lineage. They were perceived by the populace as the natural heirs of an empire that their ancestors had ruled. Zoe passed the necessary legitimacy on to the men she married so that they could be emperor. Theodora chose not to marry at all and to hold the reins of government herself. Despite some unease about this decision, the people were prepared to accept it, because of her blood line. Eudokia was not imperial in herself. She gained her majesty through coronation, when the crown was put on her head by the emperor. Her legitimacy came from him. Once she was a mother of their children and he was dead, the majestic imperial line was vested in her because her sons were under age for sole rule. In Byzantine thought, she could legitimise a different man to be emperor if she chose. The rights of the sons were then passed over, although in similiar situations they had always managed to assert themselves eventually. This was the case for Michael Doukas too. Eudokia was a mother, acting with the ideological justification of the need to protect her sons. The triumphal culmination of this ideology for women in power will be seen in the career of Anna Dalassene from 1081.[14]

The rise of the Komnenoi

The growing interest in family which this chapter has already noted cannot be overemphasised, nor its importance overstated. The difference that it made to the political structure of the empire when that ideology triumphed will be explored in Chapter 4. Here it is essential to show its beginnings through the actions of the two most prominent actors of the years 1067 to 1081, John Doukas and Anna Dalassene.

The Caesar John Doukas exemplifies the eleventh-century interest in family. He was very concerned to safeguard the throne for his

14. Hill, 'Imperial women', pp. 82–91.

nephews, not hesitating to interfere at court if he thought their interests were at risk. Faced with the marriage of Eudokia to Diogenes he retired from court, but was quick to return when Diogenes fell victim to the schemes of John's son Andronikos at Mantzikert. He managed to sway the Senate from Eudokia's side by a mixture of military force and verbal persuasion. Once Michael was installed as emperor, John stayed at his side and married him off to a Georgian princess. After he lost favour with Michael he again retired, but emerged on Michael's abdication in 1078 to engineer the marriage of the usurper Botaneiates to Michael's wife, Maria. His intention was no doubt to see that Michael's son Constantine would succeed to his father's throne. Because Michael was still alive, although retired as a monk, there were some legal problems over the marriage of Maria to Botaneiates. John showed his determination when the priest who had been engaged to perform the ceremony baulked. He produced another priest who carried his plan through. When it appeared inevitable, later in 1078, that the Komnenoi were going to triumph, John at least consented to the marriage of his granddaughter Eirene Doukaina to Alexios Komnenos, although it was his daughter-in-law Maria who suggested the alliance in the first place. This marriage healed the rift between the two most powerful families at court, guaranteeing success for the combination.

It was in arranging advantageous marriage alliances that Anna Dalassene excelled; these will be examined further in Chapter 6. The actions of Anna Dalassene and John Doukas show where the interest in family was leading. They were both primarily concerned about their families, determined to advance them as far as possible. The wedding of Alexios and Eirene welded together the two families into an unbeatable force. Two examples will demonstrate the perceived value of marriage alliances for advancement: Constantine Doukas, the son of Eudokia Makrembolitissa, attempted to persuade Alexios Komnenos to marry his sister Zoe, rather than his cousin, Eirene, and another mother, Anna the *kouropalatissa* of the Bryennios family, suggested a marriage alliance between her family and that of their political rival in the city of Adrianople to heal a schism which was threatening the success of a rebellion against the emperor Michael Doukas. The emperor Nikephoros Botaneiates recognised the nature of family ties. When he arrested the womenfolk of the Komnenos family in 1081, he arrested them all, not only Anna Dalassene but her daughters and daughters-in-law. Alexios's mother-in-law, the *protovestiaria* Maria, was also summoned and imprisoned with them: Botaneiates realised how far out the links of kin went. He himself had tried to avoid kin ties in his own marriage so that he could operate alone. The Caesar John was able to manipulate him into marrying his candidate, Maria of Alania, by reminding him that she had no kin to trouble him. In fact, that was not strictly true, for Maria had a cousin or a niece from Alania who had been married to Isaac Komnenos in 1072, as part of a reconciliation package put together by Michael Doukas after the trial of Anna Dalassene on the orders of the Caesar John Doukas. However, the Caesar's argument demonstrates that the burgeoning influence of a kin group was beginning to be recognised.

Marriage alliances were one strand in the success of the Komnenoi. They could not have succeeded ultimately in the world of the eleventh century without a measure of military talent. The problems encountered by Zoe and Eudokia Makrembolitissa had already made manifest the importance of military victory. The Komnenoi were fortunate in that there was a large family of young men who could hold the important military posts and commands.

In 1070 the young Manuel Komnenos was appointed *protostrator*, a military post, by Romanos Diogenes and sent out in command of the armies in Anatolia, modern-day Turkey. He died just before the decisive battle of Mantzikert. His brothers were too young to fight so the family once again took a back seat until Isaac Komnenos was appointed in 1073 as commander against the Turks. This sudden prominence must owe something to the eunuch Nikephoritzes, who had captured the emperor's attention by this date. Isaac was not successful against the Turks, but despite that he was then made governor of Antioch. Once again Isaac did not succeed in keeping Antioch safe and was captured in battle by the Turks. He was ransomed and returned to Constantinople in 1078. Bryennios records that Isaac, understanding the simple nature of the emperor Michael Doukas and his liking for Syrian fabrics, made him a gift of diverse sorts from Antioch. This pleased Michael so much that he promoted Isaac to the title of *sebastos* and gave him a permanent apartment in the palace from whence Isaac was able to enthral him. The title and residence are much more likely to have come to Isaac from Nikephoritzes, who had chosen the Komnenoi as his natural ally against John Doukas.

Alexios Komnenos had a much more successful military career. Sent against the turncoat Balliol, who had deserted his brother Isaac's army and escaped to assert control over part of Anatolia, he captured him and brought him back alive to Constantinople. Michael Doukas promoted him *stratopedarchos* and *strategos*-in-chief to fight the rebel Roussel who had defeated the Caesar John and his son Andronikos in battle. Alexios succeeded in capturing Roussel and brought him back to Constantinople. In 1077 he put down another rebellion by Nikephoros Bryennios in the Balkans and subdued an uprising by the governor of Dyrrakhion, Basilikes. When Nikephoros Botaneiates came to the throne in 1078, Alexios was promoted to commander-in-chief of the armies of the west. Early in 1078 Alexios was married to Eirene Doukaina, the granddaughter of the Caesar John Doukas, in a union which united the two most powerful families at court. Alexios's star was on the rise.

The coup of 1081

The coup of 1081 carries the stamp of Anna Dalassene all over it. In the years immediately preceding it, during its execution and immediately after it, Anna Dalassene is very much in evidence. The following chapters will demonstrate repeatedly that Anna Dalassene was the most powerful and visible woman of her day in areas such as titulature, power brokerage, and patronage through her fulfilment of the maternal ideal which will be examined in the next chapter. The successful revolt which resulted in the accession of Alexios Komnenos and a hundred years of Komnenian dynastic rule was the reward of Anna's political competence and appetite for risk.

Since 1059, when Anna's hopes of the imperial title were dashed, she had concentrated on building up an alliance of families by marriage. Fortunate in having eight children to use as marriage counters, Anna excelled in picking out the most prominent families whose star was rising. Until 1067, when Constantine Doukas died, Anna was not mentioned in the sources, but after Eudokia Makrembolitissa married Romanos Diogenes the Komnenoi became a major part of the bigger picture: two of Anna's children were married to members of Diogenes's family. When Romanos was deposed in 1071, Anna was tried on charges of corresponding with him, in league with the ex-empress Eudokia. This treatment may explain some of her hostility to the Caesar John Doukas who was behind the charges. Anna demonstrated her daring during that trial. As she stood before her judges, she suddenly drew from under her robe an icon of Christ, proclaiming that he was the judge and that those who judged on earth should not make him indignant by their verdicts. Made nervous by this action some of the judges wanted to acquit Anna, but the knowledge that the emperor had an opinion on her guilt resulted in a sentence of exile for the family. Anna probably was guilty as charged: she hated the Caesar John and she was linked by marriage to Romanos Diogenes.

Michael VII Doukas fell under the influence of a eunuch called Nikephoritzes, an attachment which resulted in the retirement of the Caesar to his estates. Michael recalled Anna and her family, and Isaac was married to a cousin of Michael's wife. By the end of Nikephoritzes's regime, the Komnenoi were so powerful that the new emperor Botaneiates promoted them rather than trying to destroy them. He was probably influenced by Eudokia, who was an ally of Anna Dalassene, and Anna made a marriage alliance very quickly between one of her granddaughters and Botaneiates's nephew. At the same time, she built a relationship with the empress Maria of Alania through the latter's adoption of Alexios as her son, thereby having a foot in each camp. When Botaneiates planned to groom a relative of his own as his successor instead of Maria's son Constantine, Maria's anxiety was noticed by the two brothers. Alexios and Isaac visited Maria, gaining admittance to the empress after Anna had given them a suitable pretext. This interesting titbit of information is given by Anna Komnene, but she did not enlarge on the process: it can be said that Anna Dalassene still obviously had influence at court. A little more information would have answered crucial questions about the relationship between Maria and Anna. The alliance of Alexios and Isaac with Maria was of crucial importance, for it allowed them to hear of the envy of the servants of Botaneiates in time to plan a response. Alexios and Isaac were warned by a relative of Maria of Alania that Botaneiates's advisors, Borilis and Germanos, were plotting to capture them and blind them. Alexios, as commander of the western armies, was able to concentrate a force near the city. In concert with Anna, the men of the family planned to capture the city and force Botaneiates to abdicate. The men left the city to gather their support together and the womanfolk went to Hagia Sophia for safety.

When the emperor heard of the actions of Alexios and Isaac, he sent one of his men to the great church to arrest the women. Again, Anna Dalassene showed her flair for dramatic gestures. Protesting her advanced age and that she had come to worship, she demanded to be allowed to approach the altar. On her third genuflection before it, she threw herself on the floor and gripped the altar, refusing to let go until the emperor sent a large cross as a token of his good faith. When the envoy showed her a small cross he himself wore as a token, she refused to accept it and seeing that only trouble could come from tearing a woman away from the altar by force, the envoy left to procure the cross. Under those conditions, Anna agreed to leave the church. The whole family was guarded, but their goods were not seized nor were they under arrest.

Alexios and Isaac meanwhile had secured the support of the Caesar John and George Palaiologos, the commander of the fleet. While they marched into the city from the land side, Palaiologos brought the fleet to the city walls so that the city was surrounded. Botaneiates abdicated, after attempting to strike a deal with Alexios whereby he would adopt him. At this point, by the witness of Anna Komnene, the two men wished to go immediately to their mother without securing the palace. The Caesar John, who had joined the revolt, persuaded them against this course until the city had been made safe. Their desire to take counsel with Anna reveals the extent of their dependence on her wisdom. After the capture of the city, Alexios and Anna took up residence in the Great Palace with Maria of Alania, while Alexios's wife, Eirene Doukaina, was sent to live in another of the palaces arousing suspicions among the Doukai that Alexios was attempting to throw off the Doukas connection and marry his predecessor's wife, his own adopted mother, Maria of Alania. Understanding the aftermath of the coup depends so much upon marriage alliances that it can best be discussed in Chapter 5 in the light of what marriage meant to the Komnenoi as a method.

Anna Dalassene was a model Komnenian mother: much of her justification for exercising power was as a fulfilment of this ideal role. From the sources of the time, it is possible to demonstrate the virtues and activities of the ideal Komnenian imperial woman. An exploration of this ideal woman perhaps aids understanding of the real women encountered in the historical sources.

CHAPTER THREE

Creating the ideal Komnenian woman

Introduction: deconstructing ideology

If we move from the external world of activities to the internal world of beliefs, are women any more visible as women? The discovery of the facts of people's material condition provides the bare bones of historical analysis: clothing them requires an understanding of ideology, the system of beliefs and practices by which people make sense of the world in which they live. Ideology is particularly import- ant when studying women because all societies have ideas about how men and women should behave in relation to each other. It is pre- scriptive rather than descriptive, concerned with what people should be and do rather than what they are. It is impossible to give a full treatment of women's power in Byzantium without scrutinizing the assumptions people held about women and what they should be. It is in relation to issues such as ideology that the analytic tag 'patriarchal' could be employed. However, the problems regarding the use of patriarchy as a historical analytic tool have already been discussed. Instead, the enquiry in this chapter examines how much power the dominant Byzantine ideology allowed women to exercise and in what spheres.

Ideology has four characteristics which are pertinent for this book. The first is that ideology is a human creation which does not arrive complete in society from some ultimate being or deep in the unconscious mind. It can therefore be deconstructed. It never stands alone, but is affected by political and economic factors, although their effect is slow to be seen. Ideology by its function of reassuring by familiarity necessarily changes reluctantly, but it does change. The second characteristic is that although ideology is a social entity, it presents itself as natural and universal. The world only has one true meaning, and it cannot mean anything else. A corollary of this tendency is that women are understood as having the same 'natural' qualities everywhere. The same is of course true of men, but their options are wider inside each individual society so it does not matter so much. A third characteristic is that there are different ideologies existing in the same culture at the same time because everyone's fabric is a little different owing to differences in the social processes which go into bringing up children, and the differing conditions under which people live. One of these ideologies may be dominant, 'muting' the rest, because of the power of its practitioners. It is an obvious task to search for an ideology of women which has been muted by the dominant male ideology, and this will be addressed in Chapter 8. The last characteristic is the most difficult and concerns the relation between ideology and reality. Ideology is never a mirror reflection of reality, nor is it ever a mirrored distortion of it. The relationship between the two is always complicated, and usually impossible to plot accurately for historical societies where the essential evidence is often unavailable. When the enquiry deals with women, it becomes more tenuous still. It is clear from reading anthropological accounts that women's status is notoriously hard to describe because women in many societies are often non-people who derive their status from their menfolk. When ideology and material conditions are very different, which is the real indicator of women's status? Aspects of ideology which seem to be restrictive to women may be enabling, and apparent freedom may in fact be restrictive. Ideologies which seem to condemn women's power may coexist with a reality in which women have power, and *vice versa.*

A related question is whether ideology confers or denies power in and of itself. Does being understood as a moral symbol, for example, give women power? Feminists are divided on this issue. Some feel that it does not; they are often accused of being materialistic and ethnocentric. Others believe that the realisation of the ideal can provide women with a measure of power over their lives, even when the material conditions of power are lacking, partly because they symbolise and are recreating the ideology and therefore have control over it. They contend that politics and economics are conventional sources of power but that feminists must include control over the individual psyche and ideology in their analyses. The fulfilment of the cultural ideals may bolster women's sense of worth: this has to be taken into consideration seriously and not dismissed as collusion with the oppressor.

Ideology is of particular significance in feminist historiography because gender is constructed through the workings of ideology, by means of dictating roles. There are roles for different jobs, like politician or doctor, into which the holder is expected to slide, but none of these are taught with the concentration that goes into gender role teaching, and a failure to comply rarely produces the criticism that a failure to 'be a man' or to 'know women's place' does. De Beauvoir's *The Second Sex* explored the concept that 'one is not born, but rather becomes a woman . . . it is civilisation as a whole that produces this creature'.[1] In other words, the raw material of a little girl is taught how she is to behave and what she is to expect from life. Since ideology insists on its universality and naturalness, women are not recognised as slotting into a culturally constructed role, but are seen as acting naturally according to their abilities. Feminists in the disciplines of anthropology, sociology and history study diverse social constructions of femaleness and maleness, thereby revealing the social processes involved, allowing the meaning of 'woman' in a specific culture to be deconstructed. Not only gender can be treated in this way: Barrett has worked out the influence of social processes for sexual preference.[2] To understand the social construction which is 'woman' a researcher must explore the web of meanings and assumptions which make her up.

Ideology is relevant in a study of Byzantine imperial women because ideology is a source of social power. The influence of, or better, the control of, the meanings people relate to their lives is obviously a source of power. Feminists hold that the dominant ideology of society is constructed by men, in line with male values. Women are muted, and their values are not those which are important to society at large. Ideologies grant high status on account of so-called inherent qualities or because the relevant role is considered crucial to society and the status confers power. In so far as women are included in the dominant ideology, it is a taming device. Ideologies absorb powerful images that they cannot eliminate or that threaten them. One example of this is the common image of women either as modest wife or whore. One is under the control of her husband, the other is an outcast, shunned by society. It is a no-win situation. Women's power is as difficult to gauge as women's status, because women rarely face an even restriction on their power. Men are usually allowed to have power in all spheres of human life,

1. S. de Beauvoir, *The Second Sex* (London, 1953), p. 301.
2. M. Barrett, *Women's Oppression Today: Problems in Marxist Feminist Analysis* (London, 1980), pp. 42–83.

but women may be allowed power in one sphere and not in another. For example, some Greek women are acceptably powerful in the domestic sphere, but have no part in public politics. Often women's profile is high in the family, but they have no economic status at all. Such highs and lows make it difficult to determine women's power in a wider sense, since the relative importance of each of the spheres to the society must first be calculated. But the determination of the spheres in which women are or are not allowed to take part produces a less confusing result than a method which does not explicitly deal with ideology, since it presents a clear picture of the whole. This whole can then be characterised. The question for this book is whether the whole was oppressive to women or not.

Ideology and the Komnenoi

A consideration of the ideal imperial woman will reveal inside which spheres women were allowed to exercise power. The ideal imperial woman, unlike the ideal imperial man, is not a creature who exists in a formula. No Byzantine source gives detailed, and timeless, instructions on virtues and accomplishments to be praised in a speech to an imperial woman. An imperial oration, a *basilikos logos*, one of the set pieces of Byzantine ceremony and rhetoric, was an oration to the emperor, not applicable to an empress. Yet a historically specific Komnenian imperial woman can certainly be constructed from the speeches and orations composed for or about Maria of Alania, Anna Dalassene, Eirene Doukaina, Anna Komnene, Eirene of Hungary and Bertha-Eirene. There is no obvious role model for the empress to follow, in contrast to the emperor who, in political terms, can be a second Constantine and is, of course, in religious terms, the representative of Christ on earth, as developed by Eusebius. Women are not any more to the forefront in ideological terms than they are in political terms. A weak model is Constantine's mother, Helena, but comparisons are not common. Comparisons to the Virgin Mary, which would seem to be an obvious parallel, are equally rare.

Byzantine idealisation of the emperor has a long history, at least from Menander Rhetor in the third century AD, whose advice for a *basilikos logos* set out all the areas of an emperor's life from birth which should be praised. He highlighted four qualities which the emperor should display: courage, righteousness, moderation/prudence, and good sense. Menander remained influential since he was recognised as the authority on *epideictic*, or set orations, in Byzantium. The basic elements for praise of emperors were divine favour and divine worship, and concern for subjects, shown morally in the administration of justice and economically in the protection and generous provision of property. Menander advised that the empress, if she was 'of great worth and honour', could be praised within the section on the emperor's temperance. Her character is not developed, for the suggested praise actually applies to the emperor, who made her empress and 'does not so much as know that they (the rest of womanhood) exist.'[3] Menander's brief inclusion of the empress is the sum total of the advice given about her, but it can easily be seen that any scheme comprised of such qualities as military prowess or administration of justice will show strain if it is applied to the empress, as these are fields from which she was excluded. The implicit ideology, constructed from the evidence which has survived, allows the gentler virtues to be applied to her: qualities such as generosity, piety, modesty, humility, mercy and the ultimate virtue, self-control. Physical beauty, both of face and of limbs, is also a constant.

Since the ideology of imperial women is to be found in the surviving sources it is necessary to survey them. Some sources are more useful than others in revealing ideology. Duby makes the salient point that documents can only shed direct light on the ideologies corresponding to the ruling class, who alone possessed the skills to record what they believed and who were important enough for their documents to be preserved. The historian becomes a code-breaker, 'identifying, linking and interpreting a mass of un-related signs'.[4] The sources which are most useful are those which are intended to compliment the recipient, or call to the minds of others their good qualities, especially if these are for reading aloud in a court. Examples of such sources are *encomia*, wedding songs, epitaphs, and funeral orations. They are engaged in propagating 'the ethical system upon which [their] own sense of righteousness is based'[5] and are performed in a public place. There are extant examples of all these types of speeches, but a sophisticated treatment is necessary. As well as taking into account all the rules which dictated content, it is crucial to consider the intended audience. It

3. *Menander Rhetor*, ed. with tr. D.A. Russell and N.G. Wilson (Oxford, 1981), p. 91.
4. G. Duby, 'Ideologies in social history', in J. le Goff and P. Nora (eds), *Constructing the Past: Essays in Historical Methodology* (Cambridge, 1985), pp. 151–65, p. 156.
5. Duby, 'Ideologies', p. 157.

is startlingly clear, from even a brief glance at orations, that speeches to empresses performed in the presence of the emperor, no matter to whom they are addressed, provide much more information about the emperor than about the dedicatee. On the other hand, speeches performed without a restraining male imperial presence are free to concentrate on the person to whom they were addressed. So, the funeral oration for Bertha-Eirene, Manuel Komnenos's first wife, performed in Manuel's presence, tells us little about Bertha, but much about Manuel. Where she is mentioned it is often to stress how alike their tastes were or how much in harmony they were. In contrast, the funeral oration for Anna Komnene, the daughter of Alexios and Eirene Doukaina, performed in front of friends and lacking the presence of the emperor, is concerned almost exclusively with the woman herself, apart from long sections on her parents. These describe her parents briefly and then at length how like they were to Anna, and how she had inherited their good qualities. Since we are interested in the ideal there is no need to look for 'truth' or to ask what the ladies so described were 'really' like. But there is more chance that the qualities prized by women themselves will be found in those texts performed in front of audiences which did not include an emperor.

Visual sources may be of even more use, for depending on their placing they could reach a wider section of the population than speeches performed in court and, due to their nature, they had to be less subtle than a long speech which could make its point in a sophisticated manner. The best surviving examples are the imperial panels in the south gallery of Hagia Sophia. No doubt there were more of them proclaiming their imperial ideology, in the imperial palace and in the palace of Blachernae, but these have been lost to us.

Histories are sources which must be used with great care. Unlike contemporary speeches they were usually written long after the events when the personal opinion of the author could be allowed full rein. Often the author was trying to discredit the subject; always he had his own preferences and prejudices. All can be used with care, but the evidence gleaned from them is not as straightforward as that from clearly laudatory works. The tell-tale signs of embedded ideology are off-the-cuff remarks, personal opinions expressed by the author, or constants of praise or criticism.

To discover the spheres in which women were allocated power, it is necessary to identify the ideal woman, who is a construction of the dominant ideology. There is, of course, more than one ideal woman, or rather, there are a number of roles which are made up of different qualities. These differing women appear depending on the text which is consulted. A woman can be a mother, a wife, a sister, a daughter and, in this context, an imperial consort, and each role requires a slight change of emphasis.

Mother

The ideal Byzantine imperial mother can be glimpsed through the orations of Theophylact of Ochrid to Constantine Doukas and his mother, Maria of Alania, and to Alexios Komnenos and his mother, Anna Dalassene, and through Prodromos's consolation for Eirene Doukaina on the death of her son, Andronikos, and Prodromos's birthday song for the son of the *sebastokratorissa* Eirene.

The role of mother was the most powerful ideological role for women in Byzantium from the mid-eleventh century to the end of the empire. During the middle centuries of Byzantium the denial of sexuality through perpetual virginity, by transvestitism if necessary in the case of nuns, was the route to power by choice. In the family empire of Komnenoi, the production of children for the purpose of perpetuating the dynasty was the paramount duty of women and therefore the area from which they could potentially derive most power. The law, both reflecting and encoding the ideology, considered the mother the most proper person to have guardianship of a minor after the death of the father. The widow was considered as the head of the family which entailed certain responsibilities not excused to women on the grounds of their sex. All property was under their management to be kept for their children, they had to provide education, and arrange for marriages and dowries. The children, by law, could not take away the rights of their mother and they owed her respect.[6]

In this context, it is interesting to note that Zoe was hailed as the mother of her people during the revolt against Michael V, although the intense family atmosphere was only at its beginning, not at its pinnacle. Eudokia Makrembolitissa fulfilled the role of regent for her sons, justified by this ideology. The ideal life pattern for the twelfth-century man was set out by Prodromos in a birthday speech for the son of the *sebastokratorissa* Eirene. The boy will first of all

6. G. Buckler, 'Women in Byzantine law around 1100AD', *B* 11 (1936), pp. 391–416.

excel at games, then at hunting, then in battle, a worthy wife will be found for him, he will father children, reach an old age and serve his mother until the end of his life. The importance of the mother could hardly be more clearly emphasised. In comparison, his wife is a nonentity, who must wait for her turn to come, when her sons will treat her with such reverence. Anthropologists working in modern Greek villages have encountered such a system. Consequently, there is one moral duty above all which falls to the mother, and that is care of her children to prepare them for life, whatever this involves. Depending on the status of the family, taking care of children may raise a mother to high positions in the public sphere.

There are important differences between the two orations for Maria and Anna and the other two sources. Both Maria and Anna were imperial widows, and therefore the sole parent of the emperor addressed. They had a more visible and important position than the two mothers addressed in the birthday song and consolation because they were the legal guardians of their offspring. This is important despite the differing ages of the two emperors addressed, and it partly accounts for the large amount of space devoted to Maria and Anna, in varying amounts of detail, depending on Theophylact's purpose. Eirene Doukaina and Eirene the *sebastokratorissa* are only mentioned briefly. This is also partly a function of the purpose of birthday speeches and consolations, whose rules require attention to other matters. Despite these differences in emphasis, a picture can be built up of the ideal of motherhood.

The first virtue associated with mothers is fecundity. Theophylact proclaimed that motherhood is pleasing to God and the salvation of mothers in his speech to Maria, and brought his praise of Anna Dalassene to a climax in her fertile maternity. Anna was of course more successful than Maria, bearing eight children to Maria's one. Theophylact could truly quote Psalm 112 referring to the mother gladdened by children and call her 'blessed'. Tornikes, a twelfth-century rhetor who wrote a funeral oration for Anna Komnene, stressed that children are more important for a wife than a husband, for they strengthen the indissoluble link between man and wife and restore the attachment to its former level. This production of a family, which will extend to grandchildren and great grandchildren, was how Anna surpassed and eclipsed the achievements of other women.

Not only the production of a family, but its good and wise rule is the duty of a mother. Maria was reminded that a mother must guard her children's temperance, and Anna was praised because she was the root which united all the different branches of her family and from which they drew their succour. Preparing children to meet the world meant providing proper tutors to stretch and develop their minds, and training them in temperance. Anna Dalassene instituted a moderate and prudent atmosphere in the imperial palaces, and her family was a living example of how life should be lived and an inducement to virtue to those who surrounded them. Even the birthday speech for Eirene's son, despite its brevity, expected that Eirene would prepare her son to be a soldier. Bryennios provided the information that Anna Dalassene catered for the later education of her younger sons. Another similiar duty which is not mentioned in the speech is the provision of religious guidance. Anna Dalassene fulfilled her duty in this area also: she appointed a spiritual father for Alexios to accompany him on his campaign against Roussel. The duty of providing tutors required knowledge on the part of the mother concerning suitable people for the job, who were the intelligentsia of the empire, and demanded that she be able to establish contact with them. The role of care for children was one in which women could act on their own initiative, and be praised for it. Innovation can take place inside an accepted role, as long as the innovative behaviour is not perceived as inappropriate for the role. This fact is demonstrated by the behaviour of the eighth-century empress Eirene the Athenian, who was mother of and regent for Constantine VI. Exploiting the powerful position of mother to an underage emperor, legitimised by the dominant ideology as a proper role for women, she managed to retain full power after her son reached his majority. But her actions generated unease, although her reputation as a mother to the church overshadowed her role of child-blinder to later generations. Her period of sole rule was relatively short.[7]

Anna Dalassene was probably the ultimate mother of Byzantium, in the right place at the right time to take advantage of the high ideological value of motherhood. As the legal head of the family, she had influenced the lives of her sons for many years: it was natural that they should continue to seek her help when they reached a high position whence it was too easy to fall. She was the one in whom her sons confided, she shared and shaped their plans. On the ascendance of Alexios to the throne, the pattern continued, entailing a large area of delegated responsibility for Anna; in fact the whole civil administration. Anna Komnene described her grandmother's

---

7. S. Runciman, 'The empress Irene the Athenian', in D. Baker (ed.), *Medieval Women* (Oxford, 1978), pp. 101–18.

role in full, and her narrative is backed up by the contemporary speech of Theophylact, who ended his praise of Anna Dalassene by describing the peaceful and loving division of empire between the mother and her son. That the praise was for a mother's role and not for a woman on her own is clear from the conflating of Alexios and Anna: when Alexios was absent, he was still there, for his mother safeguarded his government. The power was hers, entrusted to her completely by him, but its source was the emperor, and it was to be kept for him. Alexios had been adopted by the empress Maria of Alania, affording him legitimacy when he usurped the throne from Nikephoros Botaneiates. Anna Dalassene did not have any part to play in giving him legitimacy, so her authority came from him, for once crowned and anointed he was Christ's representative on earth. Unlike other imperial women, who are compared with regularity to the moon, Anna was equal with Alexios: they were new luminaries created by God as the second and new creation. Anna's role as head of the civil administration was obviously a summit to which few other mothers could attain, for it was a combination of historical and ideological factors which put her there.

The theory of the 'great man' or, in this case, the 'great woman' is not fashionable, nor is it sophisticated enough as a tool of historical analysis, but in this case it must be noted that when the time was right and the ideology was right, Anna Dalassene had the personality to manage the civil government in a hands-on manner. Her personal ability was perhaps the reason Alexios chose her, and we must beware of elevating one historical incident into a blueprint for action. But the limits to which the ideology of the mother could be stretched were illustrated here, and Anna knew it. She too was breaking new ground in her role as mother, but her actions were perceived as appropriate because she never attempted to set her son aside. In this she protected herself from the fate of Eirene the Athenian in the eighth century or that of Eudokia Makrembolitissa. That she was under no illusions as to the basis of her power is proved by the great care she took continually to project herself as a mother throughout her time in power. It is not necessary to suppose that such justification of her role was in any way cynical or even self-conscious. Firstly, ambition need not be individualistic. In Byzantium, as in modern Greece, the goal of an ambitious mother was advancement for her family. Anna Dalassene was an ambitious woman: the *Alexiad* makes that quite clear. But her ambition was not for herself in a personal way. The character of the woman becomes easier to untangle when it is accepted that ambition is not always personal. Otherwise, either Anna is understood as a strong woman who betrayed herself because she was a victim of patriarchal ideology, or the definition of ambition becomes confused. Secondly, conformity to rules is as much a strategy as repudiation of them, but the choice between these two strategies need not be conscious. The ideology certainly dictated that a mother scheme for her family; how much actual power did the fulfilment of the ideal allow to women in that position? The answer, in the case of Anna Dalassene, is the greatest possible amount of power for which she could ever have hoped. If the question is posed in terms of status, it could be judged that Anna Dalassene derived high status from her fulfilment of the maternal ideal.

As one would expect in Byzantium, the good mother inclined her life towards God, which involved spending much time in prayer on behalf of her children. Theophylact said that prayer and breathing were one and the same to Maria of Alania, while Anna Dalassene spent all night in prayer and tears, which guaranteed victory for her children. It was she who crowned Alexios with the laurels of his victories over the Scyths. Pious intervention with heaven was not restricted to the family alone, but the specific role of mother did not demand detailed attention to other people.

Piety could also include care for the monasteries, the serious practice of asceticism, and a denial of worldly calculation. It is therefore unsurprising that *philanthropia* for those in want was another virtue that an imperial mother could display. The particular form these virtues took was close to mothering functions: feeding the hungry, clothing the naked, comforting children, parents and widows for the loss of their loved ones. Some of these solutions required the outlay of money, with which of course the mother was no longer supposed to concern herself. The imperial mother could also display mercy by pleading for those condemned to death. *Philanthropia* and mercy were virtues in common with other imperial women and will be discussed in that connection. There was an ideal reaction to grief for the mother, which was to be steadfast and stout-hearted in the face of the legitimate sorrow of losing any of her children. Nobility of family was sometimes mentioned, but it was not itself integral to the role of mother. Maria of Alania and the *sebastokratorissa* Eirene were both credited with noble birth. Maria's was enlarged upon: Eirene's was merely mentioned. Anna Dalassene's family was not mentioned, but, since we know that it was noble, Theophylact must not have considered that her nobility was to the point in the picture of the mother he wished to present.

It should be noted that the role of mother was unique in that it did not include being beautiful. All other imperial women were described as possessing beauty, but this did not apply to either Maria of Alania nor Anna Dalassene. We know from other sources that Maria of Alania was beautiful, so obviously beauty was not one of the qualities that were indispensable in the make-up of the mother. Orators and poets praised the beauty of mothers who were also wives, like Eirene the *sebastokratorissa*, but in the two orations where the women concerned were mothers first and foremost, physical beauty was not necessary.

Wife

The ideal Byzantine imperial wife was also the ideal consort. Two epitaphs for the successive empresses Eirene Piroska (Eirene of Hungary) and Bertha-Eirene, by Prodromos and Basil of Ochrid respectively, highlight the virtues which the emperor wished his wife to be remembered as possessing. Prodromos's epitaph for Eirene Piroska was short and included the qualities of noble birth and family, fertility, and embracing the monastic life, with its connotations of humility and lack of pride and vanity. Eirene was mentioned again by Prodromos in his epitaph for her husband, John II. Once again, the wife was praised for her noble birth and powerful family, being described as the mistress of all the west. Again her achievements as a fertile child-bearer were praised, with the number of sons and daughters specified. Some of these elements were seen in Psellos's character sketch of Zoe in which her piety and her *philanthropia* were mentioned. Psellos also approved of Zoe's submissive attitude towards her husbands when they restricted her access to the court. Her lineage was a matter of great comment, being even more important since it was the source of the emperors' legitimacy.

Basil of Ochrid's oration for Bertha-Eirene is very long in comparison, but it suffers from being performed in front of an emperor and does not give the same amount of information about Bertha that is contained in the shorter epitaph for Eirene Piroska. In general, more space is given to descriptions of the grief of the emperor and the people than the life of Bertha. There is little about Bertha's noble birth, almost nothing about fertility, which is unsurprising given that in fourteen years of marriage she produced only two daughters, only one of whom survived her fourth birthday. Bertha's failure as a child-bearer was blamed by Choniates on the patriarch Kosmas who cursed her womb when he was wrongfully deposed. Instead, the virtue of being part of a family is stressed; how good it is to make one out of two, a husband and wife, or three, with the addition of children.

Bertha's ideal qualities were commitment to good works, relieving the distresses of widows, orphans, those who had not been given in marriage, those who had no money to provide dowries for their children although they were well-born, and those who were under the threat of death – all virtues which the ideal mother could also display. Kinnamos praised Bertha for her *philanthropia*, praising her because she surpassed other women in attending to the needy. Basil stressed her humility, her lack of vanity and arrogance, and made the comparisons with nature which seem to embody his ideal wife and consort. She was likened to a variety of trees. One was the cypress, well-grown and straight; there was also the cedar with its lofty foliage, and the fruitful and blooming olive. Another was the oriental plane, which with its width and height relieved weary travellers. Basil's grief was comparable to that of people who, having been sheltered by these trees, see them pulled out by the roots. Her beneficence opened all doors, her beneficent hands rendered relief and relaxation to the faint-hearted under 'the burning heat of the necessities of life'.[8] The people Bertha helped were not only of the court. Basil made it a matter of praise that she met ordinary people and visited outlying regions during armistices with Manuel. In particular, she seems to have been interested in the eastern regions of the empire, for after her death the 'Persian generals', the Muslims, came to lay presents on her tomb in recognition of the services she had rendered them. Basil did not clarify these services, and did not mention Bertha's role of mediator between her husband and her relative Conrad of Germany. A letter which survives from Conrad to Bertha-Eirene reveals that the foreign marriage had worked: political influence was not one of the virtues expected of the ideal wife, although one might have expected that a peace-bringing and unifying role would have been suitable material for praise.

Accompanying her husband in times of peace was praiseworthy in an imperial wife, but going with him on campaign was a different matter. Basil did not allude to Bertha accompanying Manuel to war

---

8. Basil of Ochrid, 'Tou gegonotos Thessalonikês kyr Basileiou tou Akridênou logos epitaphios epi tê ex Alamonon despoine', ed. W. Regel, *Fontes Rerum Byzantinarum* (Leipzig, 1982), pp. 313–14.

in the west, although the court writer John Tzetzes tells us that she did: in the course of a letter to a friend at Dristra he remarked that the rays of the empress had been cut off from him by her absence on the expedition, and lamented that she was acting against the nature of 'soft and tender empresses' probably at the prompting of some devil.[9] Tzetzes' hostile attitude to empresses accompanying their husbands on campaign was also demonstrated in the eleventh century when Eirene Doukaina travelled with Alexios. Anna Komnene related that scurrilous writings were thrown in the door of the tent of the imperial couple warning Eirene to go home.

One other virtue was expected of the ideal wife: she should be hopelessly and helplessly in love with her husband, at least in the twelfth century. This was an emotion only allowable inside the marital relationship. Until the end of the empire the destructive and un-controllable lust of women was still criticised when it was focused on any man except a legitimate husband. The twelfth-century history by Choniates is full of denunciations of women who could not control their passions and who committed adultery. But when the legalities were observed, the Byzantines were favourable to the display of emotion. Basil made much of the one-mindedness and harmony which prevailed between Bertha and Manuel. Prodromos's epitaph for Theodora from the Caucasus, the daughter-in-law of Anna Komnene, included a moving picture of love between a man and his wife. Theodora was ill, she was dying, but she made no complaint. Her only wish was to live long enough to see her husband, her breath of life, who was absent on campaign. His absence tortured her, undermining her intelligence. Then John appeared, Theodora embraced him tenderly, she wept, he groaned and wept, filling the hollows of her neck with tears, he caressed her face and stroked her gold hair, he was fainting from grief. This illustrates in detail the Byzantines' conception of the faithfulness of marital love, an ideal which was increasing in popularity during the eleventh and twelfth centuries.[10]

Prodromos's monody for the *sebastokratorissa* Eirene on the death of her husband portrayed the next stage, the grieving wife who no longer wishes to live. This monody painted a different picture from the monody for the grieving mother. There, Eirene Doukaina was praised for her steadfastness, but in this case there is no virtue in

9. J. Shepard, 'Tzetzes' letters to Leo at Distra', *BF* 6 (1979), pp. 191–239.
10. A. Laiou, *Mariage, amour et parenté à Byzance aux XIe–XIIIe siècles* (Paris, 1992), chs. 2 and 3.

suppressing grief. A wife was supposed to feel her life was over, and that the greatest tragedy of her existence had happened. Anna Komnene portrayed her mother fulfilling that role at the end of the *Alexiad*, when Alexios died. Here Prodromos showed the same emotions on the part of Eirene. There was no point in her living without him. She was distracted by grief, lamenting, crying. She thirsted for her husband, and her only hope was to die soon so that she might join him. Niketas Choniates seems to have had the same view; he revealed his opinions on good wives in several asides. He described approvingly the conduct of Alexios Axouch's wife, who threatened to kill herself not at his death, but just at his incarceration. She pleaded with Manuel to free him, but, on being refused, spent all her money on caring for her children, became deranged, and finally 'withered'. Also Andronikos's daughter Eirene 'as was fitting' loved her husband, and when her father banished him, she wept, dressed herself in rags and cut off her hair.

The ideal wife and consort was well-born, fruitful, in love with her husband, compassionate to those in need, and full of *philanthropia*, which was translated into practical good works. In this sphere the imperial wife had an outgoing role, where she was expected to speak to people and be concerned about their needs. She could interfere with the wheels of justice to a certain extent: compassion on the part of the empress could rescue criminals from capital punishment. Basil of Ochrid does not give any specific examples of Bertha-Eirene's successful interventions, but Anna Komnene records such an incident in the *Alexiad*, when her mother Eirene, by pleading with Alexios, rescued Michael Anemas at the last minute. No doubt such pleas were only granted when it suited the emperor, but in the ideal role compassion which led to a disregard for justice was a virtue in a wife and consort. The power which this conveyed is easily missed because the reports of such behaviour are subsumed under praise of philanthropy. But meddling with the wheels of justice is neither a trivial thing nor something which happens in a vacuum. Byzantine mothers and wives were legitimately allowed to do so, and their intervention was often successful, but such interference was a totally unacknowledged sphere of public power. No doubt the ideological acceptance of such meddling with justice connects with the Byzantine legal belief that women were unable by nature to distinguish between right and wrong, and therefore were not liable to condemnation except for the major crimes of murder and adultery. But this belief does not invalidate the power women exercised.

Anthropologists have noted that women are often accused of trivial or deviant behaviour which on a closer look turns out to be a political strategy. Historians are familiar with the 'power behind the throne' scenario, which is always characterised as unpredictable, informal, idiosyncratic behaviour on the part of 'strong' women. Dubisch makes the point that such behaviour should be regarded as an institutionalised, expected, predictable pattern, even if the ideology does not acknowledge or define it, because it is far from an unusual phenomenon.[11] The Byzantines did not define judicial intervention as a role for women, nor acknowledge the power it conferred, but the woman who could exercise this function became both a focus for those wishing to reverse the course of justice, and a figure endowed with power in the eyes of those who became suppliants. The Byzantine attitude to the political influence of wives is the same. It has already been noted that Basil of Ochrid ignored Bertha's influence with Manuel. One would expect that she had influence with him, but hard evidence is required to prove it, because the ideal wife was not supposed to take any part in politics. The dominant ideology did not grant wives economic power either, but they must have had freedom to spend a certain amount of money, because *philanthropia* requires funds, particularly when it involves providing dowries for well-born people who cannot provide them themselves. As ever, the source of such money is not identified, and it is impossible for us now to do so. But the control of resources, no matter from where they came, is a form of power, and one which the imperial wife was legitimately allowed by the dominant ideology, although it was entirely unacknowledged.

Sister and daughter

The ideal sister displayed the same qualities as the ideal daughter. Both were supposed to love and serve their family. Manuel Straboromanos's consolation for Eirene Doukaina on the death of her brother, Michael Doukas, is an example of the ideal behaviour expected of a sister. Eirene had nursed Michael throughout his illness, at the expense of her own health, since she had gone without food and sleep to look after him. The marks of her sacrifice were still there in her face to be seen by a casual observer, although no reference was ever made to the cause. She was mourning for her

11. J. Dubisch, ed., *Gender and Power in Rural Greece* (Princeton, 1986), p. 24.

brother, but the trouble was bravely and silently borne. Manuel had to be told by a friend what caused the empress to look so haggard: otherwise he would have thought that she was ill. There is a parallel here with ideal daughter figures, such as the three daughters of Alexios Komnenos who looked after him devotedly in his last illness. They were on hand constantly, supporting their mother, feeding their father, wiping his brow, and keeping up the morale of the family by shielding their mother from the worst. However touching and practically important the roles of sister and daughter may be, they do not confer much power on the woman. As part of the family in the Komnenian family empire, they were important as marriage partners, but there is no evidence that they themselves contributed to the choice of spouse or influenced it in any way. The potential significance of their fate did not translate into power for the agents. They had to wait for their turn as mothers.

Physical attributes

Several virtues were not specific to any role, but common to all imperial women. 'Beautiful' was the most common epithet applied to imperial women of all ages and roles, excepting only mothers. The Byzantines' relationship to beauty was complicated. On one hand, it was the most heavily used adjective in all types of addresses to women, which implies that it was firmly embedded in the minds of its users as a suitable and important quality. Menander suggests that physical beauty, which 'contributes to happiness', should be included in the propemptic talk, in the *epithalmium*, the bedroom song, where it functions as an exhortation and encouragement to a young man to go forward to fulfil his marital duty, and in the epitaph. On the other hand, the next most admired quality all imperial women could possess, and this includes mothers, was a rejection of worldly vanity. A strong emphasis on beauty as a desirable quality would seem to lead to an increase in worldly vanity unless the beauty admired was strictly of the inner or spiritual sort. However, it is clear that, in a majority of cases, the praise is directed towards physical, bodily, beauty. This beauty possessed an awesome power. Choniates laid some of the blame for the chaos which engulfed the empire after the death of Manuel Komnenos on the beauty of Maria of Antioch, which spurred many men to desire and attempt to win her. Andronikos Komnenos's measures to neutralise opposition to his own reign and dispel nostalgia included having

Maria's portrait altered to depict her as old therefore disguising her beauty. The reasoning behind this intriguing incident was the Byzantines' interest in the physical appearance of their rulers which communicated on a level beyond an aesthetic description. It is clear that Byzantines deduced inner qualities from outer characteristics, which explains the emphasis on beautiful women. Women were already handicapped by their relationship to Eve, and it was necessary that they took heed for their characters, although this theme was not enlarged upon explicitly in the imperial circles of the Komnenian era.

As far as physical beauty went, the Byzantine ideal had several well-defined characteristics. Most important was harmony of limbs, which reflected an innate orderliness in the woman. This harmony proceeded from correct proportion of parts of the body, which should be beautiful on their own and as part of a graceful whole. In both his letter and his oration to Eirene Doukaina Italikos commented on the good proportion of her body. Basil of Ochrid recalled Bertha standing in the courts of the palace, adorning and crowning them by the proportion of her limbs and parts. Anna Komnene's limbs were remarkable for their splendour, beauty and harmony; her head was set straight on her neck, her shoulders were balanced, and her feet and hands were agile; in short, her body was like a well-made lyre or cithara, a good instrument constructed for a good soul. The later orations of Choniates which mention the princess Maria who married Isaac Angelos, and Euphrosyne, the wife of Alexios III Angelos, continued the trend. Maria's figure was more beautiful than that of Aphrodite, and Euphrosyne was grace in female form.

The face of the woman was important too. Tornikes provided the fullest description of a face in his categorisation of Anna Komnene. Her face was a perfect circle, the eyebrows were arched like a rainbow, her eyes were well proportioned, not jumping about (which was the sign of an unstable soul), nor crossed and sluggish (the sign of a lazy soul), but nimble enough to follow the movements of her entourage, and steady at most times. Her nose pointed straight towards her lips, which were harmonious and the colour of roses. Her complexion was pale like wool, but her cheekbones carried the redness of the rose into old age. The imperial mosaics in Hagia Sophia are the pictorial translation of this verbal picture. Zoe's face is round and chubby, while Eirene Piroska's is slightly more oval. They both have arched eyebrows and straight noses which point down their faces. Their eyes are emphasised by black lines underneath and both stare in a thoughtful manner somewhere towards the middle of the mosaic. Each has pale skin with a circle of red on the cheekbones. Tornikes's description of Anna would seem to be what the typical eleventh- and twelfth-century Byzantine understood by beauty.

Not only did Byzantine men know what was beautiful, they demanded that such beauty be natural in Byzantine terms. Both Tornikes and Italikos laid great stress on the fact that the beauty of Eirene Doukaina and Anna Komnene was not the work of master craftsmen in cosmetics. Italikos said that Eirene did not have 'signatures' on her face, did not put on eyeshadow to mould her face nor paint beneath her eyelids. Tornikes is even more withering. He said that Anna did not smear spurious dye on her eyes, nor add foreign colour to her face, but blushed with the redness of modesty, as became women. Niketas Choniates made the same point with reference to Bertha-Eirene that she did not put powder on her face, neither eyeshadow nor lines beneath her eyes: such techniques were for foolish women. Italikos called craftmanship in cosmetics empty and worldly, a skill which destroys the image of God. The beauty of the woman should be fresh, like that of Eirene which was as much the work of the fingers of God as the heavens: Basil of Ochrid remarked with approval upon the fresh complexion of Bertha-Eirene. Comparisons with nature were often made as a justification for the animosity to make-up. The argument was that as a meadow grows and looks beautiful when it is neglected, so should a woman's beauty be something with which she is not concerned. The other favourite comparisons with women were flowers in bloom and trees. The ideal is clear. Women should be beautiful in a natural way, without the addition of cosmetics, and they should not be preoccupied with their looks.

Relating the ideal to reality is complicated. It is obvious from the detailed comments of the orators that they knew what make-up was and what to do with it. Also, the mosaics show an unnatural patch of colour on the cheeks of the women, which cannot be dismissed as lack of technique on the part of the mosaicists who were capable of achieving very subtle shading if they wished. The emphasis on pale skin is also interesting. Females only retain their pale skin if they do not venture out into the sun unless protected by a veil or headgear. The Byzantine conception of 'natural' colours was dictated by fashion, not by nature, and the patch of red on the cheekbone was also a cultural necessity, which must have been achieved with the help of rouge. The conclusion is that women had to wear make-up to look natural. Prescriptive literature is always difficult to interpret. Some feminists believe that it reflected what actually happened, others that the prescriptions were couched strongly precisely because they were being ignored. In the case of Byzantium, the reasons behind the ideal of natural beauty which required no thought on the part of the woman are easy to pinpoint; the ideal of concern for inner beauty and the denial of worldly vanity. Italikos and Tornikes were not clerics but courtly rhetors, demonstrating that the attitude was widespread thoughout society.

The inverse of physical beauty is inner, spiritual beauty, which was equally an ideal in Byzantium. Women were not preoccupied with their external appearance or assets because they were more concerned for their inner virtues. The imperial women praised for their exemplary attitude towards inner beauty were Maria of Alania, Bertha-Eirene who was more concerned with inner propriety than with hanging on to the world, holding in contempt as useless 'the deceitful information to the senses', Eirene Doukaina and Anna Komnene. Anna was wise enough to know that inner beauty is immortal, for it is of the soul. Her daughter-in-law, Theodora, who was 'celebrated for [her] beauty', was praised for making herself even more beautiful by virtues. But Tornikes exposes his understanding of the relation between physical beauty and inner beauty. He insists that Anna Komnene was physically beautiful, and did not turn to virtue through being plain of face or ugly of body, 'as others have done'. The implication is clear: if physical beauty is impossible, the lesser goal of inner beauty must become the aim. Physical beauty is the ultimate virtue that a woman can possess according to men. If the ideology of inner character shining through outer form was carried through consistently, it would be logically impossible for an ugly woman to be good. However, ideology by its nature of serving some interests above others can hardly ever be consistent, but this is never noticed by those who live it. The underlying implication is that, in Byzantium, women were judged primarily on their physical appearance, with their characters coming a poor second. Today such ideology is judged as patriarchal and sexist by feminists. Such ideology puts women who are prepared to conform under the obligation to look as attractive as possible along the lines of male prescriptions, without the obvious use of the forbidden make-up, while everyone pretends that character is really what matters. Byzantine ideology, in this area, was patriarchal and actively denied power to women, except for mothers, who were judged primarily on loyalty to the family.

If concern for physical beauty was a sin, this was partly because such concern implied vanity, which, in Theophylact's words, 'leads to hell'. The temptation to vanity followed many roads, not only thinking too much about physical appearance, but also taking the wrong sort of pleasure in doing good. All women were praised for denying the pleasures of the world and exercising self-control. The higher up the scale the woman was, the more temptations she had to face, and the more opportunities for riches that she resisted, the greater the praise. Theophylact made this explicit in his speech to Maria. He admitted that many women were forced into the monastic life, and that they were admired for embracing such a hard and rugged mode of life even if they did it in a feminine and more delicate way than men did. But Maria, who was born in luxury and brought up with soft silken garments and good food on the table, deserved even more reverence for her devotion to the ascetic life, because she did it all of her own free will and it was so far from what she was used to. Maria, following the apostle Paul, counted all things as loss so that she might gain Christ. Theophylact stressed that her philanthropy was also performed by night to avoid meriting praise which would lead to vanity. Bertha-Eirene was also in a position to wear gold to show rank and to use money for luxurious living, but she resisted such worldly behaviour with high-minded resolution, and imitated the humility of Christ. Tornikes recalled that Eirene Doukaina, with all her high position and privileges, behaved like a subject and not a ruler, except to enemies, and that Anna Komnene, although surrounded from her birth by all the trappings and temptations of the imperial life which were bound to inflame the desires of a young girl, stretched towards virtue from her youngest days. Fulfilling the ideal of unworldliness may have granted to women the power of being a moral symbol. Unfortunately, there is not enough evidence to speculate how men reacted in practice to such virtue in their women, and there is no evidence of the opinions of women about the benefits or otherwise of conforming to this ideal.

It is interesting, although not surprising, to note that one possible trend of asceticism which was neither encouraged nor valued was a spiritual marriage in opposition to a real one with a physical relationship. This would have run counter to the prevailing interest in creating a family. Virginity was a theme which was only used as a means of praise by comparison with famous virgins, not as a virtue of its own. For example, in Tornikes's funeral oration for Anna Komnene he compared her to virgins, but proved that Anna had

greater virtue for she had a husband, but always approached him
with modesty like a newly betrothed person.

Conclusion

The dominant ideology in Byzantium at this time recognised several ideal roles for women. The most powerful was that of the
mother, who had a duty to care for her children and to nurture
and prepare them for the life ahead. The law required that, once
widowed, the mother take control of property, arrange marriages,
and provide dowries, which as well as conferring economic functions which a Marxist would interpret as powers, was a licence to
set up alliances which were crucial in the public sphere of politics
in the family empire of the Komnenian era. The legitimate role
of nurturing children could be stretched to wide limits, as Anna
Dalassene proved when her justification of her control of the civil
administration successfully calmed opposition, and criticism centred on the content of her reforms and not her sex. The ideal wife
was a beautiful, well-born, fertile, pious and loving creature, whose
public role consisted of dispensing patronage to the needy and
behaving in a decorous manner. Wives did not have an overt political role, and when a hint of such a role was unavoidable it was
glossed over quickly without any detail. Both mothers and wives had
the important public role of interceding to change judicial decisions, which the ideology managed both to praise and to ignore.
Economically they controlled resources, but again this power was
unacknowledged. The only sphere in which the dominant ideology
granted overt power to women was as mothers. All other roles
involved the exercise of power either through control of resources,
or the possible symbolic power of moral force, but women as actors
were denied. It is possible to deduce from the praise lavished on
them that they had more visible, active and determining roles than
the orators are saying, but as far as the dominant ideology was
concerned, they did not possess the qualities necessary for the exercise of anything other than a gentle smile.

What has been gained in understanding about power from this
study of ideology? That women had the power of influence is
granted, but influence is rarely recorded in the written sources. It is
more significant to discover if the power of women is visible in the
dominant ideology. Byzantium's dominant ideology acknowledged
the power of the roles of widow and mother, by which a woman

could participate openly in spheres which could be characterised as public, and receive praise for it. Implicitly, the dominant ideology allowed women as wives and mothers to meddle in the workings of justice, and to control resources which were used for the relief of the needy. These activities were seen as philanthropy and were praiseworthy too, although their real significance in terms of power was minimised by concentrating on the soft-heartedness of the woman instead of on her capacity to become a focus for all those who required that the emperor change his mind. Although unacknowledged in the recital of public power, these activities were both public and powerful. Wives' political power was also played down in a similiar fashion. Not only was a political role not suitable material for an epitaph, and therefore remained unmentioned, but the historians ignored such influence if they could. Without the letter of Conrad to Bertha-Eirene, she would be written off as a political nonentity, for Kinnamos and Choniates do not relate that she had any international role at all. Without the letter of Tzetzes to his friend, we would not know that Bertha-Eirene continued the unpopular custom set by Eirene Doukaina of accompanying her husband on campaign. Immediately suspicions are aroused about Eirene Piroska and Maria of Antioch, both foreign women who were married presumably for the foreign contact, but who are not credited with any roles other than childbearers or philanthropists by the historians. They too may have played a part on the international political scene. Therefore the first thing to be noted is that the dominant ideology does allow several different spheres of power to women, but only the mother's role is openly acknowleged as powerful.

The different categories of ideal women delineated in this chapter were broadly in force throughout the whole of Byzantine history. The potential of the mother's role had been exploited several times in the past by regents determined to keep the throne for their sons or, in the case of Eirene the Athenian, for herself. The law giving to a widow the guardianship of the family was of long standing. Menander Rhetor's prescriptions for praising and denigrating through different types of speeches had been popular since the fourth century. The Byzantine insistence on physical perfection in its rulers was inherited from the Roman empire, and women on occasion were even mutilated to prevent their interference, like the fifth-century empress Marina who had her tongue cut out. The emphasis on beauty for women has such a long and well-researched history that it is nearly redundant to mention the custom of bride shows, popular during the middle centuries of the empire, where the emperor chose his wife from a line of beauties, a line which had been chosen by means of a list of physical attributes, including foot size, which the emperor considered attractive. In a Christian empire, piety and compassion for others in straitened circumstances had always been matters for praise. The Komnenian ideal was like her earlier counterparts except in the huge interest in fertility which was an outcome of the increased importance of family.

However, the political system in which this ideal woman lived was dramatically different from that of her predecessors and this too was a result of the change in the status of the family of the emperor. Alexios Komnenos devised a new hierarchy for the government of the empire which was based on the family. To signal these new posts, new titles were created. These titles were primarily created for the men of the family; their wives were called by the female equivalents. Titles for women did not follow biological categories of relation to the emperor, like sister or mother, but rather marriage patterns. This will be the topic of the next chapter.

CHAPTER FOUR

Titles for imperial women

In order to understand the position and power of women in the Komnenian scheme of government it is necessary to examine the system which Alexios Komnenos set up to govern the empire. This system was created with a specific aim in view, the aggrandisement of the family, and by a deceptively simple means, the establishment of a whole new hierarchy of titles. Since these regulated life and rank at court, as titles always had done, a grasp of who was who is essential.

In 1081, when Alexios Komnenos gained the imperial throne, the system of rewards through titles upon which earlier emperors had relied had been rendered worthless by indiscriminate use. His immediate predecessor, Nikephoros Botaneiates, was one of the worst offenders. Alexios needed to create a new system which would both reward those who had been loyal and restabilise the imperial hierarchy. As one might expect from a member of one of the new families who had a sense of family loyalty, Alexios used his family as a caste at the top of society to safeguard his own position. His reforms in this area are among the most significant for the development of the empire and their importance has long been recognised. A change in titulature was particularly effective in the Byzantine empire because correct order was believed to be a reflection of divine order and therefore to be maintained. A title conferred a place in this scheme of order, thereby attributing status and rank. The elaborate ceremonies, the religious processions, and the sophisticated bureaucracy all demonstrate how deeply the idea of order was instilled into the Byzantine *habitus*. For the same reason, innovation was seen as an evil and the maintenance of time-honoured traditions as a good. Alexios's new hierarchy broke with tradition and incurred criticism on those grounds but it endured because it was highly effective. It is important to understand that, 'Rewards and honours were not the icing on the cake of government but . . . the essence of government'.[1] Scholarly work on Alexios's new system has centred unconsciously on the males of the family. A consideration of the effect on imperial women's lives is long overdue, including whether there were any titles specifically for women, and whether their place in the hierarchy was defined by their titles. Were the titles that they held important enough to be missed if they were vacant? How visible were women by virtue of their titles?

Sources and historiography

Since the current usage of titles by the court is at stake, contemporary speeches and poems are the most revealing sources. The histories which were written long afterwards and which were not declaimed in front of the title-holders are less informative, for the authors probably used titles in a vague sense or according to a personal preference, or after the usage at the court of which they formed a part. It was a different matter when reading out a speech at a funeral, or sending a hymn for Christmas to a living woman. This analysis is therefore based heavily on the poems and letters actually received by the women from their contacts at the court. Unfortunately, one cannot be sure that the *lemmata, or titles, to the poems are authentic, and the use of them is a trifle speculative. The most reliable source for these purposes is Theodore Prodromos, for he wrote the largest single preserved body of poems to Komnenian imperial women, and his usage can therefore be compared internally. From most other authors we have only one or two pieces and consequently cannot form any idea of their awareness of titulature. This means that the women around Alexios are at a disadvantage, for Prodromos only began his career after the death of that emperor. This is unfortunate, for Alexios's situation was by far the most interesting in terms of women with a claim to power. Not only was there his mother, Anna Dalassene, and his wife, Eirene Doukaina, but also his adopted mother, the empress Maria of Alania, and his daughter, Anna, who was crowned on her betrothal to the co-emperor, Constantine Doukas. There are of course numerous other sources for Anna Dalassene and Maria of Alania and an attempt at analysis will be made on that basis.

1. P. Magdalino, 'Innovations in government', in M.E. Mullett and D.C. Smythe (eds), *Alexios I Komnenos* (Belfast, 1996), p. 146.

It is vitally important to make what may seem to be a false division between different types of sources for the success of this inquiry. One category will be designated official and the other unofficial. Official sources are those such as coins, seals and portraits. These are called official because they were in use at the time and were intended to convey something to the public which the emperor wished to have understood. Their function is perhaps best described as propaganda, the television and court newspaper of the eleventh and twelfth centuries. Unofficial sources are histories written in private, under no scrutiny from the emperor, sometimes composed many years after the events they relate. The preferences of the emperor do not impinge on the production of these sources, therefore nothing about his preferences can be deduced. Titles were official, part of the warp and woof of the system of government and their accuracy was of paramount importance for the maintenance of order.

Official sources are important because they must reflect the current usage of the time, and more than that, possibly the preferred usage of the emperor. To be able to distinguish what imperial women preferred as their title would be a huge step forward in discovering something of their self-identity and how it was formed. The most fruitful source is seals, which are created at the wish of the owner, and therefore carry whatever qualification they see as most important in identifying themselves to other people. There are some seals extant which belonged to Komnenian women, but too few to chart the changes in their self-identity. The disadvantage of seals during the Komnenian period is that individuals may tend to ignore their titles and functions in favour of emphasising their links of relatedness to the emperor. This is excellent evidence for discovering relationships, but of limited value for investigating titles.

Coins are another official source of great importance. Coinage was not only spread all over the empire, making it an unequalled medium for the spreading of information, but carried authority on two levels. Firstly, it was official, invested with the authority of the law. Secondly, it was charismatic, appealing to the values shared by the emperor and the user. Depending on the value chosen and the state of the empire, its charisma may have been more important than its legality. The perceived importance of coins in legitimisation is proved by the cases of coin distribution by would-be usurpers. The appearance or not of empresses on coins must therefore be taken seriously. For example, most eleventh-century wives of emperors appeared on the coins with their husbands with an inscription usually denoting their respective titles, like Eudokia Makrebolitissa with Romanos Diogenes and Maria of Alania with Michael Doukas. Wives who had bestowed legitimacy on their husbands usually appear on the same side as them, with either Christ or a cross between them. Alexios Komnenos, who had not received legitimacy from his wife, most often appears alone or with a heavenly personage.

Imperial portraiture is another source which reflects the titulature of the time. There are a few surviving portraits which depict Maria of Alania and Maria of Antioch. One more contemporary source which illustrates its author's understanding of titles is the *typikon*, or foundation charter, of the monastery of Kecharitomene, written by Eirene Doukaina. It would be very instructive to be able to compare this to the *typikon* of Pantepoptes, the monastery founded by Anna Dalassene. Unfortunately this *typikon* has not survived, and the *typikon* of Pantokrator, co-founded by Eirene Piroska and John Komnenos, at least the version we possess, was written by John after the death of Eirene Piroska, and so is not a direct comparison.

There has been a considerable amount of work on the Komnenian titular system pioneered in a series of articles by Stiernon.[2] Oikonomides has studied the bureaucracy before the Komnenian reforms and his exposition of the evolution of the system in the eleventh century is a clear discussion of the change.[3] Magdalino's 'Innovations in government' tackles the question of Alexios's drastic changes head on. Much interest has been shown in the changing titles of the emperor in previous centuries by Brehier, Chrysos and Shahid.[4] In contrast only E. Bensammar has devoted any attention to the significance of the titles of the empress.[5] This article, whilst a useful survey of the titles from the eighth to the twelfth centuries, is rather undermined by the indiscriminate use of anachronistic sources and the omission of some important Komnenian material. Her conclusions, that the three main titles for the empress, *augousta*, *basilissa* and **despoina*, were interchangeable and that the title *basilissa* is so overused as to lose its impact, will be explored here.

2. Published in *REB*, vols 19 (1961); 21 (1963); 22 (1964); 23 (1965) and 24 (1966). For full details, see Bibliography.

3. N. Oikonomides, 'L'évolution de l'organisation administrative de l'empire byzantin au XIe siècle (1025–1118)', *TM* 6 (1976), pp. 125–52.

4. L. Brehier, 'L'origine des titres imperiaux à Byzance *basileus* et *despotês*', *BZ* 15 (1906), pp. 161–78. E. Chrysos, 'The title *basileus* in early Byzantine international relations', *DOP* 32 (1978), pp. 29–76: I. Shahid, 'On the titulature of Heraclius', *B* 51 (1981), pp. 288–96.

5. E. Bensammar, 'La titulature de l'impératrice et sa signification', *B* 46 (1976), pp. 243–91.

The system

As well as the general problem of a break-down in the traditional system of rewards caused by the instability of the mid-eleventh century, Alexios had to overcome a strong challenge to his family's hold on the throne even before he was securely settled there. On the eve of the coup, Alexios had promised his brother-in-law Nikephoros Melissenos that he would reward his loyalty with the title of Caesar after he himself had gained the imperial throne. This concession was wrung from him because Melissenos was on the point of declaring himself emperor and marching on the city from the Asian side. Melissenos came to terms on that agreement, since Caesar was the title directly below that of emperor, with a share in imperial acclamations and a prominent place in processions and banquets. Alexios had to decide what to do once the victory was his. Melissenos still had a strong force which had to be taken into account. Demonstrating for the first time of many how well he was able to survive, Alexios granted him the coveted title, fulfilling his agreement. He then proceeded to create a whole new hierarchy above it to honour his real supporters, his family.

Stiernon's research has revealed that at the heart of the system was nearness of relationship to the emperor who was always at the centre, that rank was determined by that relation, and that status of titulature followed rank. At the top was the emperor, with the title of *basileus autokrator*, and the empress, and the eldest daughter if there were no sons. Second in rank were the *sebastokrators, a title given to sons, brothers, paternal uncles, and great-uncles. Third were the *gambroi of the emperor, his sons-in-law, brothers-in-law, and uncles by marriage. *Gambros* merely means relative: it was not a title in itself. These people were honoured by different titles according to the order in which their wives were born. The order was as follows: the title of Caesar for the husband of the first born, *panhypersebastos* for the husband of second, *protosebastohypertatos* for the husband of the third, *sebastohypertatos* for the husband of the fourth daughter. Another general title for these near relatives was *despotes*. Fourth were the nephews and cousins of the emperor. Fifth were the class of *sebastes*, a title given to the husband of a niece, who was the daughter of either the emperor's brother or sister, or the husband of a cousin, who was the daughter of a paternal uncle or aunt of the emperor (Fig. 1).

One conclusion which can be gleaned from this catalogue is that the family knew who was who on the family tree, and was very aware

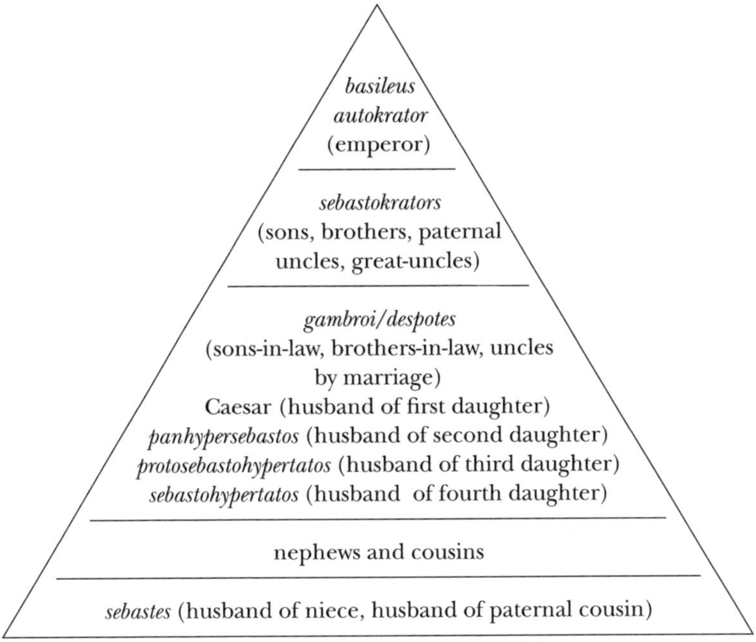
basileus
autokrator
(emperor)
sebastokrators
(sons, brothers, paternal uncles, great-uncles)
gambroi/despotes
(sons-in-law, brothers-in-law, uncles by marriage)
Caesar (husband of first daughter)
panhypersebastos (husband of second daughter)
protosebastohypertatos (husband of third daughter)
sebastohypertatos (husband of fourth daughter)
nephews and cousins
sebastes (husband of niece, husband of paternal cousin)

FIG. 1 The hierarchy of titles devised by Alexios

of the connections between them. They were also patently aware of and emphasised the difference between being related through the male line and through the female line. Being a son or a brother, or a son of a son or a brother, brought more privileges than equal affinity on the female side. Titles were described as being for the husbands of the emperor's female relatives, not for themselves. The differential weighting of importance according to sex is clear. It is difficult to say whether daughters of the emperor carried the female version of their husband's title or vice versa, since the titles were awarded on marriage as a method of raising spouses into the imperial hierarchy where they did not belong by blood. Wives of sons were in a much clearer position: their husbands already carried the title denoting their blood relationship to the emperor, and the wife merely took the female form. The family was on a higher level than the remainder of society, but inside the family itself there were different ranks. This fact will be demonstrated by the study of the title of *basilissa.* Women and their offspring were neither unimportant nor forgotten; the husband of a niece had the same title whether she was the emperor's brother's daughter or his sister's daughter. This man was related through a female and so could rise no higher, unless a higher title on the ladder of titles awarded to female relatives' husbands became free through the death of the holder. But the eldest son of a brother was privileged by a specific title of his own, that of *protosebastos*, while the eldest son of a sister had no such rank.

There are several Greek words which are translated as 'empress' in English. The three most common are *augousta*, *basilissa* and *despoina*. *Augousta* is the direct linguistic equivalent of the emperor's title Augustus, as *basilissa* is of *basileus*, and *despoina* of *despotes*. *Augousta* was a title derived from a name, and was therefore more self-conscious than the other two, which were words of varying degrees of generality. *Basilissa* meant only 'empress', but *despoina* meant the lady or mistress or ruler of a household. The word *basilissa* was used in an official sense as a title by the eighth-century empress Eirene the Athenian on her coinage after she took sole power, and by Zoe and Theodora in their year of joint rule. In the Komnenian period it was used both as a description of the person's rank and as a form of address. *Despoina* was used in an official sense by Anna Dalassene, a situation which I will discuss in detail below.

Augousta

The easiest title to analyse is *augousta*. This was the title by which the woman who had been crowned was addressed and made reference to herself, but only while the emperor who crowned her was still alive. This is because the title carried a function with it. The title *augousta* carried with it the visible honours of being imperial, such as a bodyguard, proclamations, the splendid insignia, a place in and the management of the ceremonies of the court. It was she who received the wives of the nobles when they come to prostrate themselves, as the emperor received the nobles themselves. The *augousta* was the *autokrator*'s ceremonial counterpart. Over the long history of the empire there had been exceptions and individual special cases. The eighth-century Eirene the Athenian called herself *basileus*, the male title for the reigning emperor. The ninth-century Leo VI had to crown a daughter as *augousta* because he had no wife at the time to perform the requisite duties. Zoe and Theodora during their period of joint rule were both referred to as *augousta*. Zoe had been crowned with her first husband and Theodora was crowned in Hagia Sophia at the height of the revolt against Michael

V. In their case, the *augoustai* were sole rulers, performing all imperial functions themselves. Generally, however, once the emperor died, the title passed to the wife of the next emperor. The Komnenian period was simple in one way because all the emperors married and they all had children, and the system of titles built up by Alexios simplified the precedence, since all closely related imperial women carried other titles which denoted their rank. We can therefore refer to Komnenian *augoustai* as wives of reigning emperors.

The coronation ceremony recorded by Constantine Porphyrogennetos in the tenth century may not have been the exact ceremony which was carried out under the Komnenoi, but it is the closest evidence which we have. During that ceremony the crowned woman was referred to repeatedly as *augousta*, except for once, when she was hailed as *basilissa*. The ceremony itself is worth looking at in some detail. The woman did not have to be married to the emperor to be crowned. When the marriage and the coronation took place on the same day and consequentially, the woman was promoted to *augousta* first and then the wedding ceremony followed. Her promotion did not therefore depend on her marital status. On the other hand, an emperor did not necessarily have to crown his wife, although it seems that most of them after the third century did so. There was still enough flexibility in the system to frighten the Doukas family when Alexios, at the start of his reign, hesitated over crowning Eirene Doukaina. Coronation was therefore not automatic, either before or during the Komnenian period. Although the couple may not have been wed when the woman was crowned, she still received the crown from the hands of the emperor, while he received his from the hands of the patriarch.

The emperor crowned the *augousta* because her authority derived from him, not directly from God as that of the emperor did. The empress's lack of heavenly authority was also highlighted by the fact that, if not on the same day as that of her husband, her coronation took place in the palace, not in church. The differing status of the emperor and empress before heaven is neatly illustrated in a manuscript portraying Constantine Doukas, Eudokia Makrembolitissa and one of their sons who was being crowned. Christ sits at the top of the manuscript with the three figures below him and three angels acting as mediators between the two spheres. One angel leans out of heaven to set a crown on the young child's head. The other two angels hover above the heads of the imperial couple, with one striking difference. Constantine's angel places one hand on the head of the emperor and touches heaven with the other, the angel above

Eudokia does not reach for heaven. This illustrates the different conceptions of the authority of the two. That of the emperor and the newly crowned co-emperor came from heaven, that of the empress did not. Legal sources shared this idea. According to the law code, the ninth-century *Basilika*, 'The emperor is not subject to the laws. The empress is subject unless the emperor gives to her his prerogatives'.[6] The *augousta*'s position and function was therefore set, and her authoritative space defined as deriving from the emperor who, in the context of the Komnenoi, was her husband.

Unlike the western tradition, Byzantine emperors and empresses were not anointed, at least until late in the twelfth century. Nevertheless, the emperor was regarded, and could be referred to, as the 'Lord's anointed'. The sanctity of coronation, even without an anointing by holy oil, was the source of the majesty of the empress, which she could transfer to another man if a new emperor was needed. Throughout the history of the empire empresses had chosen, married or adopted men to fill the position after their husbands died or were deposed. This procedure was amply demonstrated in the eleventh century when both Eudokia Makrembolitissa and Maria of Alania brought new emperors to power.

Augousta was a title which was passed on to another holder. The histories referred to a woman as *augousta* only when her husband was alive and reigning. Once her husband died, she was referred to mainly as *basilissa*. Contemporary letters and documents tell the same story. The inscription on the document is the crucial part. The internal text often directly addresses the woman as *basilissa* or *despoina*, but the character of the formal address has to carry the official and proper manner of addressing the recipient. Eirene Doukaina received a letter from the abbot of St George of the Mangana addressing her as *augousta*, and referred to herself as *augousta* in the title of the *typikon* for the monastery of Kecharitomene. A seal of hers survives carrying the inscription 'The Lord help Eirene Doukaina the *Augousta*', which unfortunately cannot be dated. After Alexios had died, letters, speeches, and poetry were addressed to her as *basilissa* or *despoina*, since the title of *augousta* now belonged to John's wife Eirene Piroska. A seal which possibly belonged to Eirene Piroska shows that the reigning *augousta* preferred to use that title rather than *basilissa* on her seal. It is inscribed 'Eirene the most pious *augousta*'. Two pieces of evidence suggest that a dead empress was not referred to as *augousta* even if her

6. *Basilika* II.6.1 (Groningue, 1955–74).

husband was still alive. Theodore Prodromos wrote an epitaph for Eirene Piroska, in which he referred to her as *basilissa*, carefully qualified as blessed. Secondly, in the *typikon* for Pantokrator, written by John on the completion of the monastery which his wife had helped to begin, she is commemorated under the title of *despoina*, although John had not married again. Prodromos and John could conceivably have referred to the dead Eirene as the blessed *augousta*, but instead they used a completely different title.

Contemporary evidence for Manuel's first wife, Bertha-Eirene, follows the same pattern. Two seals belonging to her have survived. Both identify her as 'Eirene Komnenos the most pious *Augousta*'. Prodromos, writing hymns for Christmas during the reign of Manuel and Bertha, referred to the empress as 'the *Augousta* Eirene' three times. Tzetzes, writing during her lifetime, called her 'the *Augousta* and our holy mistress'. On the contrary, Basil of Ochrid, writing her funeral oration, referred to her almost exclusively as *basilissa* and not once as *augousta*. There is not so much evidence for Maria of Antioch, but that which does follows the same pattern. Eustathios of Thessalonike, relating the history of Maria's attempt to rule after Manuel's death, refers to her as the *basilissa* or as *despoina*.

There is also evidence that a co-empress was not entitled *augousta* after her coronation, suggesting that there was only one *augousta* at court in the Komnenian system. This is a difference from the situation in the eleventh century when both Zoe and Theodora held the title simultaneously. In order to prove this beyond doubt it would be necessary to have documents relating to senior emperors' wives and co-emperors' wives. Unfortunately we have only one, but at least this is some indication. The document is the *typikon* of Kecharitomene, written by Eirene Doukaina before 1118, when she herself was *augousta*, as she signalled in the title of the document, and her son John was married. Eirene Piroska is identified in the document as 'the *despoina* lady Eirene, his [John's] wife'. This may therefore have been the technically correct title for the co-emperor's wife when the senior emperor's wife was still alive. All the other family members on the list are identified by their correct titles, revealing Eirene Doukaina's knowledge and her attention to detail. A document such as a *typikon* is particularly useful and reliable because by its very nature it was necessary that the people mentioned could be correctly identified so that they could be remembered in the correct way. Members of the Komnenos family expended much care on listing the members of the family whom they wished to be remembered, with exact instructions about the proper amounts of candles, ingredients of loaves and denomination of coins to be distributed. It is inconceivable that an individual's title could be unimportant in this milieu.

There is little numismatic evidence for women throughout the whole Komnenian period, in contrast to the previous decades. It is noticeable how many women are present on at least one type of coin in the years 1067 to 1081. Generally they appear on the gold coinage minted in Constantinople itself. For example, Eudokia Makrembolitissa and Maria of Alania appear with their husbands with inscriptions normally denoting their respective titles. Wives who had bestowed legitimacy on their husbands usually appear on the same side as them, with either Christ or a cross between them. Eudokia Makrembolitissa and Maria of Alania, who between them were married to all the four emperors who reigned immediately prior to Alexios Komnenos, are most prominent on the coins of their second husbands. In Eudokia's case, her title of *basilis* is more prestigious than Romanos' title of *despotes*, a device thought to signify her determination to rule him. Alexios Komnenos, on the other hand, had not received legitimacy from his wife, and neither of his sons were in need of womanly legitimisation. This shows on the coinage pattern. Komnenian emperors preferred to share a coin with a heavenly, rather than a temporal, personage. Alexios, John and Manuel minted many coin types, with Christ or the Virgin on the other face. Also popular, from the reign of John, were the military saints George, Theodore and Demetrios. There is only one coin depicting an empress in the whole of the hundred years between 1080 and 1180. This coin is the coronation coin of 1092, when John was associated in power with his father. It is very clearly a family coin, showing Alexios and Eirene on the obverse, and a beardless John on the reverse. All three are titled: Alexios and John as *despotes* and Eirene as *augousta*. *Despotes* was the most popular title for a Komnenian emperor on coins throughout the whole period. Eirene, as the wife of the senior emperor, merited the title *augousta*. Comparable evidence in the form of a mosaic in the south gallery of Hagia Sophia confirms that *augousta* was still the official title for the wife of the emperor when John II was on the throne. The panel, depicting John and Eirene on either side of the Virgin, carries inscriptions identifying the characters. Eirene's inscription is *augousta*. This panel was put in place around 1122.

The Komnenian period moved smoothly from reign to reign, with one problem. There is a lacuna of ten years in our knowledge of the *augoustai* during this period. Between the death of Eirene

Piroska in 1136 and the marriage of Manuel to Bertha-Eirene in 1146, we do not know who filled the role and function of *augousta*. There are various possibilities, ranging from no *augousta* at all, to sharing by all the daughters and daughters-in-law of John. It is quite possible that the court continued without an *augousta*. For example, the court of Basil II survived for fifty years without one. The fact that the sources do not mention the gap suggests that, despite the special pleading of Leo VI, the court did not miss its *augousta*. One suspects that the post was of little importance in the male-oriented court of the Komnenoi where males were granted titles and females took the rank of their husband. On the other hand, some emperors neglected to fill the post of patriarch of Constantinople for several years, yet it could hardly be said that that post was unimportant. In comparison to the emperor, all posts were relative and waited on his good pleasure. As for the *augousta* in this case, Eirene Piroska had admirably fulfilled one of the duties of a wife by becoming a mother eight times, and there was no lack of heirs. Another possibility is that one of the wives of those heirs fulfilled the relevant duties. This suggestion takes us back to the question of what exactly coronation conferred, and how automatic it was.

The grounds for suggesting that any or all of these daughters or daughters-in-law might have fulfilled the duties of an *augousta* during this time is that some of them were referred to as *basilissa*. So, were any of these women crowned and what does coronation confer? Since John had sons, and sons receive a higher title than their sisters and brothers-in-law, it is among the wives of sons that a replacement for Eirene Piroska should be sought. John's daughters Maria and Anna, both titled *basilissa* on contemporary evidence, can be discarded for the moment. All John's sons were married, and all were titled *sebastokrators* until Alexios was crowned co-emperor in 1122. In Prodromos's poem for this coronation, there is no mention of Alexios's wife, as surely there would have been had he been married at that stage. His first wife, called Eirene by the Byzantines, arrived from Kiev in 1122 according to the *Annales de Goustin*. Barzos suggests that Alexios was not married at his coronation but he crowned his wife upon marriage, with his own hands.[7] He quotes a poem edited by Lampros written to accompany an icon on behalf of Eirene, in which she is referred to as *basilis*. However, the *lemma* of the document does not name her as *basilis*, indeed it does not

7. C. Barzos, *Ê Genologia tôn Komnênôn*, 2 vols (Thessalonica, 1984), p. 204.

name her at all. Eirene probably was crowned, since Alexios was the heir to the empire, and is therefore also the most likely to have taken on what were to be her future duties, but in the absence of firm evidence the theory remains purely speculative. The arrival of Bertha-Eirene in 1142 was another occasion on which ceremony would have been followed. In Kinnamos's account of Bertha's arrival, there is no mention of an *augousta*, but she was met by women of the nobility, including the wife of Alexios the co-emperor, who wore imperial purple. Perhaps this is a clue that this woman was taking upon herself the duties of the most visible woman of the court.

What we know about the title of *augousta* during the Komnenian era can be summed up as follows. It was a title applied only to the living spouses of living emperors. Once the emperor died, that woman ceased to be referred to as *augousta*. If she herself died, she was no longer referred to as *augousta* in funeral orations, although there is no evidence that another woman had already been awarded the title. The title was conferred at the coronation which made her husband *autokrator* and was its equivalent. Co-empresses were officially titled *despoina* at their coronations so that there was only one *augousta* at court at any one time. Alexios therefore tightened up the use of the title, for in the tenth century it seems that there could be more than one *augousta* at one time. In the eleventh century two women held the title at the same time, but Zoe and Theodora are always special cases and should be treated more as emperors because of their acknowledged right of inheritance. Coronation, and the subsequent use of the title, was not automatic during the Komnenian period, although in all cases it seems to have been performed. The *augousta* was very dependent on her husband's willingness to create her *augousta*, for he made the decision whether or not to crown her.

Basilissa

Basilissa is a much more complex title. Firstly, it is a descriptive word which does not involve any specific function. Therefore a wider use is possible. The important question for the place of women of the Komnenian era is whether the family ethos elevated all women of the family to a dignity equivalent to that of empress. To answer this question we must first examine the usage of the history-writers to ascertain how wide a use of *basilissa* was allowed or customary.

It is particularly important to distinguish between different sources when discussing the use of *basilissa* as a title. When the word is used by historians like Zonaras it merely signals that they mean the empress. All historians use the word for all empresses: the reason for the higher numbers of references in the eleventh and twelfth centuries is that there were more high style histories concerned with that period when more women were visible. These authors do not use the word *basilissa* to indicate women who are not empresses. Very few of them mention other women at all, but when they do they identify them by their relations to other people or by other titles. Zonaras talks of Anna Komnene as 'the wife of Bryennios', Kinnamos recounts a story about John's daughter Maria without giving her a title at all, and Choniates always identifies Anna Komnene as *kaisarissa. Far from applying *basilissa* widely, the history-writers seem careful to use *basilissa* for the empress only. The internal use of *augousta* and *basilissa* by each history-writer is interesting, particularly when they are recounting the events of the early 1080s, when there were several women who either were, or had been, empress. It is very noticeable that where there is a possibility of confusion the author names the empress to whom he or she is referring. Generally the history-writers only use *augousta* when they are relating that the woman was crowned *augousta*: in all other cases they dispense with the title in favour of the word *basilissa*. There are two exceptions: Anna Komnene uses *augousta* several times to refer to her mother, and Psellos uses *augousta* to refer to Zoe. This may be because both authors are writing about a period in the present tense which they experienced at first hand. The *augousta* is never named: that was not necessary because there was only one at a time. The practice of not naming holds for Psellos and Anna Komnene when they use *augousta*, indicating a measure of respect in that in their minds there was only one *augousta*. Anna's respect for her mother is evident throughout her book and Psellos was in a position of advisor or even spiritual relation to later empresses but was young and inpressionable during Zoe's long reign.

The later reigns are simpler because there was only one woman who had been crowned empress at a time. The history-writers did not have to specify the subject of their remarks by name. Kinnamos used the names of Eirene Piroska and Bertha-Eirene to avoid confusion, since he was writing at a time when another woman was the empress, but that woman, Maria of Antioch, is not named. The only time he uses *augousta* is when he is relating that the woman was crowned or proclaimed *augousta*. Otherwise, he refers to the

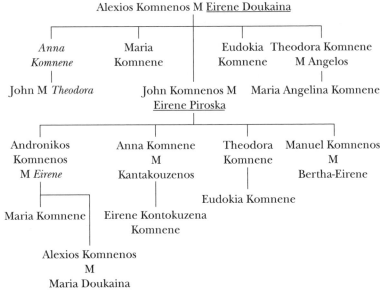

Key:

K = Komnenos or Komnene   D = Doukas or Doukaina

Women referred to as *basilissa* in italic. Women addressed as *basilissa* in the title of the poem underlined.

FIG. 2   The women in Prodromos's work

empress as *basilissa*. Choniates does not name any of the empresses he includes except for Eirene Doukaina. He leaves the identification of the empress up to the reader, who has to infer it from the reign of the emperor under discussion. He also uses *despoina* frequently for Maria of Antioch, nearly always after Manuel's death, when she was regent for her son.

Interpretation of contemporary speeches, poems and letters depends upon a careful distinction between the terms used in the title of the document and the words which may be used in the text of the document, which are much more informal. The body of work preserved from the pen of Theodore Prodromos is by far the most helpful in discovering at what point in the family lines a woman cannot be even referred to, let alone addressed as, *basilissa*. Prodromos directed poems to a vast selection of Komnenian imperial women, but only a few were referred to as *basilissa* and even fewer were addressed as such in the inscription of the poem (see Fig. 2).

Thus only Eirene Doukaina, Eirene Piroska, Anna Komnene, the *sebastokratorissa* Eirene, and Theodora, wife of John Doukas, are honoured by being included among the *basilissai*. Further, only Eirene Doukaina and Eirene Piroska are described in the inscription of their poems as *basilissa*.

Prodromos's use of *basilissa* as a title, as opposed to a word, is therefore very restricted. Eirene Doukaina, the crowned wife of Alexios I Komnenos, had the technical title of *basilissa*. Prodromos was of course writing this poem for her after the death of Alexios, so she could no longer be identified as *augousta*. By the time he wrote a funeral oration for Eirene Piroska, inscribed 'Epitaph for the blessed *basilissa* of the Romans the lady Eirene' in 1136, Eirene Doukaina was possibly dead also, so in the absence of other evidence we cannot tell whether *basilissa* was the technical and official title for the ex-empress of which there would only be one. It is unlikely that Prodromos picked this word for these women at random, since he was meticulously careful to address other women by their exact titles. Anna Komnene, for example, was 'the most wise purple-born *kaisarissa*', and the *sebastokratorissa* Eirene was 'the *sebastokratorissa*' and nothing else. The verses to Anna's daughter-in-law Theodora were addressed to 'the wife of the son of the most successful Caesar Nikephoros Bryennios, the lady Theodora' demonstrating Prodromos's knowledge and understanding of the links connecting members of the family. Had *basilissa* been such a wide-ranging term or a convenient term of flattery surely Prodromos would have used it in the titles of poems to ladies he did refer to as *basilissa* in the text of the document. Instead he uses their correct titles and restricts the title of *basilissa* to crowned empresses.

However, other imperial ladies could be referred to in the text of the poems as *basilissa*. It is interesting to plot how far down this is allowable. At the very furthest, Prodromos described Anna's daughter-in-law, Theodora, in her epitaph, as 'the beautiful *basilissa*'. The other women called *basilissa* in the text of their poems were Anna Komnene and the *sebastokratorissa* Eirene. Since Anna was married to a Caesar and Eirene to a *sebastokrator*, these women belonged to the second and third highest orders according to Stiernon's classification. Prodromos's titling of their poems has already been discussed in the preceding paragraph. From other evidence, discussed below, it seems that porphyrogenite daughters could be called *basilissa* and that daughters-in-law could be also. Prodromos adhered to this rule, too. Among the wide number of women he wrote for and about, the small number he described as *basilissa* is striking. This was because the title had a recognised field of application in the tightly-knit Komnenian system.

Another body of poems by the author known as Manganeios Prodromos (if he was someone other than Theodore), was just as careful about the addresses used. The *sebastokratorissa* Eirene, to whom the vast majority of the poems were addressed, was always addressed by her correct and technical title of *sebastokratorissa*. In poems for other members of the family, Prodromos addressed his recipients equally carefully. Maria, daughter of John, was identified as 'the purple-born first daughter of our famous emperor of the Romans, John Komnenos'. Manuel Anemas was 'the most successful son-in-law of our famous emperor and *autokrator* John the purple-born, Manuel Anemas'. Alexios's granddaughter Maria was identi-fied as 'the daughter of the purple-born lady Theodora, the sister of the emperor of the Romans, the purple-born lord John, by her husband Kammitzes'. Twelfth-century writers were aware of the cor-rect modes of address for the members of the Komnenos family and were capable of following the rules. Only one poem in the whole of the corpus identified a recipient as the husband of a *basilissa*. LVIII is a monody to Stephen Kontostephanos, who was identified as 'the son of lord Isaac the *sebastos*, by his wife the *sebaste*, the *basilissa*'. His wife was Anna, second daughter of John II. In contrast, most other poems to Kontostephanos refer to Anna as 'the Kontostephane, the wife of Kontostephanos'. In all sorts of contem-porary evidence it seems that the title of *basilissa* was not spread around without discrimination, but at its widest was applied to those who were within three degrees of relationship to the emperor.

It is now time to turn to other evidence for *basilissa* as a title for daughters of the emperor. As has already been implied, the *typika* were consistent in applying exact titles to the relatives of the em-peror, and in the lists of commemorations they did not refer to any woman, empress or otherwise, as *basilissa*. Anna Komnene is the most accessible, since there is much more evidence for her than for the other daughters of either Alexios or John. Browning noticed that George Tornikes referred to Anna as *basilissa* frequently in the funeral oration he wrote for her, and merely stated that *basilissa* was not confined to empresses alone.[8] Prodromos also referred to Anna as *basilissa*. These references are contained in the body of the text and in all cases the inscription on the document identified the

8. R. Browning, 'An unpublished funeral oration on Anna Comnena', *Proceedings of the Cambridge Philosophical Society*, 188 (ns 8) (Cambridge, 1962).

recipient as *kaisarissa*, which was Anna's correct title, since she was the wife of the Caesar Nikephoros Bryennios. Tornikes directed his oration to 'the purple-born lady Anna the *kaisarissa*', Italikos titled the prologue to her will, 'Prologue to the will of the *kaisarissa*', Prodromos's usage has already been mentioned and Tzetzes addressed his letter to 'the purple-born lady Anna the *kaisarissa*'. There is no reference to any of the other daughters of Alexios as *basilissa*. They were referred to by their correct titles at all times. Darrouzès thought that Anna Komnene deserved the title because she had been betrothed to the co-emperor Constantine Doukas in her youth, but he also noted that daughters could readily be termed *basilissa* by Tornikes's time.[9] It is not surprising that *basilissa* could be applied to more than the crowned empress under the Komnenoi, for its male equivalent *basileus* was not an exclusive title either. Anna Komnene demonstrated this and laid down the principle when she explained that she did not scruple to call Isaac the *sebastokrator basileus* although he did not wear the purple.

Darrouzès's evidence that daughters could be called *basilissa* is that Maria, the daughter of John II, inscribed the title on her seal, although this seal is the only example of Maria, the eldest daughter of John, wife of the Caesar John Roger, being titled *basilissa*. The official nature of this means that it cannot be lightly dismissed. Maria must have been recognisable as *basilissa*, but since there is no way of dating the seal we cannot say when. No other daughters of John are referred to as *basilissa* in any medium. As far as daughters-in-law are concerned, all the evidence for the *sebastokratorissa* Eirene follows the scheme of identifying her as *sebastokratorissa*. Prodromos's carefulness has already been discussed.

The monk Iakobos is another fruitful source. Elizabeth Jeffreys has examined his letters, noting that the monk referred to Eirene as *basilis* and *despoina*.[10] On the title page, these letters are addressed 'To the *sebastokratorissa*' and there is one further reference to her as *sebastokratorissa* in the title to letter 44. Iakobos's usage therefore followed the system: her title was *sebastokratorissa*, but in the text she could be referred to by the other imperial words. Manasses's history states that he was writing for 'The *sebastokratorissa* Eirene whom our emperor lord Manuel gave to his brother lord Andronikos'. Therefore at the widest possible application, evidence of the current

9. J. Darrouzès, ed. *Georges et Démétrios Tomikès. Lettres et discours* (Paris, 1970).

10. E. Jeffreys, 'The *sebastokratorissa* Eirene as a literary patroness: the monk Iakovos', *JÖB* 32/3 (1982), pp. 63–71.

and official use of *basilissa* as a title by which a woman could be addressed permitted only purple-born daughters of an emperor, and no younger than the second, to be officially referred to as *basilissa*. This was only true of John's reign: in Alexios's only his eldest purple-born daughter was even referred to as *basilissa*, still less addressed as such. This may indicate that the title was undergoing a change. Eirene the *sebastokratorissa* is the only wife of a *sebastokrator* for whom we have evidence. Nothing is known about the titles of the *sebastokrator* Isaac's wives.

An examination of the evidence leads to the conclusion that only crowned empresses could be addressed officially and formally as *basilissa* in the reign of Alexios Komnenos. Unofficially ex-empresses, for example Maria of Alania, could be referred to as such by historians without fear of confusion. In the reign of John Komnenos, according to the poems of Theodore Prodromos, ex-empresses were addressed officially as *basilissa* while the current empress was *augousta*. Other imperial women were addressed formally by their correct titles, which did not include *basilissa*. Only on other evidence can we see *basilissa* used for the first and second daughters of the emperor. Informally wives of *sebastokrators* could be referred to as *basilissa*, and in one case the niece of the emperor, Theodora. That text was her funeral oration, in which the popularity of *basilissa* as a designation has already been noted, although previously only in the case of empresses. In comparison to the width and breadth of the family tree by the early years of the twelfth century, the pool of women addressed, even informally, as *basilissa* is very small. In Manuel's reign his daughter, Maria, was designated as *basilissa* in a property document, where his wife, Maria of Antioch, was *augousta*. Maria of Antioch was the crowned empress, the emperor's wife, whereas the younger Maria was the emperor's heir, with her husband, Alexios the *despotes*. Maria was therefore very much in the same position as Anna Komnene, a generation earlier. She was the heir of the empire and a purple-born daughter. On both those counts she deserved the official title of *basilissa*.

Despoina

The Greek word *despoina* means 'mistress', she who is in charge. As a word it was used commonly by history-writers to designate the empress, and also in speeches, letters and poetry addressed to the empress. It could be used in speeches or letters addressed to living women, whether they were still the *augousta* or not, and to the dead, as in Kallikles's poem on the grave of Eirene. *Despoina* is found as an official title or unofficial reference, to an empress, alive or dead. Prodromos combined it with the title of *augousta* in his Christmas hymns to Manuel and Bertha-Eirene. Tzetzes used it as a title in the inscription to his letter, and Basil of Ochrid referred to the dead empress as *despoina* in his funeral oration for her.

An official function of this word was to differentiate between Eirene Doukaina, the reigning *augousta*, and Eirene Piroska, the co-empress, in the *typikon* of Kecharitomene, where *despoina* was Eirene Piroska's official and sole title. Other imperial women could be referred to as *despoina* also, although not addressed as such. Both Anna Komnene and the *sebastokratorissa* Eirene were referred to as *despoina*, Anna by Tzetzes in the letter he wrote to her, and Eirene by Tzetzes, Prodromos, and Iakobos. It appears that the word was particularly popular in letters. Its use in this medium was very appropriate, since most letters were asking for something from a person better placed to provide than the person asking for it. To address the recipient as 'mistress', with its connotations of possession, was therefore apt.

Two uses of *despoina* are especially interesting. First is its use as a marker of visibility as an official title for Anna Dalassene. As the mother of the emperor who had usurped the throne, Anna had no purple pedigree, and no obvious title to raise her linguistically to the political heights she had achieved. John Komnenos had been a *kouropalates*, and Anna, as his wife, a *kouropalatissa*. Bryennios referred to her as such in his history. Once the Komnenian system was in force, Anna needed a commensurate title so that all the court could both recognise her authority and show their respect. Zonaras commented that Anna did not wear imperial insignia nor was she included in the acclamations at Alexios's coronation, but that she shared in the name of empire. Presumably, it was legally in Alexios's power to create her *augousta* had he wished. This is one of the most interesting questions about the era of the Komnenoi, for there were three women to be considered and nervous supporters to appease. Whether Alexios did not create his mother *augousta* because he was considering marrying Maria of Alania or because he could not afford to offend the Doukas family will never be known. In the event, Eirene Doukaina was crowned *augousta*, and Maria of Alania slid gently out of the political picture. Anna Dalassene was created regent by Alexios with *despoina* as her official title. Anna Komnene comments that everyone called her by this title because

Alexios wanted his mother to be so known. *Despoina* is the word used in the several property exchanges carried out on Anna's orders, where her men described her as 'our holy *despoina*', and 'the *despoina* and mother of our emperor', and themselves as 'the men of our holy *despoina*'. Alexios described her as 'my holy *despoina* and much-loved mother', and St Christodoulos, in his instructions for the monastery of St John, called her 'the blessed *despoina* and mother of our emperor'.

However *despoina* was more than just a way of identifying Anna among the women of the court. Oikonomides was the first to notice and comment on the title to a property document of 1087 issued by Anna categorised as a '*pittakion* of the *despoina*'. Oikonomides noted that in this document Anna wrote as though she were the emperor with the phrase 'my majesty'.[11] Although more people than the crowned emperor had majesty, only crowned emperors and empresses used it of themselves. Alexios referred to his majesty in documents relating to property given to the monk Christodoulos, as did Eirene Doukaina in her *typikon* for Kecharitomene. Anna Dalassene had the authority of an emperor, and was officially enough in charge of affairs to have her own authority defined as different from, although equal to, that of Alexios. In her case her title expressed her power: she was the *despoina*. Anna's *pittakion* is the only instance of a **pittakion* of the *despoina* in Byzantium: Anna Dalassene had visible authority far beyond that of any other regent in Byzantium. This visibility is the most important facet of her power; all women have influence, but it is too private and informal to quantify. A visible woman with authority (even if given to her by her son) is worth noting.

The reality of the exercise of the authority conveyed by Anna's title is made manifest by a consideration of the military campaigns which Komnenian men fought. Alexios himself was rarely in the city for the first twenty years of his reign, the years when Anna made the decisions as regent. When Alexios left the city, many of his male relatives accompanied him, since they all had military commands. In 1081, 1082, 1083, 1087 and 1091, Alexios and his commanders campaigned on the western borders of the empire. In 1094 the army was fighting the Cumans, in 1097 they were at Nicaea in Asia Minor and a year later deep in Asia Minor at Philomelion

11. N. Oikonomides, 'The donations of castles in the last quarter of the 11th century', *Polychronion, Festschrift Franz Dölger zum 75 Geburtstag* (Heidelberg, 1966), pp. 413–17.

on their way to Antioch to relieve the beseiged crusader army. The early years of the twelfth century saw the army once again on the western side of the city in the Balkans, fighting against the Normans once again.

The family character of Anna's authority is illuminated by the way in which her granddaughter Anna Komnene referred to her mainly as *despoina*, but in the occasional references to her as *basilissa* took care to remind the reader that Anna Dalassene was the emperor's mother. Theophylact of Ochrid, writing a double *basilikos logos*, or speech to the emperor, to Alexios and Anna, used no title at all for her, but referred to her exclusively as Alexios's mother. Anna Komnene also referred to her grandmother as 'mother of the Komnenoi', a phrase which Anna Dalassene adopted as a semi-official title during her years in power; a seal survives inscribed with the phrase. Her use of the word as a title demonstrates the readiness of the Komnenian regime to use whatever was already there for its own ends. When required, a word which had been used of the empress, although in an informal capacity, could be transformed into an official title for a character otherwise without one. This is another example of the fertile mind of either Anna Dalassene or Alexios, or both, and the versatility of the Komnenian system.

Conclusion

Owing to the lack of systematic evidence for women in the Komnenian system the most that can be said is that under it only crowned empresses were dignified with the title of *augousta*. Crowned empresses were more likely to use *augousta* than *basilissa* to identify themselves on their seals. Any imperial lady above the rank of *panhypersebastos* could be referred to as *basilissa* informally, but only crowned empresses could receive poems with the word as a formal title at the top. By the reign of John II, purple-born daughters could use the title on a seal. Any lady above the rank of *panhypersebastos* could be referred to and addressed as *despoina*, a title which was official only in the case of the co-empress and Anna Dalassene. This possibility was completely different from the situation before Alexios implemented his system. Then, only the crowned emperor and his immediate family could use words which implied imperial majesty.

This study of titles under the Komnenoi has demonstrated how the system was set up, showing the difference between women and men. There were advantages for women in that they were visible and had a recognised place in the hierarchy which was the organising structure of the Komnenian court. Certainly there is more evidence for women of the family than in any earlier century. To be related to the emperor was good, but to be related on the male side was better. It entailed higher ranking from birth, since brothers and sons of emperors were *sebastokrators*, the next thing to emperors, and daughters were a degree down, *kaisarissas* or *panhypersebastes*. Sons were given titles on their own account, but daughters only got titles on marriage, so that their husbands would be elevated in the hierarchy. When men were promoted, their wives moved up too, but women were not promoted on their own account, even the daughters of the emperor.

The extension of the title of *basilissa* can be plotted accurately to above a certain rank precisely because daughters did not receive titles on account of their birth. Alexios and John each had four daughters, but only two of them in each case qualified for the title of *basilissa* since their husbands were Caesars or *panhypersebastoi*. It is clear that the system did not privilege women members as women, or on the same terms as the male members of the family. The titles were particularly important for men who were engaged in arenas where precedence was a factor. They were primarily granted to men as men, to sons by birth and to sons-in-law on their marriage. Purple-born daughters held titles as wives and had a lower rank than the women their brothers married. The one title from pre-Komnenian times which was granted to women as women, the *zoste patrika*, or belted patrician, seems to have declined in importance and certainly in visibility. Only one patrician, Maria Melissene, is known for the twelfth century and she is only known from her seal.

We are without evidence which would show us how imperial women related to one another in daily or ceremonial life. Even Anna Komnene does not provide this sort of information, for she refers to the women in her history mainly by their relation to herself, such as 'my sister Maria'. Eirene Doukaina is referred to as 'the *augousta*' or 'my mother' but these references come in general descriptions of life and not a part of a description of ceremonies. If this had been available, the prestige and importance of the titles would have been clearer. From the existing evidence one can say that there was a distinction between official and unofficial titles for imperial women which was recognised by the court and considered of sufficient importance to be adhered to by the majority of writers.

But it is hard to escape the impression that the system was based on male privilege, for the rank of the females was a consequence of the rank of their husbands. After the death of the husband, the wife kept his rank, but she could never rise any higher, with the exception of course of Anna Dalassene. Her case is a specific historical incident, dependent on unique events, and in no way influenced the system. However it does serve to highlight a change which took place between Alexios's reign and John's reign. Anna Dalassene was visible and active with a title of her own which meant something to the rest of the court who were obliged to call her by it. Thirty years later John's wife, the *augousta*, died, and no chronicler thought it important enough to mention who took her place during court ceremonies. This exploration has shown that the system that Alexios set up privileged the male above the female inside the family on the basis of sex and that this had far-reaching consequences for the power of women. The regression from visibility to disappearance for the women of the family will be encountered again in the following chapters.

CHAPTER FIVE

The method of marriage

The previous chapter considered the hierarchy of titles set up by Alexios Komnenos and its effect on the lives of imperial women. It is now time to investigate the principle that lay beneath the new use and invention of titles. Alexios created titles for his kin: kinship determined the relative position of each individual on the ladder from the *basileus* at the top to the numerous *sebastoi* who occupied the bottom rung. It has long been recognised that the empire that Alexios Komnenos bequeathed to his successors was quite different from the one which he won in 1081, and his use of kin is one of the explanatory concepts. This chapter explores the significance of a kin system for women in two ways. Firstly, it analyses the period along anthropological lines of enquiry to determine the status of women in this new system, thereby still treating women as the Object. Anthropologists consider factors such as descent, inheritance, marriage patterns, guardianship of minors, residence patterns and kin terminology when analysing societies. These categories are useful for studying women in Byzantium. Marriage alliance as a system has been understood to work by exchanging women, thereby reducing them to the level of pawns in a man's game. I will argue that Komnenian marriage was not an exchange of women. Secondly, the chapter changes focus to make women the Subject and shows how women acted to achieve their own goals by the manipulation of marriage alliances.

Alexios, John, and Manuel Komnenos were all concerned with kin. The general scholarly understanding of the system of titles and honours invented by Alexios is that it created an echelon above the traditional honour of Caesar for the members of his family, transforming them into a class all on their own, access to which was by birth or marriage alone. To achieve this necessitated a change in mentality to the clan spirit, where high posts were occupied only by the relatives and friends of the emperor. This was only possible because of the shrinkage in territorial terms of the empire. Paul Lemerle is scathing in his judgement, claiming that the system of the Komnenoi was a family affair where the superior interest of the state was subordinated to that of the family.[1] This was due to the management of a narrow-minded adventurer, Alexios Komnenos, who by chance became emperor, and, unable to handle the width of the majesty of empire, reduced it to his own horizons. As a land-owner, he had a sense of what was due to his family, and therefore ran the empire like a private estate, a solution which was only of short-term benefit to the empire. Other scholars are less critical: Angold credits Alexios's 'close-knit network of relatives' with his survival as emperor through a series of failures and mistakes which would have brought a more isolated ruler down. He sees the regime as an alliance of powerful families, whose power was guaranteed by the emperor, who made them his priority.[2] Kazhdan mentions the change from the nuclear family to the extended family in the late eleventh century, resulting in the growing importance of lineage, which determined the status and power of an individual, and the related interest in genealogy, as every family tried to prove that its roots were noble and far-reaching.[3] Margaret Mullett, investigating the later career of Maria of Alania, shows that the system was a family empire, and that the domestic virtues were paramount.[4] The fullest statement of the kin-dominated empire of the Komnenoi is by Paul Magdalino, who illuminated the 'heavy atmosphere of family intimacy and family tension which surrounded the Komnenian emperors' and explored what contemporaries felt about it. The Komnenian system was a family regime, in which closeness of relationship to the em-peror determined rank, the emperor ran and perceived the state as his own property, and gave his kin a real share in it, not just in name but in fact. He remarks that Alexios Komnenos did not *create* the concept of kinship, with its inevitable 'in-people' and 'out-people' but merely organised in a systematic way what had always been 'the real basis of rank and privilege', even before the Komnenoi.[5] Laiou's study of marriage through the legal record reveals how important

1. P. Lemerle, *Cinq études sur le XIe siècle byzantin* (Paris, 1977).
2. M. Angold, *The Byzantine Empire, 1025–1204. A Political History* (2nd ed., London, 1997), pp. 146–8.
3. A. Kazhdan and A. Epstein, *Change in Byzantine Culture in the Eleventh and Twelfth Centuries* (Los Angeles, 1985).
4. M. Mullett, 'The "disgrace" of the ex-Basilissa Maria', *BS* 45 (1984), pp. 202–11.
5. P. Magdalino, *The Empire of Manuel Komnenos, 1143–1180* (Cambridge, 1993).

marriage alliances were to the power base of the Komnenoi. Throughout these two centuries, the state and the church constantly fought
over regulations and control of marriage alliances, with the power
of the state often succeeding in making and breaking marriages
which were forbidden by the church.[6]

Scholarly understanding stems from the comments of the contemporary sources. Concerning the change in the hierarchy, Anna
Komnene gives the fullest explanation of her father's 'statecraft'.
As a Komnene, she approved of the scheme, and considered that it
illustrated Alexios's ability to improvise on behalf of the state. The
critical viewpoint was also represented. Both Zonaras and John the
Oxite singled out the tendency on Alexios's part to favour his family. Zonaras accused Alexios of inventing titles and honours for his
relatives and giving them cartloads of the state's money, enabling
them to live in houses like palaces. He concluded that Alexios ran
the state as if it was his own property and in the manner of a private
gentleman. The contemporary patriarch of Antioch, John the Oxite,
in a speech to the emperor in 1091 said bluntly that the emperor's
relatives were a plague on the state. The more general importance
of kin from the eleventh century is widely expressed in contemporary sources from Psellos to Choniates. Psellos found it necessary to
excuse Isaac Komnenos for electing Constantine Doukas as his successor rather than his brother John Komnenos. He made Isaac say
that Constantine's qualities have a greater claim on him than even
the ties of kin, but that he has the support of his kin in this choice.
Anna Komnene talked of the dignity of Maria of Alania, living
alone in Constantinople, bereft of kin, and how Maria assumed
that to be alone without kin was trouble enough without needing
any more. Zonaras in slandering Michael V said that 'his will was
deceptive, his soul unfeeling and ungracious, respecting institutions
neither of kin nor of friendship'. John II Komnenos was pulled up
short by John Axouch when he wished to give Axouch the property
he had confiscated from Anna. Axouch advised John to return the
property to Anna and John realised that 'I would be unworthy to
rule should you be deemed more merciful than I towards my family'.
Choniates made the issue quite clear when describing the return of
the *sebastokrator* Isaac to his brother John II after his self-imposed
exile among the Turks. He said 'For love of kin is a strong emotion,
and should it ever be slightly injured, it quickly heals itself.'

6. A. Laiou, *Mariage, amour et parenté à Byzance aux XIe–XIIIe siècles* (Paris, 1992),
ch. 1.

Anthropological analysis of the Komnenian system

The Komnenian kinship system is too complicated to be understood in terms of the simple societies for which kinship analyses are usually carried out. In contrast to societies which are dominated by kinship rules today, Komnenian Byzantium had no positive prescribed or even preferred marriage rules, nor named descent groups necessary for such a system to work. Medieval western kinship analyses may be more useful, since both western Europe and Byzantium were largely shaped by Christian ideology and both sprang from the ancient Mediterranean civilisations of Greece and Rome. But attempts to compare Byzantium and the west are plagued by the inevitable use of terms such as lineage or clan, which were derived from an understanding of the way the west worked by western anthropologists and still bear the marks of their origin; like feudalism, they are used widely, but if applied to Byzantium must be hedged around with copious explanations. For example, 'clan' in anthropological terms is an inaccurate characterisation of the Komnenos family, since a clan is a large unit whose members acknowledge common descent without being able to specify the exact ties. The Komnenoi, on the contrary, were well able to specify exact ties out to six degrees of kinship. The disadvantage of 'lineage' is that a lineage is a male system, whether used in its most restricted sense of a narrow line of *filiation, or of a 'house' which views itself as a collection of related men (agnatic), handing down a name from male to male, practising *primogeniture and endowed with a sense of genealogy. The Komnenoi possessed a sense of genealogy, but the other criteria are open to dispute.

Perhaps it is wiser to employ the term used by the Byzantines themselves, the *oikos*, the household, which has no implications of unilineal descent reckoning. Recent sociological work on kinship in modern western societies may be of more use for it enables us to see Byzantium as a kinship society despite the differences between it and the previously mentioned simple societies. The work of Christopher Harris, for example, is in no danger of relegating kinship to the private domain even when dealing with capitalist societies which ostensibly run on economic principles. As well as making a very good case for the continued significance of kinship in capitalist society, he produces a method for determining whether a society is dominated by kinship principles or not. Kinship is understood as a set of beliefs, values and categories which structure social action, rather than the sum total of a number of facts about who is related to whom, and in what degree. To decide if this set is central to a society the researcher must discover to what extent three categories overlap. These three are biological relations, social relations and kinship terms. If there is extensive overlap, then kinship is central to the workings of that society.[7] We can talk about kinship 'structuring' Byzantium under the Komnenoi since this set of beliefs and values was paramount and dictated social status and rank, power, employment, income, prestige, and marriage partner. Kinship terms were used to describe religious relationships like 'spiritual father', social relations certainly followed biological relations, which in Manuel's time were equivalent to titles, and spiritual relations like godparents were mapped onto existing biological relations. The imperial world of Byzantium can therefore be considered a kinship-dominated society under the Komnenoi.

Marriage

The favoured method whereby kin were created in the Komnenian period was by marriage alliance. This was not for lack of alternative available methods for creating kin. Ritual and spiritual kinship were other ways of achieving the same aim, and in some cases did it better, since bonds of spiritual kinship were understood to be superior to those of physical kinship.[8] But during the era of the Komnenoi, bonds of spiritual and ritual kinship seem to have been underplayed in favour of marriage alliance. There are few references in the sources to any but physical bonds of kinship. This may of course suggest exactly the opposite conclusion, namely that ties of spiritual kinship were working so well that they did not show in the sources, which normally only mentioned them when they went wrong. It was still the case that every infant required a sponsor to 'lift them from the font', and it is also the case that baptismal sponsors were chosen on the basis of friendship where any reason was specified. But in at least one documented case during the Komnenian era, the sponsors were the maternal and paternal uncles of the infant. Ruth Macrides concludes that the family probably played a much larger role as a source of baptismal sponsors than the sources indicate, thereby

---

7. C.C. Harris, *Kinship* (Minneapolis, 1990), p. 27.

8. R. Macrides, 'The Byzantine godfather', *BMGS* 11 (1987), p. 141 and n. 14.

merging the ties of physical and spiritual kinship together. Marriage as a method may appear more important than it actually was in the minds of Byzantines because there were many western marriages in the Komnenian period as a result of the fact that other ties of kinship, like baptismal sponsorship or adoption, were not practical because of the distances involved.[9] Certainly, the Komnenoi used all bonds of kinship, skilfully interwoven, to an degree exposed by the magnitude of their success. This observation is not new. What has not received so much attention is the place of women in the scheme.

Since marriage alliance was the privileged method in the Komnenian system, it necessarily involves women. Does marriage as a method give significance to women or does it exploit them? Most certainly, prestige is not conferred automatically because of the crucial importance of women to the system. A look at the relative prestige of women in any historical period or place will prove that it is possible to be vital yet treated like a chattel. In the eleventh and twelfth centuries Byzantine girls were married off without any choice in the matter and at a very young age. However, the same was true of boys. The system may have been exploitative, but it was not sexist: both sexes were married at their parents' discretion and betrothed at as young an age as possible. Unfortunately, the necessary evidence concerning the woman's point of view about arranged marriage has only survived in one text. Anna Komnene seems content with arranged marriage, and presupposes that love and affection will be found inside it. Both her parents' marriage and her own are described in terms of love and tenderness between spouses. Marriage for love and free choice of partner are relatively recent developments. A more useful question is whether a system of marriage alliances operates by exchanging women, a method which would imply that they had little power and were considered as pawns.

In *The Elementary Structures of Kinship*, Claude Levi-Strauss viewed marriage alliance as exchange of women, necessitated by the universal incest taboo, in which the spouses are not equal partners, since the women function as objects of exchange between men. This exchange of women creates kin, which as a concept stands between nature and culture, partaking of both. It is natural because it is created from a physical union between a man and a woman, a union which in certain respects is a biological imperative. But

9. R. Macrides, 'Dynastic marriages and political kinship', in J. Shepard and S. Franklin (eds), *Byzantine Diplomacy* (Aldershot, 1992), pp. 263–80, pp. 269–70.

kinship is also created by culture, by the laws and rules which a society invents to regulate and operate it. Animals mate by biological necessity but they do not thereby create relationships between the families of the mating pair. The human institution of kin relationships is therefore what separates man from animals, the concept which makes men human, which turns nature into culture. These views are the bases of Levi-Strauss's theory of kinship and marriage. The kinship structure operates around the relationship of brothers-in-law, for even in systems of matrilineal descent it is the hand of the father or brother of the woman which reaches into the son-in-law or brother-in-law's village. Women lose their identity because the act of exchange is what is significant, not the value of the goods exchanged.

The radical feminist and psychoanalyst, Juliet Mitchell, has added this theory to Freud's Oedipal theory to produce her own theory of how patriarchy is built and perpetuated. She understands women to be exchange objects in all kinship systems, accepting uncritically Levi-Strauss's ideas.[10] As a non-anthropologist, she is aware of but unconcerned with the serious methodological and conceptual difficulties in Levi-Strauss's work which have been the subject of anthropological criticism since they were written. The first point that could be made is that the incest taboo is not universal, since in Ptolemaic Egypt brother-sister marriage was encouraged. One general area of criticism is Levi-Strauss's assumption that women almost lose their identity when they are exchanged because the exchange is all. Jack Goody believes that the emphasis on the exchange of women distorts reality by stressing affinal relationships too much, and reduces the incest taboo to brother-sister relationships only.[11] These effects reduce its applicability for Byzantium, where the tie between brothers was stronger than between brothers-in-law, evidenced by the system of titles, and where the incest taboo extended as far as the definition of kin, that is, to the sixth degree.

The most potent argument against marriage-as-exchange in Byzantium is the extensive marriage prohibitions which forbade intermarrying with kin at all. Marriages must be made with outsiders, but once a connection is made, there can be no exchange, because

10. J. Mitchell, *Psychoanalysis and Feminism* (Harmondsworth, 1974), p. 370. On the theoretical shortcomings of an approach which assumes that women are pawns, see A. Weiner, *Women of Value, Men of Renown* (Austin, 1976), p. 17.

11. J. Goody, *Comparative Studies in Kinship* (London, 1969), p. 46. For a general criticism of Levi-Strauss's theory see E. Leach, *Levi-Strauss* (London, 1974), pp. 95–111.

the family of the outsider becomes kin too and therefore is subject to prohibitions. For most of the period marriage was prohibited inside six degrees of kinship, both by blood and affinity. Manuel Komnenos changed the situation slightly in 1166, legislating that marriage could not take place between consanguines within seven degrees of kinship. However, in 1175 he passed another law more or less abolishing the Tome of Sisinnios, which had prohibited marriage between affinal kin out to the sixth degree since the end of the tenth century.[12] These strict regulations were not always up-held, but anyone wishing to marry inside the prohibited range had to apply to the patriarch for permission, which was often given, depending on the status of the petitioner.

There is only one instance within the three generations of Komnenoi studied in this book where exchange looks likely. This is in Alexios Komnenos's own generation, when his brother Manuel and his sister Theodora were both married to Diogenoi in the same year, 1068. The Komnenoi therefore received a woman from a family and gave one back to the same family. An attempt to marry two brother-sister combinations from the Petraliphas and Komnenos families was vetoed by a synod in a later generation. There are other families which marry into the Komnenoi several times over the three generations, but they are always spread out in time, due to affinal prohibitions and there is no direct correlation of males and females. On the contrary, in general the Komnenoi take males from other families and do not take the corresponding females. This is the case with the Botaneiates, Bryennios, Kantakouzenos, Batatzes and Kontostephanos families. One male and one female Taronites married in, and the female was a Komnene Taronitissa, eight degrees removed from her husband; and one male and one female Synadenos. It is impossible to arrange these instances of inter-family marriage into a system. The operating principle behind choice of spouse did lie in reciprocity, but not of females.

If women are exchanged, the women of the family have to leave, in some sense, their natal family. However, the evidence does not show that Komnenian women ever considered themselves as leaving their family of birth and becoming part of another. Seals belonging to Alexios's sisters show that they took their identity from being his sisters rather than their husband's wives. His sister Maria owned a seal proclaiming its owner as 'the *sebaste* and sister of the emperor' and his sister Eudokia, the wife of Nikephoros Melissenos, owned

12. Magdalino, *Empire*, pp. 214–17.

two. The first featured her rank, which was the female equivalent of her husband's rank and her family name: 'Mother of God, assist Eudokia Komnene the *magistrisse*'. The second, while retaining her rank and family name, included her relation to the emperor: 'Mother of God, assist Eudokia Komnene the *Kaisarissa* and sister of the emperor'.

Anna Komnene certainly considered herself to be an imperial Komnene all her life. Her husband, Bryennios, while he appears in her history, does not fill her life in the way that her father did. Of course, the *Alexiad* is a biography of her father, but by its witness Anna spent her life as part of her natal family while her father was alive, and afterwards retired to her mother's monastery of Kecharitomene, to which she was heir. There is no hint that Bryennios provided for her upkeep, or that she even knew his family. He spent most of his time fighting for Alexios and, after him, John. The Bryennioi were based in Adrianople: there is no evidence that Anna ever went there. On the contrary, spouses of Komnenian women became part of the Komnenos family, to be rewarded with the appropriate title and to fulfil the appropriate job, as the previous chapter demonstrated. Their children were part of the kindred that the emperor had at his disposal, and were considered as Komnenoi.

Events which blood kin would construe as insults were felt by affines to dishonour them too. John Kantakouzenos joined with his brother-in-law John Komnenos in enmity against Andronikos when he took John's sister, Eudokia Komnene, as his mistress. The case of the Caesar John Roger, the husband of Maria Komnene, daughter of John II, illustrates to what extent the Komnenoi swallowed up the individuality of outside men who had married in. After the death of Maria, Manuel considered John Roger as a possible bridegroom for Constance of Antioch. Even after the death of his Komnenian wife, the Caesar was still considered as part of the family who could be used to further the family's connections in spite of his spotted record of loyalty. The same marriage alliance demonstrated beyond doubt that women of the imperial family retained their loyalty to their natal family. When Maria heard that her husband was plotting revolt she demanded that the men of the city take action to preserve the throne for her brother or she would take action herself. Maria did not consider that her destiny was bound up with that of her husband: instead her loyalty to her brother was uncompromising. It is hard to sustain the notion of exchange of women in the absence of any third party, and evidence for a third party in the form of a family into which these Komnenian women were received is missing. If exchange of women operated at this time, the question is, with whom?

A possible marker of exchange or otherwise is a study of residence patterns after marriage. Although physical removal is only one aspect of exchange, relocation to another residence reveals inherent tendencies in the structure of the society. It is also one of the factors that feminists take into account because the experience is deemed to be traumatic for young girls. Evidence for this period is slight, since the sources usually refer to the court as a whole and do not divide it into its components. The city as a whole was usually opposed to the provinces, not investigated at the micro-level. Zonaras relates an episode which gives a clue to residence after marriage for the daughters of the emperor. He says that Iasites did not treat his wife, Eudokia Komnene, with the respect due to an emperor's daughter and was thrown out of the palace, by his mother-in-law Eirene Doukaina. This implies that the couple were living there prior to the incident. The Great Palace was a conglomeration of buildings spread over a large area, so close proximity need not be assumed, but it was very much the imperial dwelling of the emperor's family, and as such, Iasites was an outsider moving into the territory of his wife. On the other hand John Komnenos, the emperor's son, had a house in the city. Anna Komnene at the conclusion of the *Alexiad* describes a nuclear family gathering of her mother, herself, and her sisters around the death bed of her father in the Mangana. One of these was the aforementioned Eudokia, now widowed, who presumably lived in the palace. The other was Maria, married to Nikephoros Euphorobenos Katakalon. Does her presence imply that she too lived in the palace with her family, or at least in very close proximity? The youngest sister, Theodora was also there. She too was a widow, and presumably had a residence in the palace.

Prior to the Komnenian consolidation there were two other instances of residence removal on betrothal. Before the coup the grandson of Nikephoros Botaneiates, who was betrothed to Manuel Komnenos's daughter, came to live with the Komnenoi. Several years after the coup Anna Komnene herself went to live with her future mother-in-law, Maria of Alania, on her betrothal to Constantine Doukas. The connections may be too complex and personal to be reduced to principles in these cases. A theory depending on movement of women is obviously not correct. Prestige is equally hard to calculate. Would the grandson of the emperor, even if not by the empress, have more or less prestige than the granddaughter of a private family, albeit a powerful one? She was twelve, he was probably about the same age. Anna Komnene was the daughter of the reigning emperor, but Constantine was the co-emperor. Perhaps he had more right to have his betrothed move to his house. Or perhaps the reasons were incidental and personal. Alexios was fond of Maria of Alania: perhaps he did not want to deprive her of her son. The only other hint of living arrangements for the imperial family comes in the funeral oration by Theodore Prodromos for Theodora, the daughter-in-law of Anna Komnene. Prodromos praises her for following the lead of the great empress Eirene Doukaina, who was the gardener of the garden they all lived in. This is possibly a reference to the way in which imperial ladies spent their time: in close contact with the rest of the family in one physical *oikos*, the Great Palace. While the positive evidence is slight, it is enough to state that residence patterns in the Byzantine empire under the Komnenoi were not virilocal, but again may have been dependent on status, the imperial line dictating residence.

Women have been understood as 'bundles of rights' in relation to exchange. Physical removal is only one aspect of exchange which may or may not operate. At marriage some rights in women are transferred to her new family, but never the whole quantum of rights that her natal kin have. Two such 'rights' are reproductive services and sexual services. Given the use made of children of Komnenian women, whose marriages were arranged by the emperor for his dynastic or security purposes, the reproductive services of the women remained with their natal family. Sexual services were exclusive on account of Christian ideology, which conceived of marriage as a partnership of one man and one woman, whose bodies belonged to each other, backed up by law, which laid penalties on women who lost their virginity before marriage, made proven adultery a cause of divorce for either partner, allowed a woman to divorce her husband if he imported another woman into their house, and allowed a man to divorce his wife if she spent three consecutive nights outside their home at any other location except her parental home. Sexual rights were vested in the conjugal family, while reproductive rights remained in the imperial family. Women marrying Komnenian males transferred their reproductive rights to their family of marriage. Their children were also at the disposal of the emperor, sometimes against their preferences. The prestige of the imperial *oikos* therefore is the deciding factor in relation to rights in women and there is no structural reallocation to the non-imperial family.

Although so much else of Levi-Strauss's theory seems inappropriate, his ideas on kinship and reciprocity are useful for an understanding of the kinship system of the Komnenoi. The operating principle behind choice of spouse was one of reciprocity, but not of female for female. Given the way in which Alexios Komnenos gained the throne, and the type of autocracy he was attempting to perpetuate, support from others was vitally necessary. As only one of a number of families who were rich enough and ambitious enough to aim for the throne, the Komnenoi needed to neutralise the rest and bring them all into line behind them. Even when the throne was won, it was not secure, as the history of the eleventh century had demonstrated. Support from other powerful people was still necessary, and the best way of ensuring this support was to create kin obligations. Harris's definitions of kin relationships demonstrate why. The most pertinent points are that kin relationships are always significant in every situation, the parties have no choice but to fulfil their obligations, the genealogical relation in which they stand is the most important thing about their relationship, and an overt calculation of personal interest is inappropriate.[13] The usurpations of the eleventh century had shown beyond doubt that notions of loyalty for the good of the state were insufficient. Personal benefit was no doubt ideologically inappropriate, but it was effective in practice. By the time Manuel was on the throne, it was normal for the emperor to arrange or at least approve all marriage alliances of members of his family. This was necessary because a marriage changed the balance inside the *oikos*.

The family tree (see page 221) shows that Komnenian emperors wanted males from important families as spouses for Komnenian women: the reason was because the full weight of kin obligations fell on them in marriage. These men were often given military commands, which was the most sensitive area of security, because a disloyal commander was in the best position to usurp the throne for himself. The emperor could not be everywhere, especially given the amount of military activity in which the Komnenian emperors indulged: loyalty in a commander was therefore the paramount virtue, even above military competence. Trustworthiness and loyalty were the coin in which the inmarrying men paid for the prestige of being part of the imperial family. In fact it could be said that women were not part of the exchange at all, for the men did not really possess the woman except by the subjective and unforcible bonds of affection. The identity of the woman was paramount: if she was not who she was the exchange would not be able to happen.

---

13. Harris, *Kinship*, pp. 49–65.

A better expression of the situation may be in Annette Weiner's words about the Trobriand Islanders that men did not receive women on marriage, but the value of womanliness, which opened up to them a whole new world.[14] The reciprocity set up by a kin relationship need not have been immediate, and may have consisted of nothing more than quiet support, but once it was entered into, it endured until death or beyond, unless a momentous event occurred to break off the links.

We are ignorant of the details of the economic side of marriage, which might constitute one indicator of exchange. By law women in Byzantium received dowries, which were preserved to be handed on to the children of the marriage. The number of marriages and the number of daughters who were married suggests that either the emperor had so much money or movable goods that he had no objection to dowering all his daughters, or that he had found a way to prevent the daughter's inheritance leaving the *oikos* in any real way. The original dowries of their mothers cannot have covered the spread of obligations. Eirene Doukaina had goods given to her by her family, which she spent on Alexios's military campaigns. Unfortunately there is no evidence to show what the imperial daughters' dowries contained, but favourite imperial gifts given to foreign rulers included cash, court titles, silk and jewels. It is reasonable to suggest that the dowries of Alexios and John's daughters were comprised of these in the appropriate amounts. The benefits of becoming part of the family, receiving a title and its income, would have been sufficient attraction for most men. Recovering the facts about the dowering of daughters would reveal much more about women in marriage than merely the possessions she brought with her. For example, if the dowry included worked silk which the daughter was supposed to have embroidered herself, we would know more about how imperial daughters spent their time and what skills they were supposed to possess.

Inheritance, descent and naming strategies

Having established that Komnenian marriage did not work by exchange of women, it is time to turn to other anthropological concerns. Feminist anthropologists have used a definition of patriarchy closely linked to the specific practices which perpetuate it, such as

14. Weiner, *Women of Value*, p. 230.

inheritance rules, methods of reckoning descent, and naming strategies. In patrilateral societies property is passed down from father to first son intact, with the other siblings being provided for out of movable goods. In Byzantium, by law parental property was divided equally between sons and daughters, whether a will had been made or not. Inheritance in Byzantium was therefore not patrilateral but bilateral. Daughters on marriage received a dowry which was subject to very strict controls. It did not become the property of the husband. He could manage it, but in the case of mismanagement he had to make reparation, for the dowry was handed on to the children of the woman and had to be preserved complete. By law only widows or those whose dowry property had been mismanaged by their husbands had full control of that property. Ownership in law does not always mean economic freedom in practice, and again we are faced with the lack of evidence for Komnenian daughters. However, there must have been other sources of income for powerful women which were not under such strict control, either by law or from their spouses, for Maria of Bulgaria used her money to get Alexios and Eirene married, Eirene Doukaina founded the monastery of Kecharitomene, which entailed endowment with property for its upkeep, while Alexios was still alive, and Anna Komnene may have paid the expenses of a literary circle while still a wife.

The most favourable position in law was that of wealthy widows. They had full control of the whole property, as opposed to nominal ownership. They were the preferred guardians of children, with the concomitant responsibilites of educating them, arranging marriages for them and providing dowries. As long as they did not marry again they had all the freedom which was denied to wives. Second marriages were viewed as unfair to the children of the first marriage, since there was the possibility of more siblings. Usually the widow lost control of the property left in trust for the children and retained only her *morning gift. There was every incentive for rich women to remain widowed, but the situation was very different for poor women without property.

The most important type of inheritance in an empire is succession to the imperial throne. Immediately patrilineal succession is assumed in Byzantium because of the obsession with sons in the west at all periods of its history. It has been noted that it is necessary to differentiate between different types of inheritance, and that where succession to office is involved there are often different rules due to the nature of office. Office, unlike property, is not partible.

Alexios at least, as far as was possible, did divide office. The position of emperor might have been considered as indivisible before, but by the grant of a hitherto imperial title to his brother, including him in imperial proclaimations and acting as if Isaac was nearly as much emperor as he himself was, Alexios split the office. This was not the same as creating a co-emperor. Alexios did this also, firstly for the Doukas heir, Constantine, and then for his own son, John, but that was a safeguard for the future. The position of Isaac was in the present. *Affines were also granted high titles and lands if their status merited it, for example, Nikephoros Melissenos, who was made Caesar and granted Thessalonike. John Komnenos did something similiar. He compensated richly all the sons who were not his designated heir with the high title of *sebastokrator* and gave them lands in abundance, even considering creating a separate appanage for Manuel. Such actions demonstrate the high value placed on kin by the Komnenos emperors by demonstrating their assumption that even the office of emperor was not the preserve of one person. Due to the success of this policy, which diluted the emperor's prestige, Manuel had to reverse the trend by taking much more authority into his own hands when he became emperor in 1143.

The fact that succession to office is agnatic does not mean that the whole system works on patrilineal clans or lineages. Agnatic succession to office and bilateral inheritance of property can exist in the same system. In Byzantium agnatic succession was preferred. Sons inherited the empire if at all possible. Choniates put the opinion into Alexios's mouth that all the past rulers of Byzantium would mock him if, having a son perfectly capable of inheriting the empire, he should choose his son-in-law instead. In the absence of a son, the first choice was a daughter. The only Komnenos, Manuel, who faced this situation made provision for this eventuality by giving careful consideration to her husband, in contrast to Basil II and Constantine VIII who gave it no consideration at all until it was too late. Unlike a truly agnatic system, a more distant male relative was not the obvious choice for a successor, nor was the heiress married to a male relative, although it should be noted that the emperor's cousin, Andronikos, complained that she should be married to a Roman, not a foreigner, and Choniates remarked that Manuel overlooked all the possible Roman nobles in favour of a western spouse. Rather, Manuel Komnenos looked for men of a sufficiently high family not to disgrace his daughter Maria, but not so powerful that they would demand that she should leave Byzantium and reside in their countries, implying that the empire had fallen under the rule of another dynasty. This resulted in a series of betrothals for Maria before marriage to her eventual husband, Renier of Montferrat. Manuel's choice of heiress was not dictated by lack of choice of close male relatives. On the contrary there were many Komnenian males within three degrees of kinship who would have been suitable as his heir if he had chosen that solution, like the Angelos cousins who did eventually inherit the throne. Maria was his heir because there was no impediment to a woman occupying the imperial throne. But once her brother was born, her own claim was waived in favour of his.

Guardianship of minors is another legal area which may illuminate the place of women inside a kinship system. In Byzantium the system changed over time. According to the law-making emperor Justinian, children were born into the authority of their father, and he preferred agnatic kin as guardians for children where no specific appointment had been made by will. By the time of the *Basilika* in the ninth century the mother of the children was preferred above all others as guardian, a legal situation borne out in practice certainly in imperial circles, where the mother of a minor had the guardianship of the empire also. The rules of guardianship discouraged second marriages, but, as with other imperial situations, the status of the widow sometimes nullified the law. Eudokia Makrembolitissa, wife of Constantine X Doukas, left as guardian and regent, married Romanos Diogenes. She should therefore by law have forfeited the guardianship of her sons by Constantine. However, she remained in control until the defeat of the emperor when, after a short period of joint rule, she was removed by force by her first husband's relatives. Once her powerful protector had gone, her affines closed in. They did not, however, appeal to the law, but threatened violence instead. The most famous guardian of the Komnenian era was of course Anna Dalassene, who explored and exploited the possibilities of her position in gratifying her ambition for her family.

After inheritance, descent is an important criterion. The family under the Komnenoi cannot be analysed as a patriclan, where members trace their descent exclusively through the father, or a matriclan, where decent is traced through the mother exclusively, because descent was traced through the Komnenos parent, regardless of sex. This is not technically bilineal descent, which traces descent through both parents, because often only one line is important, that of the imperial parent. Nor is it unilineal, in that only one line counts, for it is often a different line, neither male nor female consistently, but dependent on the prestige of the parent's family. Such a situation is not of course surprising but it does lead to difficulties in characterising the system.

Naming practices illuminate the process of descent. Surnames were not passed through males exclusively. To talk of 'patronyms', which normally reveal patriliny, is misleading. Females of the family held their name after marriage, and transmitted it to their children. The criterion for choosing a surname was prestige, not paternity.[15] A glance at family names, which made their appearance in Byzantium in the tenth century for the first time, reveals this clearly, although the law, at least in an earlier age, counted children as part of their father's family. Justinian's *Institutes* ruled that children were in the authority of their father, and counted inside their father's family. This implies patrilineal descent, but faced with the identification of children of Komnenos females with their mother's family, the law, if still technically in force, seems disregarded in practice.

The poems of Theodore Prodromos and Manganeios Prodromos are an excellent source for identifying the family connections of the people to whom they were addressed. Usually the poet describes the ancestors of the recipient, a practice which intimates that genealogical connections were both well-known and significant. The recipient is connected to the emperor if possible and often this involves tracing descent through the mother. If the father's family was also prestigious, paternal descent was sometimes specified as well. Children of Komnenos males usually only carried the name Komnenos; they did not add their maternal name to it. In the Komnenos family tree, the children of daughters as well as sons usually took the name Komnenos, although they sometimes added the family name of their father to it. This tendency was not a Komnenos invention, although the longevity and fame of that family probably gave it impetus: the first Manuel Komnenos, Alexios's grandfather, was known by his mother's name of Erotikos; Anna Dalassene took her mother's name rather than Charon, which was her father's, because of the prestige of her mother's family.

There was certainly no rule, or even tradition, forcing people to adopt a patronym rather than a matronym. Names could also be chosen from alternate generations, and where this is the case suspecting a personal attachment is feasible. Anna Komnene's daughter

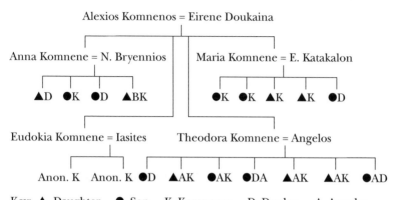

Key: ▲ Daughter   ● Son   K Komnenos   D Doukas   A Angelos

FIG. 3   Genealogical connections

preferred her maternal grandmother's name of Doukaina to either
her mother's prestigious name of Komnenos or her father's less
important name of Bryennios: she had been named Eirene after
her grandmother and therefore is the second Eirene Doukaina.
None of Anna's children included their father's name at all, except
perhaps the last daughter, Maria Bryennaina Komnene. The sons
divided the surnames, the firstborn being called Alexios Komnenos
and the second John Doukas. Alexios's second daughter Maria was
married to a Euphorbenos Katakalon, one of the largest families in
the empire besides the Komnenoi. None of their children took their
father's name, the two sons and two of the daughters choosing
Komnenos, and one daughter choosing Doukaina. Both of Eudokia
Komnene's children were called Komnenos. Only Theodora Komnene's children chose to include Angelos in their names, and not
one of them chose Angelos alone. The possibilities are demonstrated
by Manuel Kamytzes Komnenos Doukas, the son of Maria Angelaina
Komnene and Constantine Kamytzes, born in 1150. Considerations
of prestige led to maternal and paternal surnames being piled up,
until in the fourteenth century people carried five or more. Thus
the genealogical connections until the end of the empire can be
roughly plotted (Fig. 3).

Another criterion for analysing any system in anthropological
terms is terminology. In the simple societies of Levi-Strauss maternal and paternal kin are differentiated and identified by different
terminology, which is precise in indicating the genealogical relationship. Therefore there are precise terms for mother's brother,
father's brother etc. The use of such terminology suggests that it

is important to know whether any given person is related on the maternal or the paternal side. In Byzantium the terms are the same, implying that there was no difference in how such kin were perceived. The all-important role of mother's brother does not seem to function in Byzantium. There may have been a role for him, but it does not appear in the sources. All uncles, whether maternal or paternal, were identified by the term *theios*. Byzantines were aware of connections by marriage, indeed very aware, being capable of prohibiting marriage with affinal kin to the same degree as with consanguinal kin. A brother-in-law was *gambros* whether he was a wife's brother or a sister's husband. The same term was used for son-in-law, which suggests that generation was not stressed either. Father-in-law and mother-in-law were *pentheros* and *penthera*, a daughter-in-law was *nymphe*, a term which also applied to any marriageable girl. The Byzantines therefore had terms for affines as well as for consanguines, but did not distinguish in terms of the side by which they were related. This suggests the lack of clearly defined groups which intermarry. It also suggests that exchange of women in marriage was not a concept held by the Byzantines. If women were exchanged, whether this refers to physical removal of the woman to another locality or transfer of rights in the woman to another man or set of men, surely there would be different terms to indicate whether ego was the wife-giver or the wife-taker. In cultures which do identify these two roles, there is usually a difference in status between them, although which is the more prestigious is subject to cultural norms. Greek is the only European language which gives an early indication of 'lineal' terminology, which is said to indicate a change from the extended to the conjugal family, the introduction of testamentary inheritance and bilateral prohibitions on marriage when it is discerned in other languages at a later date.[16]

The Komnenoi were very successful both at propagating a huge *oikos* and neutralising opposition from outside. The family started by John Komnenos and Anna Dalassene ruled the empire until the end in 1453, with enough *oikoi* to ensure that it never died out (see page 221). This is in stark contrast to the west, where lineages died out, or had to resort to distant relations. The other long-lasting lineage of Byzantium, that of the Macedonians, also died out, despite having more strategies for survival than were available in the west. This lack of provision does require an explanation, for in the end

16. J. Goody, *The Development of the Family and Marriage in Europe* (Cambridge, 1983), pp. 263–4.

the emperor had to resort to a hasty marriage which could have been organised earlier. Neither of the emperors Basil or Constantine would have sent their nieces and daughters out of the empire by marriage but they could have married in a noble but inferior man to serve their purposes as Manuel Komnenos did later with his daughter Maria. The very different attitude of the Komnenoi, who married off all siblings in all generations, usually not long past the earliest age at which marriage was legal, accounts for the fact that the family never died out. Not only the attitude to marriage was different: that towards children must have followed suit, for Alexios and John Komnenos produced more purple-born heirs between them than their tenth- and eleventh-century predecessors put together. The question is how far was this deliberate policy? Did they produce more children to perpetuate the *oikos*, or was the interest in the *oikos* fostered by the need to provide for all the children?

That the policy of many children was deliberate is suggested by the exceptions in the Komnenos family. The only imperial woman in Byzantium who had few children was the western Bertha, Manuel's first wife, who bore two children only, beginning in 1152. There had been fears that Eirene Doukaina and Alexios were not going to have children between 1078 and 1083. This may have been part of the reason that Alexios was considering divorcing her, and marrying the fertile Maria of Alania in 1081, although lack of offspring was not a legal cause for divorce. Eirene Doukaina may have been particularly fond of her first-born child, Anna, because she justified her position and proved that she was not barren. This was especially important in the 'era of the mother', the 1080s. As a more general survival strategy for the family, the kin-based system of relationships ensured that Alexios, John and Manuel never had to face the kind of rebellion which had brought the dynasty to power, although minor conspiracies were frequent. Most of the young men were loyal: few considered replacing the reigning emperor. The Doukas brothers-in-law of Alexios fought for him; there was only one failure at that level, when Michael Taronites joined a conspiracy with Nikephoros Diogenes.[17] Only one nephew-in-law, Alexios Axouch, conspired against the emperor.[18] Inclusion in the imperial family could even break natal family loyalties. For instance, Gregory

17. Anna Komnene, *Alexiad*, trans. E. Sewter, *The Alexiad of Anna Comnena* (Harmondsworth, 1969), pp. 278–98.
18. John Kinnamos, *History*, trans. C. Brand, *The Deeds of John and Manuel Comnenus* (New York, 1976), pp. 199–202.

Taronites was opposed by his cousin, John Taronites, who was a nephew of Alexios Komnenos.[19]

In fact, consanguinal loyalty was more problematic. At the beginning of the era, the family was bound together by the knowledge that the disloyalty of one would overthrow them all. By the end of Alexios's reign, the dynasty was so firmly set on the throne by the diminution and absorption of the best of the rest that it was breaking up into smaller groups. The rivalry between Alexios's daughter Anna and his son John is one example. Manuel had the opposition of his brother, of his nephew and of his cousin to deal with. Only one brother-in-law considered revolt, and this case demonstrated the value of a sister. In 1143 at the changeover of power to Manuel, John Roger Dalassenos, of Norman descent, desired the throne. His wife, Maria Komnene, getting wind of his intentions, informed on him and demanded that he be turned in to her custody, or that the men take other preventative measures. John Roger was imprisoned awaiting Manuel's arrival in Constantinople. His later career shows that Manuel continued to trust him to a certain extent. Marrying potential troublemakers into the family could be a way of keeping them under close supervision, or as a reward for personal loyalty. Michael Anemas had been the ringleader of one of the most serious revolts against Alexios Komnenos. A generation later Manuel Anemas was part of the family. Either John Komnenos wished to incorporate him for preventative reasons, or as a reward for not following in his relative's footsteps. Inclusion into the imperial family carried obligations as well as privileges, and in reciprocation for the honour of a marriage alliance the recipient gave loyalty and trustworthiness.

Thus far, women have been discussed as passive cogs in the Komnenian kinship machine. The emperor was the operator of the machine, because supreme power and authority was his to use. He was not only in control of women in the system, but of men. As part of the machine, women were not necessarily more respected. The imperial family occupied a rung above the remainder of the aristocracy, which was still an aristocracy, proud of its traditions and exclusive in its alliances. As members of that imperial family, women partook of its prestige. As kin, they were accorded respect by their own menfolk because of their blood, not because of their usefulness as marriage partners. Marriages sometimes failed, but the women were still Komnenoi. Men respected their mothers because they were related to them, not from some sense that they had, in their

19. *Alexiad*, Sewter, pp. 386–8.

day, fulfilled their destiny as marriage partners. However, inside the kin group, as members of it, women could have influence because of their birth. An imperial woman remained a Komnene in name, through the reproductive services which remained with her family, and probably by residence too. Komnenian women as brides were not at the bottom of the pecking order, but were the source of their husband's exercise of power.

Woman as subject

One feminist strategy used most successfully by anthropologists is the refusal to treat women as pawns. The area of marriage alliance is a fruitful one for a feminist because this is one area where women can be seen pursuing goals by definite strategies. As arrangers and manipulators of marriage alliances they can be analysed as Subject. However, a biological determinism trap awaits the unwary. Alexios's choice of *modus operandi* has been alternatively blamed or credited to his mother, Anna Dalassene, depending on whether the author approves of the system or not. Magdalino speculates that concern for kin was a female trait, and that the influence of women on Alexios can be judged from his policy of dependence on kin. However, as soon as he has made the point, Magdalino recollects the Caesar John Doukas, who was a family strategist too. A glance back in time suggests the resolution of the difficulty.[20] It is striking that there are greater numbers of visible women in the histories dealing with the years 1025 to 1100; this reflects the heightened profile of 'aristocratic' women. Women, as well as men, understood how kinship worked, and can be seen operating networks to extend their repertoire of kin. This has been described as the 'aristocratic principle'.[21] Chapter 2 has demonstrated the extensive use of kin and trust of kin which was developing. The manoeuvres of the Komnenoi therefore fit into a long tradition. Anna Dalassene was the direct inspiration for her son's policies, since she brought him up, but her own views came from her upbringing as a member of one of the great families of the eleventh century. The Caesar John was a product of the same milieu, where the prevailing wisdom recommended creating kin as a method of survival. It is probable that Alexios, having seen the effects of his mother's strategy prior to his

20. Magdalino, P., *Innovations in Government*, pp. 151–2.
21. Angold, *Byzantine Empire*, p. 155.

coup, would emulate it, as other offspring of the time were doing. An accident of death has given Anna Dalassene too much credit, concentrating attention on her sex, rather than her society, adducing biological rather than social causes. Had John Komnenos lived, he would no doubt have followed the same policy, since before his death two of Alexios's sisters were married to Michael Taronites and Nikephoros Melissenos. Anna Dalassene has been considered the ambitious half of the couple, partly due to the words put into her mouth by Bryennios during the incident where Isaac I Komnenos offered the throne to his brother, but ambition on John Komnenos's part should not be entirely discounted.

Our treatment of woman as Subject concentrates on the period of the Komnenian coup. This was one of the high points of visibility of women in the eleventh century, and has been discussed briefly in Chapter 2. Once the Macedonian dynasty had ended, the throne was the possible goal of four families, the Komnenoi, the Doukai, the Melissenoi, and the Diogenoi. The Komnenoi reached the pinnacle first, but failed to hold it, through neglecting to operate the kin principle, a lesson not lost on Anna Dalassene. The throne then passed to Constantine Doukas, in 1059, and remained in the hands of the Doukas family until 1078. Laiou describes this period as the 'increased interference of a whole class of women in public life'.[22] It is more accurate to regard it as the increased interference of a very specialised set of women, namely mothers. In the 1080s respect for the domestic virtues was at its height. The two double *basilikoi logoi*, one for Constantine Doukas and Maria of Alania, and one for Alexios Komnenos and Anna Dalassene, performed in that decade indicate this clearly. This period could be described as the triumph of the mother, always accorded an honourable place in Byzantine theory, if not in practice. If motherhood was ever 'the greatest and most glorious function of a woman',[23] it was now. Mothers had always had a part to play in the handing on of power as they were the legal guardians of underage emperors and had the right to rule until the emperor came of age. Motherhood was the most glorious function of a woman in a different way perhaps than the builders of the ideology of the empire intended. Being a mother and a widow was the most powerful position of them all, for the *imperium* rested in imperial widows and could be passed on by them, even if there were sons of a previous emperor still alive. This situation was short-lived. Crisis points are often revealed when the observer is

22. Laiou, 'Role of Women', p. 250.   23. Ibid., p. 236.

given a glimpse of the internal workings of a system which seems to be running smoothly. The two crisis points of 1081 and 1118 reveal how women were manipulating kinship and how much the reign of Alexios I Komnenos diminished the power which they could wield.

In 1081 three women manipulated succession to the imperial throne by playing the kinship game with consummate skill. The Caesar John appears as an amateur beside the three women, all of them widows to all intents and purposes. These three were Anna Dalassene, Maria of Alania, and Maria of Bulgaria. The beneficiary was Alexios Komnenos, and one secret of his success could be the fact that he had two mothers: his biological mother Anna and his adopted mother, Maria of Alania.

Anna Dalassene is the most obvious example of the good Byzantine mother acting to elevate her family. The important people of the time can be judged from a glance at the family tree of the Komnenoi, because they are all there, with the exception of the Palaiologos family, married to Anna's children. Anna and John had five sons and three daughters. One son, Manuel, and one daughter, Theodora, were married into the Diogenes family in 1068, a good insurance policy at a time when the emperor was Romanos Diogenes. Anna's daughters Maria and Eudokia had been married, possibly by their father, into the military families of Taronites and Melissenos since the early 1060s. Nikephoros Melissenos had enough support and popularity to make a bid for the throne himself in 1081, but came to terms with Alexios and was created Caesar. Isaac was married to the niece or cousin of the empress Maria of Alania, and therefore had access to her, a critical component in the survival of the Komnenoi at court under Nikephoros Botaneiates. Alexios himself made the crucial Doukas connection possible by marrying Eirene Doukaina: he had previously been married or at least betrothed to a daughter of the wealthy and landed Argyros family. Adrian Komnenos married the daughter of Eudokia Makrembolitissa, Zoe, in 1081, a connection which by that time did not have obvious crucial importance. Perhaps it was a long-standing promise to keep the tacit support of the ex-empress, who was favoured by Botaneiates, during the critical days when Alexios and Isaac were in danger at court from the enmity of Borilos and Germanos.

Thus the Komnenos family was allied with all the possible contenders for the throne. No matter who was raised to power the Komnenoi would stand close to the throne. That the Komnenoi were better or more successful than everyone else has been recognised:

the architect of these alliances has not. The head of the Komnenoi was Anna Dalassene, and as a widow and therefore the head of the family, she did the arranging. Hers was the astute mind which guided the family through the years when power was changing hands rapidly until it was in a position to revolt. Her speed and dexterity can be seen in the match she made for her granddaughter, the daughter of Manuel, for whom she arranged a match with the grandson of Botaneiates, in 1081. Since Botaneiates was on the throne it was wise to create some alliance with him. In the end it did not matter, for the Komnenoi were successful, but the safeguard was there. She managed to do this while simultaneously allying her sons with the opposing camp, that of the empress Maria, who intended her own son to succeed.

Maria of Alania was trying to ensure that her porphyrogenite son succeeded to the throne, but without instant means of carrying this out. She was a foreigner with few compatriots in Byzantium; her affinal kin were the Doukai. Anna Komnene tells us that the Caesar John had influence with her after talking Botaneiates into marrying her.[24] Maria possibly began to create new kin for herself by marrying her niece or cousin to Isaac Komnenos. Anna Komnene says the marriage was made by Maria; Bryennios maintains it was the work of Michael Doukas as part of the reconciliation package after Anna Dalassene's trial and exile.[25] There is no way to choose between these two conflicting accounts. As far as Maria's own future was concerned, marriage with the new emperor was the best way that Maria could keep her son near the centre of power. The story of that marriage is always told as if it was the Caesar's brainchild, but who suggested the marriage to him in the first place? Probably Maria married Botaneiates gladly, despite his age. When it became clear that Botaneiates was going to try to elevate one of his own relatives to the throne, Maria gave her support to Alexios and Isaac, after receiving oaths from them that Constantine would not lose his throne through them. Isaac was already a relation of hers by marriage. Having gained as much as possible from marriage, Maria turned to motherhood, adopting Alexios as her son in the time-honoured ceremony. This forged strong links between the empress and the Komnenos family.

After the accession of Alexios in 1081, it is possible that Maria, Alexios or Anna Dalassene had further plots to marry Maria and Alexios. Zonaras reports the gossip and Anna Komnene is very

24. *Alexiad*, Sewter, p. 107.   25. Ibid., p. 74.

quick to justify Maria's continued presence in the Palace at length.[26] As expected, her justification is Maria's concern for her son, despite appearances to the contrary. In such a marriage, Anna Dalassene would have seen the end of the Doukas alliance, Alexios would have had the extra claim to the throne of marrying his predecessor's wife, and Maria would have secured her son's accession to the throne. The adaptability of marriage alliance as a method can hardly be demonstrated more clearly. In the event, the marriage of Alexios and Maria did not happen, but Maria, before retiring, ensured that her son's rights were protected, that he was included in proclamations, had the right to wear purple buskins, and was co-emperor. Later, Anna, the first daughter of Alexios and Eirene, was betrothed to Constantine, thus sealing the alliance.

The Doukas family had a strong claim to the throne, and no doubt thought that power would pass to Constantine Doukas after the death of Botaneiates, who was an old man. The Caesar John had done his best, marrying Constantine's mother to Botaneiates, who was too old to have a son, leaving Constantine, the son of the previous emperor, to step into his shoes. The Doukai must have thought they were safe. They also had a useful connection by marriage with the Palaiologos family. The Caesar John was the head of the family, but seems to have been slow to see the most important connection of all. According to Bryennios, the Doukas–Komnenoi connection was the inspiration and work of his daughter-in-law, Maria the Bulgarian. She decided that the family needed a protector, since her own husband was dying, her eldest son was dead and her youngest was too young, and she chose Alexios Komnenos. The Caesar approved, Alexios agreed depending on his mother's approval, the emperor Michael Doukas disapproved, and the emperor's brother wanted Alexios to marry his own sister. Despite the obstacle of Anna Dalassene's hostility to the Doukai, Maria did not rest, nor did she spare her money until Alexios and Eirene were betrothed. This is the only account we have of the betrothal, and it is the only betrothal of the time for which there is any information. Andronikos Doukas proposed the marriage to Alexios one day while he was visiting the Doukas house. Given the famous hostility between the two families, it is likely that Alexios had an inkling of what was in the wind, but there is no evidence to enlighten us. From this account, betrothals were arranged orally, with written documentation following, at least in the case of foreign marriages. The exact manoeuvres

26. *Alexiad*, Sewter, p. 104.

in which Maria engaged are a mystery. The only hint is in the comments of Bryennios that she did not spare her money, and that she told all the servants. Would Anna Dalassene back down before a rumpus created by adverse gossip among servants if she refused to allow the match to go ahead? What kind of money was involved? Eirene was young, only fifteen years old: Anna perhaps decided that a young girl would not be able to replace her, which was the truth for many years, and that it was better to unite the two families for political success. United, the two families would be nearly invincible.

One more alliance by marriage was crucial in the revolt. The master of the fleet was George Palaiologos, who was married to Anna Doukaina. This was one connection missed by Anna Dalassene which favoured the Doukas family to a great extent. At the time of the victory, George, who had only joined the rebels on the insistence of his mother-in-law, Maria of Bulgaria, insisted that the proclamations by the sailors include Eirene's name as well as Alexios's. Since Alexios needed Palaiologos to secure the city, he had to agree to the joint proclamations. Because George was a kinsman of the Doukai it was vital for his own safety that Eirene Doukaina should be proclaimed as empress, and that all credit should not go to Alexios Komnenos.

The tangled web of alliance uniting these families is not simple, but it is clear that it was the way forward in the late eleventh century, when so many had a chance of gaining the throne. None had any previous tie or claim to power; they had all grown up since the time of Basil II. The Komnenoi triumphed partly because their network was superior and partly because there were children of the right age at the right time to be married and to fight. Despite the connections built up by the strategy of Anna, the Komnenos family could not have succeeded in taking and holding power without the military abilities of its menfolk. While the Caesar John and his sons were defeated and captured by Roussel, Alexios Komnenos was bringing to heel not only Roussel, but Bryennios the Elder,[27] making himself useful to the emperor. This type of fame, however, generated the envy which the servants of Botaneiates displayed, and against which it was necessary to guard by the support of the powerful at the centre of power, in this case the empress Maria. The Doukai also had the hostility of their own kin, the ex-empress Eudokia, to contend with, so the family was neither so large nor so cohesive as the Komnenoi. Nikephoros Melissenos was a good

27. *Alexiad*, Sewter, pp. 37–46.

general and a military man, but he did not have a sufficient network of support to succeed alone and his interests were best served by acquiescing in Alexios's command of power and using his military threat to extort a title from him. No one family could act against the Komnenoi, for if they did they would be bringing disaster on their own heads. Too many families had their destiny tied up with that of the Komnenoi for an alliance of families to unite against them. Such was the culmination of the policies of Anna Dalassene. She was clearly the most skilful transformer of human resources into kin at the time.

Other Komnenian women cannot be seen pursuing their goals in this way. Eirene Doukaina is visible mainly through the witness of the *Alexiad*, but apparently had no part to play in the marriage alliances of her children. Anna Komnene does not hint that she was involved in them and Zonaras states that Alexios arranged the marriages of not only his own children, but those of his brother Isaac after the latter's death. Eirene as a wife therefore had no perceptible role in the important power-building activity of marriage alliance. She did look out for her daughters' welfare inside the marriages that their father arranged for them, in one case even breaking a marriage up because it was proving unsuitable. But the crisis point of 1118 illustrates her impotence as a mother, which contrasts with the power of the women of 1081.

In 1118 Alexios Komnenos died. Immediately a power struggle became evident between Anna Komnene and John Komnenos for the throne. Anna was the oldest child and had been proclaimed empress when she was betrothed to Constantine Doukas in the 1080s. After Constantine's death and the birth of John in 1087, Alexios's plans changed. John was proclaimed co-emperor in 1092. Before Alexios's death, Eirene Doukaina attempted to persuade him to appoint Anna and her husband as his heirs. Alexios refused to do this. When Alexios became so ill that he handed power over to Eirene, she put Anna's husband Bryennios in charge of affairs. When Alexios died, John seized the Great Palace with his supporters and succeeded in establishing himself on the throne. Anna's revolt failed.[28]

Both protagonists in this contest were of the Komnenos family, because by 1118 there were no other individuals capable of challenging a Komnenos. But inside the family itself there were fissures,

28. B. Hill, 'Actions speak louder than words: Anna Komnene's attempted usurpation', forthcoming.

and kin lined up on each side. Eirene, Anna and Andronikos Komnenos were on one side; Alexios, John, and Isaac on the other. Eirene Doukaina's attitude as the mother of both claimants is interesting. She must have brought Anna up to have imperial expectations, even after her imperial fiancé had died, and on the evidence of Zonaras and Choniates, felt able to meddle with the succession. Zonaras says that she wished her son to be subject to her, and Choniates relates that she favoured Bryennios. Yet she failed to place her candidates on the throne. As far as we can ascertain from the sources, Eirene did not mobilise her Doukas connections as an alternative base of support, but concentrated on trying to change Alexios's mind. The revolt the following year did not have her support. Anna seems to have been *persona non grata* for the remainder of her long life, which she spent in the monastery of Kecharitomene. Eirene, on the other hand, appears to have survived with her credit intact. The evidence is slight, but Italikos felt that an appeal to his service with his mother would move the emperor's heart to generosity towards him, and Prodromos, writing a wedding song for the wedding of Anna's two sons in 1122, was fulsome in his praise of Eirene. John may not have been present, and Prodromos's early career seems to have been spent with Eirene Doukaina, but he was not banished from court and court favour by John after her death; on the contrary he was employed by him. Prodromos was still naming Eirene the great *basilissa* in 1140 when one of those brides died. John may have been suspicious of Eirene immediately after his accession. A letter of Italikos complaining about Eirene's assessment of his capabilities loads on psychological guilt by reminding her that the emperor is angry with him because of her. But the very fact that he expected her to be able to obtain him a job shows that she was not entirely without influence. However, she never performed the same tasks for John that Anna Dalassene did for Alexios. For her part, Eirene did not hold any grudge against John. He is described in the *typikon* of Kecharitomene as a dearly-beloved son, and is commemorated in the same way as Andronikos, Isaac, Bryennios, Anna, Maria and Eudokia. This is not because Eirene treated all her offspring equally. The designated ceremonies for Theodora and Constantine Angelos consisted of fewer commemorative loaves and coins of a smaller denomination. Eirene's fate is another example of Choniates's comment that the love of kin is a strong emotion which quickly heals itself. But it also suggests that the heyday of power through motherhood was over.

The same point is illustrated by the rest of the Komnenian mothers, but may be partly due to historical accident. Two of those mothers, Eirene of Hungary and Bertha-Eirene, died before their husbands. Eirene of Hungary bore eight children and spent her time and money on her children and the poor.[29] She was dead at the time of the succession crisis of 1143, so her attitude and influence cannot aid the enquiry. Bertha-Eirene practised philanthropy,[30] and took care of her daughters' education, but she died too soon to have any influence in the marriage of the one who survived. Maria of Antioch was little heard of while Manuel was alive, but she came into her own after his death since she was regent for their underage son. These women hardly figure in the sources at all, in strong contrast to Anna Dalassene and Eirene Doukaina.

This imbalance has led to the theory that Alexios was weak and led by his mother and wife,[31] while by implication John and Manuel were strong characters who kept their wives in their places. An alternative theory is that only women with a kin group could oper-ate at a power level when it was required. John's Eirene was from Hungary, Manuel's Bertha-Eirene from Germany and his Maria from Antioch. Transportation into a foreign land must have robbed these women of both confidence and a close kin network. Eirene Doukaina had the powerful family of Doukas behind her, ready to see and complain about any slight. Bertha-Eirene arrived in 1142 and was not married until 1146. Bertha's kin did eventually ensure her future, for Manuel married her on hearing that Conrad of Germany was on his way to Byzantium, but the physical distance between her kin and herself meant that they could not protect her as the Doukas family did Eirene. A geographically close kin network provided more than protection: it conferred power. The Doukas family was more like part of the core of the Komnenian network than of the periphery, and a Doukas woman had powerful relatives to influence. Unfortunately, there is not enough evidence to show how well Eirene used the network or to what ends, but the coincidence of less general visibility for women at the same time as they come from foreign lands suggests that the lack of relations was one factor which influ-enced it. Another argument for the importance of the kin network is the career of Manuel's sister-in-law, Eirene the *sebastokratorissa*,

29. *History*, Brand, p. 17.   30. *History*, Brand, p. 154.
31. Lemerle, *Cinq études*, p. 298; P. Magdalino, 'Innovations in government' in M.E. Mullett and D.C. Smythe (eds), *Alexios I Komnenos* (Belfast, 1996), pp. 146–66.

who was also almost certainly a foreigner. Although the details are obscure, she was certainly exiled twice for getting in Manuel's way: would exile have been her fate if her kin were the Doukai?

The *sebastokratorissa* Eirene provides positive evidence of the change which was taking place between the days of Alexios and those of Manuel. She disapproved of her daughter, Theodora, being married to Henry of Austria and wrote to Manuel about it, fulfilling her motherly duty. The result of her petition is instructive: she was ignored. By Manuel's time the emperor took a greater interest in marriage alliances than ever before, and either arranged them himself, particularly if they were with foreigners, or gave his permission if they were internal.[32] Manuel arranged more marriages with other powers than any emperor before him, and needed to use his nieces as brides. He did this in the teeth of parental opposition. The other end of the spectrum had been reached. In the crisis days of 1081 it was mothers who did the arranging, but by the reign of Manuel, all arranging was in the hands of the emperor, and where mothers complained they were ignored.

Conclusion

The study of the kinship system of the Komnenoi illuminates the position of women of the family in relation to one of the most vital parts of the system. They shared in the prestige and pride of the family as an echelon above the rest of society, they inherited goods from both parents, and a name from either or both, depending on the prestige involved. They remained part of their natal family in all important matters, bringing their husbands into the family circle rather than moving out to join another family. They passed on their name to their children, who were also members of the imperial family to be used to further dynastic and diplomatic schemes. If the inheritance was the empire itself, there was no bar to women exercising authority in their own right. Although they were of the elite, and their number is small, the fact that it was possible for such women to play a sometimes crucial part in the politics of the empire, and to appear in the records as doing it, reveals Byzantium as less patriarchal than one might expect from the very male-dominated lists of emperors. The significant point of Anna Komnene's revolt was that she, as a woman, felt able to challenge

---

32. Magdalino, *Empire*, p. 205.

her brother's supremacy as a result of an inheritance system which did not denigrate women as women but treated them as equal heirs with men. But despite the fact that we can see women pursuing their goals and deciding the fate of the empire, their ultimate power depended on influence on their menfolk, for their power was not designated to them automatically nor by law.

Byzantium was a male-dominated society, partly due to its military character, and the Komnenoi were among the most military of emperors. Attitudes to women in power were ambivalent, and justification was necessary in order to escape slander. The most potent justification during the Komnenian era was the mother's role of protecting her young. Anna Dalassene, arguably the most successful mother of the Byzantine empire, projected herself as a mother, using 'Mother of the Komnenoi' as a semi-official title during her period in power.[33] It is as mothers that most of the visible women are acting, not as liberated or independent females. The variables governing how much power an individual woman exercised cannot be fully investigated because the necessary evidence about the internal workings of the kin group is too slim.

The existence of a kin group may be important: Anna Dalassene and Eirene Doukaina were native Byzantines, while Eirene of Hungary, Bertha-Eirene and Maria of Antioch were foreign. Personality also seems to matter. A defined domain for powerful women is identifiable by examining fluid spaces, gaps, through which those women with the intelligence and strength of personality could slide to positions of extreme importance. There was nothing in the prescribed role of a mother that forced Anna Dalassene to take over the running of the civil administration. There was nothing which forced Eirene Doukaina to take an interest in the succession. Both these women had the inclination to participate in politics. Anna Komnene was clearly a confident woman, in no sense giving the impression of relying on her husband for anything. On the other hand her sister Eudokia was mistreated by her husband, and needed her mother to resolve the situation. She perhaps did not have the same confidence in dealing with men. Anna Komnene remains an exception by her actions, and even Anna is careful to present her powerful grandmother in terms which will be acceptable to her society. She uses the conventions of sainthood, and removes Anna Dalassene from womanhood as far as possible by omitting any physical description of her, the only major character treated in this

---

33. See below, ch. 7.

fashion.[34] Anna Dalassene ended up in retirement, blamed by the people for any faults with Alexios's reign.

The power that these women exerted was temporary, because although there was a space that they could occupy, there was no legal position upon which they could rest. As a consort to a man, they could join in as far as their personality took them. As mother of an underage emperor, there was precedent and position, but it was only a matter of time until their wings would be clipped. As an aristocratic mother, or even more as widow, there was position and a job to do, but again, the amount of licence taken depended on the personality of the woman. The external political situation was crucial. The account of the power of women to arrange marriage alliances reveals a great change over the period in question, from mothers as marriage brokers to protesting mothers cast aside by an emperor who arranged all alliances himself. This is due to the consolidation of the system from a period of crisis in male authority, where women were to the fore, to a restoration of male authority, where women were pushed back into the background. We have already seen how this system was set up and consolidated by the system of titles and ideology. We will see it illustrated again by a consideration of patronage.

34. See below, ch. 7.

CHAPTER SIX

Power through patronage

The evolution in the visibility of women which can be noted through a consideration of imperial titles and kinship is equally clear when the same women are investigated as patrons. This book has already chronicled the metamorphosis from 1080, when there was a woman with an official title of her own who overtly arranged marriage alliances, through the twelfth century when the absence of an *augousta* was not thought worthy of note, to the reign of Manuel when mothers' protests about the marriage of their children were ignored. A study of imperial women as patrons reveals the same pattern. But why address the question of patronage? Firstly, Byzantinists are unanimous that the Byzantine empire worked through personal patronage in the absence of an impersonal state machine of education and promotion. In Angold's words, 'A man's standing in Constantinopolitan society depended upon his his rank at court and the clientele that his largesse secured.'[1] Since patronage was so important in the running of the empire, the power of women as patrons is an obvious area of enquiry. This book has already considered the effect of rank on the power of women of the court: the clientele is the subject of this chapter. Patronage was also the visible practice of the imperial virtue of *philanthropia*: more than a personal inclination, it indicated the concern of the ruler for the people. It is particularly pertinent for the second reason: all the women included in this book have been credited by Byzantinists with being either personal or literary patrons. No study to date has brought them together as members of one elite and one dynasty in order to compare them.

1. M. Angold, *The Byzantine Empire, 1025–1204. A Political History* (2nd ed., London, 1997), p. 147.

Patronage as a concept has not been subjected to rigorous theoretical analysis by feminists in the way that names and kinship have, but some anthropologists have understood it as a 'kind of power'.[2] That is invitation enough for a feminist searching for spheres of women's power. This chapter, as far as the evidence allows, will examine the relationships between imperial women and their clients to show how wide their network was and how well they manipulated it. The difference between the early years of the period and the later ones will become clear, suggesting once again that the power of imperial women declined over these hundred years.

Those Byzantinists who are interested in patronage have used it without developing a theoretical foundation which others can use to explore hitherto ignored patrons. The exception is Margaret Mullett, who has made the most use of the concept as a tool to analyse both the activities of the aristocracy of Constantinople, and the wider society of Byzantium in the eleventh and twelfth centuries. Mullett has identified networks as the vital component of the system, and as 'the very power structures of the eleventh century'.[3] Her research has concentrated on those lower on the social scale than the imperial family who were interested in creating networks of influential people to aid their endeavours, but it is reasonable to assume that the influential people they were petitioning regarded the networks as important too. Indeed, for what other reason would they have entered into them?

The state of our knowledge about relationships in Byzantium is far from complete in comparison with the Roman Republic and early empire, and general conclusions about the workings of patronage in Byzantium will not be possible until there is much more information gathered and distinctions made between patronage, friendship and spiritual kinship. Mullett sets forth a series of leading questions designed to aid this project. They are as follows: who knew whom: a definition of types of relationship and multiplexity, a distinction of links of kinship from those of teaching, of spiritual parentage from literary patronage, of instrumental friendship from patronage. Once patronage relationships are isolated, they must be examined to find out how each was made to work: finally, the intimacy factor, the indicator of the quality of a relationship, must be assessed. Answering these questions will reveal a network which can

2. E. Gellner, 'Patrons and clients', in E. Gellner and J. Waterbury (eds), *Patrons and Clients in Mediterranean Societies* (London, 1977), pp. 1–6, p. 4.

3. M.E. Mullett, 'Byzantium: A friendly society?', *P and P* 118 (1987), pp. 3–24, p. 14.

be used to answer further questions. Personal, political, literary and artistic patronage all have their advocates among Byzantinists like Paul Magdalino, Michael Angold, Robin Cormack, Michael Jeffreys, Elizabeth Jeffreys and Rosemary Morris. Before we can understand how imperial women fitted into this general scheme of patronage it is necessary to define the concept and explain why it is useful in a book about power.

Defining patronage

There is general agreement among sociologists on the meaning and characteristics of patronage as a relationship. The classic definition, incorporating three vital elements, was coined by Boissevain: patronage relations must be reciprocal, must be personal and of some duration and must be asymmetrical.[4] The personal aspect distinguishes patronage relations from commercial or market relations and the assymmetrical aspect from friendship relations, which may be between equals or not. Later voluntarism was added. This element distinguishes patronage relations from master–servant or landlord–serf relations. Patronage is therefore founded on reciprocal relations between a person called a patron, who has and uses his influence to assist or protect some other person, who willingly becomes his client and in return provides certain services to his patron. The nature of the services rendered on each side varies from society to society.

Thus far, there is agreement. The problems arise when an attempt is made to understand a society in terms of patronage. It is possible to see patron–client relations everywhere. Even in the most impersonal of modern bureaucracies, where patronage is not supposed to exist, relations like these can be seen. The tool thereby loses its usefulness: it becomes ahistorical. Therefore it is meaningless to say that a society is held together by, or runs on, patronage, because it is possible to see such relations everywhere. This is obviously true; those who use the concept must be careful to contextualise it. One method of avoiding such traps is to compare patronage to other systems of resource allocation. If patronage networks are the dominant mechanism by which resources are distributed and power relations maintained and reproduced, then the society can be characterised

4. J. Boissevain, 'Patronage in Sicily', *Man*, n.s. 1 (1966), pp. 18–33.

as a patronage society.[5] This is all very well as theory, but the links between individuals in Byzantium are still far from clear. Before the system can be characterised, the raw material must be collected: this chapter aims to contribute to that goal.

The relationship of patronage to kinship, friendship and spiritual kinship is another area of debate among theorists which ranges from Davis's contention that these phenomena are secondary forms of patronage to the opposite opinion, stated by Pitt-Rivers and Campbell, that patronage is an extension of some or all of them.[6] Mullett has strong opinions on keeping these concepts apart. She analyses the nature of friendship in Byzantium, concluding that friendship regarded in a practical way is very close to patronage, and strict definitions are necessary to facilitate understanding and prevent confusion.[7] Both friendship and patronage involve the reciprocal exchange of goods and services and a personal relationship of some duration. The only way to keep these two apart is to insist on asymmetry in the relationship before it can be classified as patronage. Some theorists have called for an end to considering relationships between individuals, in favour of concentrating on the system as a whole. This is unwise for Byzantium since looking at patronage as a system without differentiating kinship, friendship and patron–client relations from one another will result in the bland conclusion that there was nothing new about the Komnenian way of doing things, which at the broadest level may be true, but which misrepresents the empire as its contemporaries saw it: they were convinced that there had been a change and we must retain the vocabulary with which to describe it.

Another question of interest for sociologists of patronage is whether patronage is official or unofficial. Gellner sees it as always outside the 'official' ethos of a society. Patronage for Gellner can never be the official morality; it is always unofficial and knows it.[8] An 'unofficial' patronage smacks of corruption, illegitimate operations, underhand dealings, the parasitical behaviour of the underprivileged, the deceptive conduct of the weak. Illegitimacy, deception,

---

5. T. Johnson and C. Dandeker, 'Patronage: relation and system', in A. Wallace-Hadrill (ed.), *Patronage in Ancient Society* (London, 1989), pp. 219–41.

6. J. Davis, *People of the Mediterranean* (London, 1977), pp. 146–8; J. Pitt-Rivers, *The People of the Sierra* (Chicago, 1961), p. 140 on lop-sided friendship; J.K. Campbell, *Honour, Family and Patronage* (Oxford, 1964), pp. 100–2 on assymetrical friendship. On spiritual kinship in Byzantium, see R. Macrides, 'The Byzantine godfather', *BMGS* 11 (1987), pp. 139–62.

7. Mullett, 'Aristocracy and Patronage', pp. 180–1.

8. Gellner, 'Patrons and clients', p. 3.

and underhand conduct are accusations often levelled against women, particularly when their methods are effective. A feminist feels impelled to defend imperial women in Byzantium against the negative connotations this conclusion brings. Indeed, understanding patronage in Byzantium as corruption is anachronistic, as the fine work by Saller on the early Roman empire demonstrates. The greatly different conditions of life in the empire, where 'work' did not carry the positive ideological load that it does for twentieth-century capitalists, must be taken on board.[9] The classes concerned with patronage of every sort in the empire were the leisured classes who did not work and would have considered it beneath their dignity to do anything for money. Even the begging poets of Byzantine times who sound as if they were destitute had alternative means of support. The qualities emperors were looking for in every job were those of the good aristocratic gentleman: honour, integrity, charity, loyalty. These could best be inculcated by an education of horse-riding and practice with arms. Promotion by the good graces of a patron was not a method of escaping rigorous intelligence tests or a series of interviews. Personal testimony was, in fact, best. But accepting that patronage is not illegal or illegitimate does not equate it with the state. The state is usually assumed to be a network of legal and constitutional rights and limitations. Patronage, on the other hand, was a moral relationship without legal ties. The only legal relationship that could be considered as patronage, that of the master and serf in the Roman empire, is usually excluded from discussions of patronage precisely because of its legal character. Patronage differs from law or justice because it is never codified and it is therefore less confusing to keep it apart from the state. In any case, the emperor stood at the top of both of these networks as supreme lawgiver and judge and as the patron blessed with the most command of resources.

A consideration of the position of the emperor necessarily involves power. As Gellner stated, patronage is a 'kind of power' for two reasons. Firstly, power is always 'power over' someone else. Patronage involves an element of submission on the part of the client, who puts at least a part of their present or future well-being into the hands of the patron. There is also necessarily a measure of trust. Second, being a patron confers status and prestige in society and these are powerful. Saller comments on the ideology of the early empire which considered that a man's status was reflected in the size of his following. The honour system of modern Greece

9. R. Saller, *Personal Patronage under the Early Empire* (Cambridge, 1982).

emphasises the importance of prestige for men, and patronage is one of the elements which contributes to it and is governed by it.[10] Prestige as a value has an advantage for the powerless in that it does not always reflect material power because a reputation takes on an existence of its own.[11] Therefore women whose material power is small may exercise great ideological power through a reputation which rests on small foundations or even on the intention to be generous.

The emperor's prestige was unassailable because he had the reputation for generosity which he could fulfil. His power as a patron was ultimate because there was no one to whom he was a client. All other persons could be patrons in one relationship and clients in another, but the emperor and his family were at the top of the pyramid. The range of *beneficia* at the emperor's command included the distribution of all offices and statuses, privileges, immunities and money. The distribution of these things was taken so much for granted that the author of the *Historia Augusta* dismissed the emperor's appointments and promotions as trivial and worthy of no more notice than his diet and clothing.[12] Emperors could create disorder and conflict (though not between orders) by channelling *beneficia* through lower order men, thereby making them powerful. However, emperors who used this method, for example Gaius, Nero, Galba, Domitian, Commodus and Caracalla, seem to have survived less well. The most successful emperors were those like Augustus who, in Saller's view, managed to distribute the *beneficia* at their disposal in a way that created cohesion. Both political and literary patronage could be used by powerful men to build up support groups in which the clients were expected to be loyal and to parade their patron's qualities before those who held a vote, but this function faded with the cessation of public politics after the republic. Even where the Komnenoi fought within themselves, they tended to seek kin support,[13] which cannot be patronage because patronage by definition operates between people of unequal status.

Patronage as power for women is a more obscure issue. Even authors, like Saller, who describe women's roles in dispensing patronage do not enlarge on the results of such roles. Although the role

10. Campbell, *Patronage*, ch. X, 'The values of prestige', pp. 263–316; Davis, *People*, p. 132.
11. S. Ortner and H. Whitehead (eds), 'Introduction: accounting for sexual meanings', *Sexual Meanings: The Cultural Construction of Gender and Society* (Cambridge, 1981), p. 14.
12. Saller, *Personal Patronage*, pp. 41–58.
13. See Chapter 5, The method of marriage.

of patron has not been theorised by feminists, some have investigated the social organisation of prestige as a determinant of gender
conceptions, reaching the conclusion that prestige is one of the
most meaningful elements in the construction of gender.[14] This is
an important point for, given their high social position, it might
not seem valuable for imperial women to gain prestige. Patronage
also fulfilled one of the ideals held of imperial behaviour, that of
philanthropy. Praised universally by all authors of the period, from
bishops to court poets, the importance of philanthropic acts should
not be underestimated. Philanthropy had a long tradition as an
imperial virtue, exercised by all who were rightfully crowned as
emperor, and its value was high. In particular, the foundation of
monasteries and the feeding of poor monks and holy men deserved
extra prayers of intercession by those so aided. The prayers of monks
and holy men were believed to pass more quickly to heaven and to
receive a special hearing by the heavenly deities (God, Christ and the
Virgin Mary). It was in search of extra heavenly intercession that so
many imperial women eased the earthly lives of holy men, thereby
freeing them from the irksome tasks which would have hindered
their praying. In many *typika*, or foundation charters of monasteries,
there are explicit rules set out for the number and frequency of
prayers to be said for the founder and their families. This investment
in the afterlife is evident in the patronage patterns of imperial women
over the entire period, although the amount of and type of aid given
depended on the economic resources of each individual woman.

Literary patronage in particular offered a further advantage which
might have been attractive to imperial women: it kept their memory
green. One major problem in perceiving literary patronage, which
represents a large part of Komnenian imperial women's activity, is
that the sources are usually not explicit enough to know whether
work was commissioned or not, and even where it is stated that one
person was patron to another, this may simply be an elaborate
literary construct. The issue revolves around the value to be placed
on dedications. Some Byzantinists accept dedications as solid evidence of patronage: Mullett does not. There are two approaches to
the workings of literary patronage which lead to very different conclusions. One way is to look for a patron and find a following (a
circle). The other way is to look at the writers and look for the links
between them. The first approach is that used by Elizabeth Jeffreys,
who postulates that the *sebastokratorissa* Eirene was the patron of a

14. Ortner and Whitehead, 'Introduction: accounting for sexual meanings'.

circle which included all those who ever dedicated a work to her.[15] This allows her to suggest that the novels of Prodromos and Manasses were sponsored by her because she had come into contact with western forms,[16] despite the fact that they are not even dedicated to her. Mullett adopts the second approach, the writer-centred one. Having examined the dedications on eleventh- and twelfth-century productions, Mullett concludes that writers are not dependent on one patron, but accept patronage wherever it may be found. This operates to such an extent that it is more accurate to group the patrons round the writers than *vice versa*. Therefore the influence of a dedicatee on the other works of the writer cannot be assumed and his entire production cannot be credited to the patronage of the dedicatee. This makes a difference in the prestige that can be calculated for any one patron. Artistic patronage is no easier to quantify. Enamels are a case in point. Although there are enamels featuring imperial women, the artefact itself does not proclaim who commissioned it or presented it or received it. At least a dedication on a manuscript may represent a relationship between two people, and the manuscript might disclose in detail the people involved.

Imperial women were able to exercise patronage because of their proximity to the emperor. Saller's analysis of the early empire shows that those who had access to imperial *beneficia* were those who were physically close to the emperor. The male members of his family had priority but personal friends and skilled men, such as doctors, writers, rhetors and teachers, also numbered among those with close contact. Two categories of women could also exact *beneficia* from the emperor. The Vestal Virgins, who came into contact with the emperor during ritual, had enough influence to procure posts from him. The female relatives of the emperor were more influential. Specific acts of patronage include education of daughters and provision of dowries, for example, by Livia. It is not surprising to find that emperors could be criticised for allowing their wives access to imperial *beneficia*, like Claudius who was criticised because his wives sold offices, honours and verdicts. Perhaps it was too blatant an exercise of power in this case for not all emperors whose wives were alleged to have exercised patronage were bad emperors. Trajan and Marcus Aurelius were 'good' emperors, but their womenfolk

15. E. Jeffreys, 'Western infiltration of the Byzantine aristocracy: some suggestions', in M. Angold (ed.), *The Byzantine Aristocracy, IX–XIII Centuries* (Oxford, 1984), pp. 202–10.

16. E. Jeffreys, 'The Comnenian background to the *romans d'antiquité*', *B* 50 (1980), pp. 455–86.

are recorded as securing posts for those who petitioned them.[17] Crediting influence to women is not only or always a subtle way of criticising emperors, although it can be used in that way.

Imperial freedmen and slaves illustrate the importance of proximity to the emperor even more strongly. They were resented by those of good birth, and control over his freedmen became one of the attributes of a good emperor.[18] The idea was still current in the twelfth century when Anna Komnene and Zonaras criticised Botaneiates for the influence his Bulgarian 'slaves' had over him. Imperial women were not castigated in the Komnenian period, not because they were powerless, but because they were considered inside the frame of the family. Patriarch John the Oxite denounced the influence of Alexios's whole family, men and women, as a plague on the state. Proximity to the emperor therefore was crucial, and imperial women were in a prime position to influence him. Characterising the use of influence in this case as the action of the weak is not useful, for since the emperor was the ultimate patron, all other people in the empire must necessarily be weak in comparison to him. Such a forced division rejects the analytic tools with which to differentiate between all those that are left.

Influencing the emperor was not the only way to be a patron. Patrons could also use their own money or goods to alleviate misery or enrich a client. Imperial women can be observed doing both, although this statement begs the question of women's economic resources, which cannot be satisfactorily answered for this period. It is clear that imperial women had money, but it is not clear where they got it from. If this could be answered, we would know so much more about the position of women in Byzantium. The issue of economics will be addressed below.

Individual patrons

ANNA DALASSENE[19]

In the light of the conclusions of the previous three chapters one would expect that Anna Dalassene would be the most visible patron

---

17. Saller, *Personal Patronage*, ch. 2.   18. Ibid., pp. 58–69.
19. My analysis starts with Anna Dalassene rather than Maria of Alania because M.E. Mullett in 'The "disgrace" of the ex-Basilissa Maria', *BS* 45 (1984), pp. 202–11, has already explored Maria's relationship with Theophylact, which is the most sustained one for which there is evidence. Maria's appearance on enamel and manuscript is as ambiguous as that of the others which will be discussed where they appear.

and that her political position as regent for Alexios would afford her opportunities denied to other imperial women. Both these expectations are justified. Anna Dalassene was interested in monks and holy men and as regent it was on behalf of these two groups that she used her administrative powers. As head of the family before the coup she used her influence and authority to appoint spiritual fathers for Alexios and introduce monastic advisors and writers such as Little John and Euthymios Zigabenos. Unfortunately Anna cannot be assumed to have been their patron since nothing more of the relationship is known. She need not necessarily have known these men personally for they could have been recommended to her by someone else, like her own spiritual father, Cyril Phileotes, whom she visited for advice and current news.

A monk who may have been a client of Anna was Eustratios Garidas, who became patriarch in 1081. On the testimony of Anna Komnene her grandmother favoured and visited this monk and came to depend on him. This argues a personal relationship of some duration. However she had no qualms about deposing him when he proved unfit for his post, although of course it is unknown if she compensated him well afterwards. Anna Komnene drops other hints of her grandmother's fondness for monks, like the open table at which there were always some monks and holy men, but there is not enough evidence of any further relationship to postulate that they were all her clients.

One more piece of evidence confirms the direction in which Anna used her powers. The monks of the monastery of Docheiariou had difficulty in 1085 with Xiphilinos, a state tax-collector, who was about to take away part of the holdings of the monastery and add it to the state revenues. This was forbidden by Anna, probably when Alexios was away on the frontiers. Alexios came back, disagreed with his mother and instructed Xiphilinos to take the village of Atouble, whereupon the monks panicked and addressed a request to him. He changed his mind and signed a decree, which is resumed and 'interpreted' in an ordinance of Anna's. When Alexios went away again, Anna, at the request of the monks, sent out the ordinance, which was signed in March 1089. Xiphilinos carried out his orders in April 1089, giving the monks a copy, signed by him. This example testifies to the amount of authority which Alexios had invested in his mother, for she was able to countermand his wishes both by personal discussion and by interpreting his decrees in legislation of her own to follow her own policies. Although this episode spanned four years, there is no suggestion that any of the monks in question ever met Anna, let alone had a personal relationship with her. This incident does not prove Anna's patronage of these monks, but it does indicate to what lengths she was prepared to go for them. Her inclinations were exploited by the most troublesome monk of them all, Christodoulos.

Christodoulos is most famous for the foundation of St John of Patmos, but he spent time before that on Mt Latros and on Kos, where he founded the church and monastery dedicated to the Mother of God. It is clear that the donations to this church and that on Patmos were due to the goodwill of Anna Dalassene. Christodoulos visited Constantinople, in 1087, in order to protest and prove his innocence in relation to charges of mismanagement of the monastery of the Stylite on Mt Latros. It is a fair assumption that he met Anna Dalassene then, since his visit fell during the years when she was exercising the authority invested in her by the *chrysobull of Alexios. Christodoulos asked at this time for the whole island of Lipso and other landed properties including half the castle of Pantelion on the island of Leros. Anna gave him these properties by chrysobull unconditionally: they were inalienable and for ever, tax-free and not liable to any exactions, such as the requirement to provide animals, ships, or soldiers. In the same chrysobull Anna ensured that neither the Myrelaion nor the monastery of Pantepoptes, both of whom had been granted these same properties in the past, could ever claim them back. A decree of Alexios followed confirming her decisions. Anna was leaving nothing to chance. She subsequently supported the monks of Kos in defending their newly-received properties, after they had written to Christodoulos. The chain of events suggests that Christodoulos might still have been in Constantinople, where he could contact Anna immediately upon receipt of the letter from his monks. Even if his petition was not made in person, it is clear that she was his first court of appeal. Later on, Anna ordered that the other half of the castle of Pantelion was to be given to Christodoulos and the inhabitants of the island could have the other castle of Lepida for their protection. This grant was eternal, in contradiction to the imperial *prostaxis* which ordered that castles should only be granted for the lifetime of the recipient. The most interesting question is Anna's source of information that there was another castle on the island. The most obvious source of her knowledge is the monks of Christodoulos themselves, once again presuming on the favour of Anna to ask for what they wanted.

This pattern continued when Christodoulos became interested in Patmos. Having achieved his aims in Kos, Christodoulos feared the advent of the encircling Turks. He proposed to Alexios that he would present Kos and all its associates back to the state and in return take the island of Patmos. Alexios agreed and Christodoulos was granted Patmos, in 1088, completely exempt from tax. In his *diataxis* of 1091, Christodoulos says openly that he received Patmos through the intercession of the blessed *despoina* and mother of the emperor, who negotiated on his behalf with the emperor. The relationship between Anna and Christodoulos endured over a space of six years, during which time Christodoulos was receiving from the imperial bounty what he required, and the order of events proclaims his contacts with Anna. Her part in his acquisition of Patmos is stated explicitly: the surviving documents for the donations for Kos reveal the extent of his obligation to her quite as clearly.

Anna Dalassene was a personal patron. Her political position allowed her to offer greater benefits to her clients than other imperial women, and her correspondence was in the form of official governmental documents. Some of her contacts were face to face, for example Eustratios, perhaps Christodoulos and the nameless but numerous monks who visited her in Constantinople. Other relationships were conducted by letter, like that with the monks of Docheiariou, to whom she responded by ordinance. For other incidents there is no evidence of personal contact. The relationships for which there is evidence lasted over a space of years; Christodoulos's needs spanned six years, the Docheiariou case four. Eustratios was patriarch for three and Anna had been visiting him before Alexios came to the throne. All were reciprocal.

The benefits that Anna as patron derived from her patronage of monks was their intercession for her and her family in the heavenly courts to which they were believed to have special access. The monks of Docheiariou exchanged prayer for her temporal protection, as did all those who feasted at her expense. Her explicit aim in ensuring peace from any sort of disturbance for the monks of Christodoulos's monastery on Kos was that they could pray more for her and her family. The general importance of intercessory prayer is revealed by the custom of non-imperial founders to have prayers said for the emperor in their foundations too. A popular image of the period between death and the Last Judgement understood it as a series of gates, guarded by an official, through which the soul must pass. The prayers of the holy still on earth assisted the soul on its journey. Monks had an advantage over other people when it

came to gaining their desires, given the heavenly-looking attitude
of the Byzantines, but a patron like Anna Dalassene can explain
why some monks were better off than others.

Anna also founded a monastery herself, that of Christ Pantepoptes,
which seems to have been a male monastery. Monastery-building
is perhaps the most visible sort of patronage, and visibility may
have been part of its purpose. The community would be very aware
of its patron because of the frequent readings of the *typikon* and
especially the elaborate commemoration services carried out weekly
for the founder and her family. Unfortunately we do not know who
apart from the community was allowed entry into the monastery to
be enlightened by the reading of the *typikon*. Although it is not
possible to specify how many people knew that Pantepoptes was
Anna's monastery, it is likely that many people at court did know.
The amount of prestige that was generated by such a foundation is
amply proven by the efforts of Manuel Komnenos to prevent his
relatives founding large monasteries in the city.[20] Anna Dalassene
can therefore be described as a visible and powerful personal patron
of holy men, monks and monasteries.

<h2 style="text-align:center">EIRENE DOUKAINA</h2>

The next woman for whom there is evidence is Eirene Doukaina.
There is visual evidence for Eirene, which is lacking for Anna
Dalassene, in the form of an enamel piece belonging to the Pala
d'Oro in Venice, but in all the theories relating to the commission
of this piece of art, there is no suggestion that Eirene herself might
have been involved. She too was involved in the highly visible and
prestigious work of founding monasteries, and was virtuously imperial in her *philanthropia*. She founded the monastery of Theotokos
Kecharitomene and co-founded the monastery of Christ Philan-
thropos Soter with Alexios. The considerations of prestige that
applied to her mother-in-law applied equally to her. Her contacts
were much more wide-ranging than those of Anna Dalassene for
they included ecclesiastics, writers and officials of the court, but her
powers were limited in comparison. Some contacts suffer from the
same lack of evidence that was encountered when dealing with
Anna Dalassene, especially her relationship with Theophylact, bishop
of Ochrid. He sent a letter to an unnamed *despoina* thanking her

20. P. Magdalino, 'The Byzantine holy man in the twelfth century', in S. Hackel
(ed.), *The Byzantine Saint* (London, 1981), pp. 51–66.

for her kindness in visiting him in his illness. The letter conveys the information that imperial ladies were able to visit their contacts freely.

For other contacts there is only one record, insufficient evidence on which to analyse the nature of the relationship or even to state whether one existed. It is possible that Eirene commissioned poetry from Manuel Straboromanos; she received a consolation from him, one of the duties of a client, on her brother's death. Straboromanos also wrote verses to accompany an icon which Alexios and Eirene sent to St Demetrios. Eirene may therefore have been his literary patroness. There is no direct evidence of a sustained and personal relationship between Straboromanos and Eirene, but it is reasonable to postulate that there may have been from the fact that he wrote a consolation for her and that he is mentioned by Theodore Prodromos, who compliments his poetry and iambics. Prodromos was certainly part of Eirene's circle and it is possible that he had heard Straboromanos's poetry in that milieu. Another single record is the letter written by the abbot of St George of the Mangana to Eirene because of money problems. The bishop of Kitros, who may have been her brother, who had owned a vineyard and paid the wages of its workers, had died, and the abbot needed someone else to take over this responsibility. There is no hint of previous involvement between the abbot and the empress. He is not noticeably personal, and he does not remind her of her past generosity but of Alexios's. The abbot obviously knew that the way to solve his problem was to apply to the empress for aid. It is unclear whether he picked on her because her brother had been the previous benefactor, therefore on kinship criteria, or because she was the emperor's wife and likely to have the money or some way of obtaining it. The abbot claimed to know both men. Eirene also commissioned poetry from Nicholas Kallikles, and he wrote a burial speech on her death. He was well known to the imperial family, but there is no information about his personal contacts with Eirene in the years before Alexios's death.

One contact about which there is more information is Michael Italikos. Two works from his pen addressed to Eirene have survived: one a letter, the other a speech. The evidence for Eirene as patron consists of the letter that Italikos wrote to her, which is his reply to her invitation to take up a post as *didaskalos*, or teacher, of the doctors.[21] It has been suggested that he had been teaching in a

21. Michael Italikos, ed. P. Gautier, *Michel Italikos, Lettres et discours* (Paris, 1972), pp. 92–8.

private school and that Eirene's offer related to an official post. This raises questions about Eirene's ability to fill official posts after the death of her husband, especially since her relationship with her son was allegedly strained. Gautier suggested that Eirene was appointing Italikos to one of the hospitals in which she had an interest. Since Pantokrator listed a *didaskalos* of the doctors among its personnel, it is possible that some of the other large hospitals did so also, perhaps St Paul. Unfortunately, we are only shown one side of the transaction: Italikos's reply. The method Eirene employed to make her offer is unknown: did she detain him after a literary gathering, did she write a letter, did she send a message through someone else? Answering these questions would provide information about the operation of networks by imperial women. As it is, we do not even know if Eirene acted on her own initiative, or if Italikos petitioned her for promotion. He was certainly not shy of lauding his own abilities later in life when he wrote to the emperor John.

This transaction alone does not constitute a relationship, but other evidence is extant in the speech which Eirene requested of Italikos at one of her *theatra or literary gatherings. From this, and other references made to the same *theatron*, it appears that their relationship spanned several years, although neither letter nor speech can be precisely dated. It cannot be claimed that Eirene was Italikos's only patron. Italikos's literary output was large. Some of his correspondents, like Anna and Bryennios, frequented Eirene's *theatron* in Kecharitomene, so it is reasonable to postulate that Eirene may have bolstered his career to a great extent. He reminds John II that he had been a member of the circle of John's mother as part of a supplication to John.

Italikos's gains from the relationship are clear, but those of Eirene are harder to quantify. Certainly any return was not in material terms, and it might be thought to be prestige. But how much prestige did a retired ex-empress in a monastery need, and what good did it do her? If she had been out in the court, a following of devoted litterati might have given her standing and status, but although she was not in any way secluded nor had she lost her interest in affairs of the outside world, her life in the monastery seems less in need of that kind of prestige. Perhaps Italikos was grateful and respectful and kept her profile high with his fellow intellectuals. The other return is pleasure, and friendship, but the intimacy factor is difficult to prove on the small amount of evidence that we have and requires an exhaustive study of Italikos's normal forms of greeting and address. The relationship can be described as patronage in so far as the status of the two was asymmetrical, but even this case does not supply sufficient information about the exercise of patronage by an empress.

Another possible client of Eirene Doukaina was Theodore Prodromos, one of the most famous twelfth-century poets of Byzantium. Prodromos seems to have started his career of writing 'for the court' around 1118, and his early works are all connected with Eirene Doukaina. He says openly in a poem to Manuel that he only knew one court and one patron, that of Eirene. To Eirene herself he wrote a poem of consolation on her brother's death and another on that of her son Andronikos. The existence of these works might indicate that Prodromos was Eirene's client. More evidence of Prodromos's connection with Eirene is found in his speeches written to other people and for ceremonial occasions in which Prodromos's praise for Eirene goes beyond what is demanded for a member of the imperial family, particularly one who was in retirement. In a marriage poem for Eirene's grandson, Alexios, the son of Maria Komnene and Nikephoros Phorbenos, written perhaps in 1122, six of the bridegroom's relatives are included. Of these, only Eirene is named. She is called best of mothers and empresses by Prodromos. Alexios Komnenos, the bridegroom, is described as a shoot of the Doukas and Komnenos trees. It might have been expected that the uncle of the bridegroom, the ruling emperor, or his grandfather, another emperor, would have been the object of most praise, but instead it is his grandmother, Eirene. In a wedding song for the sons of Anna Komnene and Nikephoros Bryennios, Prodromos again has much praise for Eirene Doukaina. He praises both grandparents, starting with Alexios for his victories, and brightens up the spirits of the company by direct praise of Eirene, who seems to have been present. The parents of the bridegrooms are praised for their learning, and the boys themselves are praised. Eirene is praised for her generosity, pity and compassion. Were these qualities which Prodromos had special reason to appreciate? She is named as the origin of the race, which is unsurprising since Alexios was dead. Another member of the family gets a mention: Eirene Doukaina the second, the daughter of Anna and Bryennios, who is called beautiful and the envy of all. The emperor John is mentioned in his role of leading the party to the altar, but his wife Eirene, the current empress, is ignored.

This is not the only family occasion on which Eirene Doukaina receives inordinate praise. In Prodromos's epitaph for the death of one of those brides, Theodora, she is described as a sprig planted in a garden, of which the gardener is Eirene Doukaina, 'the eminent empress herself', whose generosity is bottomless, who is the crown of virtues, mistress of herself as well as of the empire. In a set of hexameters to Anna, Prodromos refers to Anna's role as a mediator for him with the 'greater lady'. If the reference is to Eirene, here is a hint of one method used by Prodromos to approach her. The combination of all these small indicators results in a supposition that Prodromos was dependent on Eirene Doukaina, most probably because she was helping him in his career. It was only in the early thirties of the twelfth century that Prodromos began to write for John, and it has been suggested that this was after Eirene had died, when Theodore needed another patron.

Even if Prodromos was Eirene's client, the crucial questions remain unanswered. She may have been very generous to him, promoting his career by ensuring he was the poet chosen to write marriage songs when required. However, the poems themselves do not explain how their relationship was conducted, or indeed how they got in contact. We are not shown any transactions, only respect poured out presumably in return for aid, whether simply financial or in terms of goodwill. He might have been grateful for membership of the *theatron* in Kecharitomene where he would meet many other members of the imperial family and other litterati, while Eirene enjoyed the status that came from counting a famous poet among her associates.

ANNA KOMNENE TO EIRENE *SEBASTOKRATORISSA*

Anna Komnene was not in a position to be a great patron. Living in genteel retirement in the royal apartments of Kecharitomene for most of her life after the accession of her brother John, she was outside the immediate circles of the court. When Eirene Doukaina retired to Kecharitomene she took her daughter Anna and her granddaughter Eirene Doukaina the second with her. Both these women were involved with the circle that Eirene gathered around her. Italikos wrote the prologue to Anna's will, probably because she knew him already. The long funeral oration by George Tornikes reveals Anna's activities after her mother died, but evidence of an independent circle of her own as distinct from Eirene's is lacking. Anna did have access to money from her estates which John restored to her on the advice of his right-hand man, Alexios Axouch. This money seems to have been spent on continuing her well-known literary interests. She was interested and involved in commentaries

on Aristotle, and may have encouraged and organised the commentators, of whom several are known, including Michael of Ephesus,
Eustratios of Nicaea, and possibly James of Venice. Tornikes's funeral
oration for Anna ends with a short eulogy of Eirene Doukaina the
second, and may conceivably have been commissioned by her, since
she too lived in Kecharitomene and would have known the men
around her mother and grandmother.

Anna probably knew these men over a length of time. Her involvement may have consisted of interest and financial aid, which would
have been very important for Eustratios of Nicaea at any rate, since
he was probably writing these commentaries when in disgrace and
suspended from his post. Prodromos wrote a set of hexameters to
Anna asking for her aid, but again, these may have been elegant
literary exercises and not a genuine plea to which Anna was intended
to respond. But at least these are indicators that Anna carried on
the relationships she had forged with her mother's circle. Anna's
patronage did not include philanthropy, which was associated primarily with empresses. Anna could not plead for the emperor's
indulgence on behalf of those who were under judgement. Even if
the Aristotelian circle did operate under the auspices of Anna, her
patronage was on a very small scale compared to that of her mother
and grandmother. Part of the reason for this was her own early
disgrace and retired life in Kecharitomene, and part can be attributed to the smaller resources at the command of a *kaisarissa* in
comparison to those of an empress.

Hardly anything is known of Eirene Piroska of Hungary, the
empress of John II, except that she was involved in founding
Pantokrator, and her image is enshrined in mosaic in the south
gallery of Hagia Sophia. John was left alone to complete the monastery, and in the introduction to its *typikon*, he mentions his partner
and helper in life, who was involved with planning, construction and
completion of the monastery, but who was torn from him before
the complete establishment of the task. Kinnamos wrote of the
empress that everything that was given to her by her husband was
given away, rather than spent on adornments or her children. The
list of property which Eirene assigned to the monastery, a small list
compared to that of John himself, included monasteries, houses,
and rights in villages. There is no evidence to indicate who was
responsible for the installation of the mosaic of John, Eirene and
Alexios. It is an imperial donation in the style of the Zoe panel to
its left and depicts John and Eirene presenting gifts to the Virgin.
That nothing else is recorded is perhaps as significant as positive

evidence would be. Did Eirene not interest herself in patronage, has the evidence disappeared, or was it becoming less profitable to be a client of an empress?

Manuel I Komnenos's first wife, Bertha-Eirene, certainly commissioned works from the grammarian John Tzetzes, namely the *Iliad Allegories*, which were intended to explain Homer to the western-born empress. Evidence of specific commission is extant in the work itself, which demands several times to be told the empress's requirements. The reciprocal nature of the exercise is equally clear: Tzetzes asks for more pay for a summary of the *Iliad*, because a summary requires much work for a small result. In the course of the writing, Bertha-Eirene died and Tzetzes feared that he would lose his payment but a new patron came forward with the necessary money. The death of the empress was not the only problem Tzetzes encountered with the writing of the *Allegories*. Money quarrels dogged the production. Tzetzes had agreed a price with the empress for his work, but it seems that he decided to use bigger and more expensive sheets, hoping to get more money. The treasurer of Bertha refused to pay any more than had been agreed and Tzetzes, feeling that Bertha did not know how to appreciate his work at its full value, stopped writing and tore up the part of the *Chiliades* he had dedicated to her. In the *Historiae* he comments on his troubles, and specifies that he was to receive twelve gold pieces for each page.

Bertha and Tzetzes presumably knew each other because they both operated in the same court, but we do not know how personal the relationship was. Tzetzes did not write directly to Bertha, but to her treasurer, and we do not know how she made her wishes known to him, whether by letter or in person. Most certainly, they do not seem to have been friends. Not only was there the quarrel over the *Allegories*, but Tzetzes wrote to a secretary of the court, consoling him on the empress's failure to reward him, and hoping that God will prick her heart so that she will reward him suitably. Bertha seems to have had problems with money. Theodore Prodromos wrote her hymns for Christmas, probably in his capacity as 'court poet'. The only other surviving piece of evidence for Bertha's contact with the literary men of the court are the verses written by Prodromos to accompany the gift of a gilded dove to the Theotokos, which mention an Eirene, the spouse of Manuel. This must be Bertha, but as there is no other evidence at all for a relationship between these two, we cannot use the verses to answer any probing questions.

Although the more interesting questions about patronage cannot be answered from the Tzetzes–Bertha evidence, the case does deserve to be classified as such, because paying for a work which would not have been written without a specific commission, for which there is also evidence, constitutes the minimal role of a patron. Tzetzes perhaps really did live by words and writing, as he claimed, and was thus more financially dependent on a patron than the men of independent means who were writing in the earlier era. The most that can be said about Bertha's role as a patron was that she was in contact with the most visible men of the court, and interested in the production of literature. Given her obvious problems with money, she should not be seen as an important patron of literary men. It is very noticeable that her gifts to the church are small objects, not large gifts of money or property.

Even less is recorded of the activities of Manuel's second wife, Maria of Antioch, as a patron. She may possibly have been the inspiration, and perhaps the financial support, behind the poem of welcome for Agnes of France. Verses of dedication survive, written to accompany a gift to the church of an icon from the 'western-born Maria, the wife of Manuel'. This is obviously Maria of Antioch, but we know nothing more about her contacts with anyone. The manuscript of the five acts of the Council of 1166 depicts Manuel and Maria, but there is no reason to suggest that Maria commissioned it. Other portraits of Maria were in existence: Choniates relates that Andronikos Komnenos had one redone to disguise the empress's beauty. The same sort of church patronage was extended by Maria as by Bertha: small objects which may have been very precious, but which did not represent the visible and prestigious patronage typified by Anna Dalassene and Eirene Doukaina.

The great literary patron of the reign of Manuel was his sister-in-law, the *sebastokratorissa* Eirene, with whom several of the writers of the twelfth century are connected. Her relationships with John Tzetzes, the Manganeios poet and the monk Iakobos merit more detailed study than the others. She certainly specifically commissioned the *Theogony* of Tzetzes, which ends with the sentiment that her loan is repaid and he has met his obligation. Their relationship appears to have been more personal than that between the empress Bertha-Eirene and the writer: Tzetzes wrote to the *sebastokratorissa* directly, and to two of her grammarians with general advice. His letter to her complains that another rhetor had handed out his, Tzetzes's, expositions to his friends, pretending that they were his own, and she had either not noticed or not reprimanded the guilty one as Tzetzes felt she should have. He is surprised and hurt that her clear-sighted mind had not realised that here was a Jacob masquerading as an Isaac. The unanswerable question is whether this mistake resulted in the unnamed person receiving pay which Tzetzes thought should have been his. From this letter, it seems as if Tzetzes was in the habit of having his work seen by Eirene, perhaps in a circle. Tzetzes seemed to work in response to pay, and financial aid, rather than influence, is the benefit exchanged on the imperial side.

The second relationship is that of Eirene with the Mangana poet, who was possibly part of her household and may even have followed her to Bulgaria when she was exiled there. He wrote innumerable occasional poems for her on birthdays, on her return to health, on the marriages of her children, or to accompany gifts, such as altar cloths, that she made to churches. Their relationship was long-standing and surely personal, although the specific evidence of contact between them is absent. Eirene's third relationship, with the monk Iakobos, is interesting. He certainly wrote letters to her offering advice and spiritual counsel, perhaps spread over two years from 1142. As far as the facts of Iakobos's life can be ascertained, he had a career in Constantinople and then retired to the otherwise unknown monastery of Kokkinobaphos, writing his sermons in the 1130s, and producing a second manuscript a couple of decades later. It is likely that Iakobos was Eirene's spiritual father, offering her strong advice on keeping control of her household and imploring her to desert the secular learning with which she was engrossed. There is less detail for Eirene's other contacts. Constantine Manasses dedicated his *Synopsis Historike* to her, indicating that she commissioned it. In the preface he refers to her desire for knowledge, and accepts the task of supplying her need, also referring to the size of her presents and her generosity. The *sebastokratorissa* did not suffer from whatever deprivation caused Bertha's meanness, and was very prepared to reward her literary contacts. A doubly attributed astrological poem, either to Manasses or Prodromos, is dedicated to her. Prodromos wrote four occasional poems for her, none of which carry hints of specific commission: she was probably one of his patrons, rewarding piecework when required. He also supplied her with a grammar. Apart from the mere facts of works dedicated to Eirene, there is no evidence on how or where the contacts were made, or any way to assess the intimacy factor.

Eirene appears as an active patron of literary men. Her relationship with Tzetzes seems to have been closer than aristocratic woman and grammarian. Chalandon goes so far as to say that she pulled him out of misery, which indeed she may have done after his disastrous dismissal from his secretarial post. The Mangana poet seens to have had a long-lasting relationship with her too. Even though, as Mullett remarks,[22] she cannot be seen as the literary inspiration of all the men with whom she was connected, since the level of education required to understand some of their work does not square with a need for a grammar, she does seem to have been personally involved with some of them. In return for financial aid, she received pleasure and perhaps prestige. She also acquired an apologist. One of the poems of the Mangana poet is written to Manuel as from Eirene, complaining of his marriage plans for her daughter. One type of patronage she did not extend, or at least not on the same scale, was the philanthropy for which the empresses were so much praised. Eirene may have provided for her own servants and perhaps those who were brought to her notice by them, but she had no role as a bringer of mercy to those who were under the condemnation of the emperor.

Patterns of patronage

The preceding discussion has divided patronage up by individual patrons. An interesting pattern, demonstrating again the decline in women's power through patronage, becomes visible if types of patronage are compared over the period. For example, the personal patronage which was so much a part of Anna Dalassene's activity disappears in the later period, to be replaced by literary patronge, for which she did not have the time. Anna Dalassene, and Eirene Doukaina to a lesser extent, brought men to the emperor's notice, bettering their circumstances, getting them jobs. Eirene became highly interested in literature after her retirement to Kecharitomene, and the later empresses all exhibited an interest in literature, albeit of widely varied standards. This was the area in which they have left behind evidence of their activity for the historian to see. They all practised the virtue of *philanthropia*: only Maria of Antioch is lacking praise in this area and this could be due to the fact that she was bundled off in disgrace and did not receive the honour of a funeral oration.

The highly visible practice of founding monasteries disappears over the period. All the early empresses from Maria of Alania to Eirene Piroska founded or co-founded monasteries. Anna Dalassene

---

22. Mullett, 'Aristocracy and Patronage', p. 179.

in particular influenced the wealth of monastic holdings even where she had not founded the monastery. Manuel's wives donated small gifts to existing monasteries, in obedience to Manuel's above-mentioned veto on founding more. Women's power was being deliberately curtailed in this area because of the prestige it generated. The emerging pattern reveals Anna Dalassene as the most powerful patron, a conclusion which is unsurprising given her position as head of the civil administration.

Two more points are relevant in a study of women's patronage. Firstly, Eirene Doukaina's assumptions about who is of importance in her monastery and about its future are those of her society and milieu. The *typikon* is clearly concerned with her family: a phenomenon not confined to women. Two other *typika* of the same era, those of Gregory Pakiouranos and Attaleiates, and the will of Eustatios Boilas show the same concern. In the *typika* of Attaleiates and Eirene and in the will of Boilas, only the limited circle of the immediate family is concerned, not the wider kin network. Eirene's concern with her immediate family has been seen as gender-related by Magdalino,[23] in contrast to the *typikon* for Kosmosoteira by Isaac Komnenos, which was concerned for servants as well. Isaac may be operating under special circumstances: he had quarrelled with his family and was living far from the capital. The existence of the family feeling on the part of Attaleiates and Boilas points rather to something which is part of the culture at the time than a gender difference. Both Attaleiates and Boilas belonged to the immediate pre-Komnenian era, and can be seen more as exemplars of the importance of family to the individual, which was certainly part of the Komnenian mentality.

Secondly, Eirene Doukaina prearranged the inheritance of her monastery in the same manner that emperors did. It has often been noticed that founders were very concerned about ownership after their death: they usually specified the heirs to prevent the property passing out of the family. Eirene, too, was preoccupied with inheritance. The line through which Kecharitomene was to pass was set out, with provision made in case one line died out. All the lines envisioned were female: this is a case of patronage from woman to woman. Originally Eirene's daughter Eudokia was to have the management of the monastery, but she died and Eirene changed it to Anna's family. This was perhaps because her favourite granddaughter was Anna's daughter: Eirene specifies that the

---

23. Magdalino, 'Innovations in government', p. 151.

younger Eirene Doukaina was to follow her mother in the position.
A more interesting question is why she left it to Eudokia in the first
place. I suspect that Eirene was very conscious of leaving all her
daughters well provided for, and Eudokia was the unfortunate spouse
of Iasites, whom Eirene threw out of the palace and had tonsured
for treating her daughter like a common woman and not the daughter of an emperor. Since Eudokia was therefore perhaps in need of
future support, Eirene made sure that she would always have a home
and a sphere of power after her powerful mother was gone. This
suggestion of course raises questions about the sources of support
and income and dependency of imperial daughters who were married, which will be addressed below. In the event, Eudokia's death
rendered Eirene's plans unnecessary. Eirene had already decided the
destiny of her elder daughter: no less than the imperial throne was
to be Anna's inheritance. This may explain why Eirene did not leave
the monastery to her eldest (and some would say, favourite) daughter
Anna in the first place. Maria was to be allowed to enter Kecharitomene without hindrance or a probationary period if she so desired.

Economic resources

Patronage demanded money in most cases. What were the resources
at the command of imperial women? The striking change in the
pattern of monastery foundation, for example, demands an explanation. Manuel's wives could not found monasteries because members
of the family had been forbidden to, but they also neglected to
refurbish old foundations, of which there must have been many in
Constantinople, and which carried the same sort of ideological load.
One reason for their failure to do so could be lack of resources.
The whole question of wealth is pivotal in the context of patronage
and power because a woman who had independent sources of wealth
and the control of it would have been in a stronger position vis-à-vis
other people, including men, than a woman who depended on someone else for her survival. Control over resources is one measure,
and sometimes the meaning, of power in sociological analyses. Is
the evidence of the spending of money by some of these women
evidence for their economic independence? This cannot be assumed:
the art historian Robin Cormack has argued that it is one thing to
see women as connected with the establishment and decoration of
monasteries and quite another to identify this as a simple indicator

of their legal and economic freedom in society.[24] It is a common practice of societies to extend a privilege to women when it no longer carries the weight or significance which made it desirable in the first place. Unfortunately, the precise sources of imperial women's wealth are obscure. Anna Komnene relates that her mother used the gold and silver inherited from her parents to help Alexios's war effort in the 1080s. Did Alexios compensate her when he could? Maria the Bulgarian had money. She used it to good effect to get Alexios and Eirene married, but Bryennios does not give its source. She also rebuilt the Church of the Chora. Anna Dalassene was perhaps unique: she after all, was not only head of a family, but had imperial authority as Alexios had, and correspondingly greater resources.

Eirene Piroska was co-foundress with John II of Pantokrator: the *typikon* mentions properties that came to her by gift, but not how or from whom. Some of Eirene's money may have been given to her by John, since Kinnamos comments that whatever was given to her she gave away. Her resources alone were not enough to support the monastery: John endowed it also. Tzetzes' sad experience at Bertha-Eirene's hands suggests that she was not well off, but the information is ambiguous and of limited use due to the unanswerable questions about the transaction. Did Bertha consider that the price of his work was too high, as opposed to not being able to pay it? What part did the treasurer play? Was he merely the unfortunate messenger of the empress sent to inform the unhappy writer that his demand would not be met, or was he the ruling voice in the affair, either advising or even compelling Bertha not to pay up? All we can say is that it is possible that the empress did not have the money. Maria of Antioch perhaps had the money to commission the very beautiful *eisiterioi* for the arrival of Agnes of France, but the whole question of her involvement is not secure, let alone the source of her finances. Eirene the *sebastokratorissa* had enough money to pay for her literary interests without encountering financial difficulties, but there is no information in the texts as to its source.

The obvious place to look for money in the hands of women in Byzantium, especially if they were royal princesses, is to a dowry. No doubt all these ladies did bring a dowry with them when they came to Byzantium, but there is no evidence at the moment to suggest how large it was, what it consisted of, or how much access imperial women had to their dowries. Another possible source of ready money

---

24. R. Cormack, 'Patronage and new programs of Byzantine Iconography', *Major Papers of the 17th International Byzantine Congress* (Washington, 1986), pp. 609–38.

was the morning gift which women received from their husbands upon marriage. This could be in the form of money, jewellery or property. All of these goods were suitable for donation to monasteries or could be used to pay for literature. The paucity of the evidence prevents us from calculating how economically independent these women were of the men in their lives.

The effect of marital status

Although economic independence cannot be quantified, it is clear that some of these women did have money and influence. In so far as control over resources is power, they held it in differing measures. Several different factors are significant. Anna Dalassene held authority by chrysobull from Alexios, and her patronage was on a grand scale. She was able to use both her authority and her influence to procure posts for her favourite monks, and to sort out the financial problems of both communities and individuals. Her patronage was on the scale and of the kind that the emperor dispensed. Anna's patronage proceeded from the power that she held and her prestige came from her relation to the emperor. She therefore had access to means that none of the other Komnenian women had. Eirene Doukaina is seen working in small ways for her contacts. She had money, it seems, from the request of the abbot of St George to her for aid, and she was able to found and endow Kecharitomene. But her activities seem to be concentrated later in life and particularly after her retirement to Kecharitomene, which perhaps suggests another answer to the differences between the patronage of Eirene and Manuel's wives. Bertha-Eirene and Maria of Antioch hardly appear as patrons at all, and are far outshadowed in their era by the *sebastokratorissa* Eirene.

The key factor seems to be that Anna Dalassene, Eirene Doukaina and the *sebastokratorissa* were all widows, while Bertha and Maria were wives. Bertha died before Manuel, so missed the opportunity to branch out on her own in the way that imperial widows did, and that Maria of Antioch certainly did, although in her short career she was more concerned with wielding political power than patronage. Eirene Doukaina began her patronage of literary men after the death of Alexios, when her standing as a widow would have both protected her reputation and given her more freedom; perhaps her status also released the income from her estates into her own hands. The *sebastokratorissa* Eirene was in disgrace for a part of her life, yet she managed to protect her household and took some of them with her into exile. Her activities seem to start after the death of her husband in 1142, when again, the status of widowhood was her protection and her release. Anna Komnene, a widow, but not an empress, did not have the resources to found a monastery and no need to, for she inherited Kecharitomene, so she spent her money and time in literary pursuits. Eirene of Hungary began to fulfil what was perhaps, by that time, one of the main occupations of the empress, but died before its completion. She did not indulge in literary activity, perhaps because she was never a widow. If she had outlived John, she too might have spent her time with texts and writers. The patronage of imperial women seems to corroborate what one might suspect about the place of women in Byzantium. It was an excellent thing to be a widow, and a bad thing to be a wife. Widows had much more fun.

Conclusion

This chronological survey of the patronage of Komnenian imperial women documents a shift in patronage patterns. Monastery foundation is one obvious example. Monasteries were founded by Maria of Alania, Anna Dalassene, Eirene Doukaina, and Eirene of Hungary. It is not surprising that Anna Komnene did not found a monastery, since she had inherited Kecharitomene. Maria of Bulgaria, who was not an empress but only the mother of one, rebuilt the Chora. But the later empresses of the period did not found monasteries as a result of Manuel's deliberate policy of preventing such foundation because of the prestige it generated. Although his policy explains why there was no new foundation by his wives, it does not explain why they did not refurbish older monastic foundations, which would have achieved the same goals.

The net result of their restraint was that women were less visible and had less prestige as patrons in the later period than before. These mid twelfth-century women were exclusively literary patrons, if patrons at all. There is no evidence that Bertha-Eirene or Maria of Antioch were approached by members of the court requesting help. Bertha-Eirene did exercise *philanthropia*: her funeral oration lauds her generosity to the destitute and the condemned, but of course does not include information about her actual contacts. The *sebastokratorissa* Eirene may have been the personal, as well as the literary, patron of Manganeios Prodromos, for he requested entry into the monastery of St George of the Mangana through her. Literary patronage does not argue the same influence at court as personal patronage does, for the patron can aid the client from their own resources without requiring political influence with the emperor. The *sebastokratorissa* managed to maintain her household despite being out of favour with Manuel, but she was not the patron to choose to aid a young aspiring courtier.

Anna Dalassene had been the first choice of patron for any monk or holy man in her day: her special resources of course mark her out. Eirene Doukaina was the object of supplicants from abbots to poets, although she did not possess the legal powers held by Anna Dalassene. Her influence must have been visible to those of the court who clearly considered her worth cultivating. Eirene Piroska of Hungary was in the process of founding a monastery which would have given her prestige, but died before she could reap the benefits. Manuel's wives were non-starters in the political stakes, and are only visible as literary patrons, if that. They made gifts to the church, but these were small, even if valuable, icons and gilded ornaments for which they themselves had the resources to pay. Eirene the *sebastokratorissa* is visible as a literary patron, and as a woman with money, but as she was exiled at least once and perhaps twice, her presence at court would not have been visible at all, and her scope of action limited. Her exile by Manuel of course raises questions about her ability to oppose him, but in the absence of any indication as to why she was out of favour, all speculation is merely that.

The trend of declining visibility is as noticeable through a study of patronage as it is through titles and kinship. It may be objected that Anna Dalassene, the most visible, had special powers which make it unfair to compare her to the rest, but the question remains, why did she have special powers? The answer is the same as before: Alexios needed her because of the crisis through which the empire was passing, but Manuel was stamping out all power in the hands of his family, because he could now stand on his own, and needed to if he was going to control the vast imperial *oikos*. Influence is not in question here: it is accepted that all women had influence but that it is impossible to quantify it. The criterion is visibility, and when men's power and authority were weak, women were visible as patrons with power, but when men established themselves firmly, they made women invisible.

CHAPTER SEVEN

A women's ideology

The ideal woman from a Byzantine man's point of view has been described earlier through a consideration of speeches and art which survive from the period. That woman, whether mother, wife, sister or daughter, exhibited piety, charity, and love for her family. None of these virtues, however good in themselves, require any intellectual ability at all. This is where the possibility of another ideology must be considered. No woman can conceive of women who embody only the qualities revered by this dominant ideology. Were other qualities praised, and if so, where? Theorists of ideology believe that more than one ideology can exist in a society simultaneously, one of which may mute others because of the power of its practitioners. The ideal woman delineated in the earlier chapter represents one powerful ideology, that which revolved round the emperor first and foremost. Women featured in other ideologies too. That of the hard-line monks, exemplified in the twelfth century by Neophytos the Recluse, viewed all women as the deceitful Eve, whose mission in life was to mislead men away from virtue and into sin by her very nature. This ideology denied power to woman by concentrating on her nature rather than on any conscious choices she might make.[1] It is an equally unsatisfactory area of exploration. Can we find traces of an ideology for women held by women during the Komnenian period? Four pieces of evidence suggest that we can. Two of these are orations, one is a letter and the fourth is the *Alexiad*, the history/biography of Alexios I Komnenos written by his daughter Anna Komnene.

1. See discussion by Catia Galatariotou, 'Holy women and witches: aspects of Byzantine conceptions of gender', *BMGS* 9 (1984/5), pp. 55–94.

One oration was written by the courtier Michael Italikos, who was part of the circle of Eirene Doukaina in the monastery of Kecharitomene and a teacher of philosophy. The other was a funeral oration for Anna Komnene written by George Tornikes, another courtier who wrote several pieces of poetry for the court. He included a large section on both Alexios and Eirene Doukaina as part of the oration. These two orations are so different from the rest in feeling and in content that, although the sample is small, the difference must be accounted for. Several factors besides content separate them from the others which were considered in Chapter 3. Firstly, they were addressed to women who had lost their husbands, who had lived a large part of their lives in a monastery which they directed. Secondly, there was no emperor present when either of these orations was performed. Italikos's speech was composed at Eirene Doukaina's request, if Italikos is telling the truth, and was certainly performed in the monastery of Kecharitomene before Eirene's circle of friends. As is the case with all speeches, it was gauged to be pleasing to the ears that heard it, and where it differs from other orations performed at court will describe Eirene's ideal imperial woman. Tornikes stated that his oration was written at the request of Anna Komnene's daughter, Eirene Doukaina the second, who also lived in Kecharitomene and shared in the literary pursuits of her mother and grandmother. The letter was written by Italikos to Eirene Doukaina. Since the virtues he selected to praise Eirene are the same as those of his oration, the two will be discussed together.

The two orations do differ in major ways from those in Chapter 3. They are preoccupied with the woman to whom they are addressed, and they praise qualities which are not mentioned by the other orations. These qualities are all to do with the mind and the will, unlike the dominant theme of the others, which was concerned with beauty and mercy. Both orations do mention beauty, both physical and spiritual, but such passages are a small part of the whole, and are applied to prove different points. For example, when Tornikes stated that Anna Komnene ignored the temptations of the imperial life and displayed virtue, this was not an end in itself, but a means to attain wisdom, both secular and divine. When Italikos praised Eirene Doukaina for concentrating on inner beauty, he did so to demonstrate her *sophrosyne*, her self-control. Menander praised the emperor in the *basilikos logos* for possessing self-control. It was a quality highly admired by the Byzantines, and is found in all descriptions in the narrative sources. The accusation of intemperance, or rashness, or excess, was the worst insult a Byzantine could make.

The forms intemperance took differed in men and women: men could be rash on the battlefield, or in anger; women could care too much for their clothes. They could both be guilty of sexual intemperance and greed. Moderation in everything was the formula for health. Self-control was never credited to women in the other orations even when they practised controlled behaviour. A certain highmindedness, the Greek **phronema*, was the most they could achieve. But both Eirene and Anna were credited with this *sophrosyne* by Italikos and Tornikes. In this alone, these two orations proclaim their difference from the rest.

Tornikes emphasised that no one practised *sophrosyne* better than Eirene in his description of her as part of the oration for Anna. It led her to the perfect resolution of the main difficulty experienced by an empress in public: the gaze of the male. Believing that the male gaze penetrated the soul of those upon whom it alighted, Tornikes was concerned for Eirene, but she, with her marvellous self-control, arranged and controlled her own glance, so that the ogling stares were reflected back at those who gave them. In this way, she was in control of them. Anna's *sophrosyne* was given concrete expression in relation to the vices of lust, anger and greed. Anna had such self-control that she could not be moved by anger, but remained decorous. Not all the spices in food could make her greedy, nor did the sweet smell of Arabian wood make her weak. Her control also showed in her sex-life. Although not of course a virgin, Anna rivalled the virgins for true integrity of soul and won, because although she had a husband she never approached him with boldness, but always as a newly-betrothed person. Anna's control was of more value because she was under more temptation since she had legitimate normal marital relations. Eirene and Anna, or the younger Eirene, valued the quality and believed that women were capable of it.

Other qualities which are not mentioned in the other orations are those of the mind. Perhaps unsurprisingly, Tornikes's oration for Anna Komnene dwelt extensively on her intelligence. References to her skill in letters, philosophy and medicine were frequent. Both Eirene Doukaina and Anna Komnene were also praised for being wise and shrewd and having quick understanding. These were qualities which the ideal mothers and wives did not display. Eirene's wisdom led, when she was empress, to the more equable distribution of imperial largesse. Her quick intelligence showed itself in intellectual pursuits, such as contemplation, and in practical ways such as transacting business; all in all she had an active mind which meshed philosophy and commonsense together for the purposes of action. Her commitment to the monastic life was praised but not in the context of the denial of vanity. Rather, she showed how to live both lives to the best, finally choosing the superior and heavenly one to which she rose like an eagle flying through the air. Italikos concluded his praise by insisting that even the arguments that the circle of friends used were inspired by Eirene and that they, the people, were but tools that she used. Her intellect was above all; her mind was the best.

Both Eirene and Anna reasoned. This logical ability is not attributed to any of the ideal wives discussed in Chapter 3. Eirene knew what to say and what not to say, and when and where, by reason. She added reason like a wall around herself, in addition to the walls of nature. Anna allowed only some of the things she heard to penetrate her ears, by the exercise of reason. That ability was the reason why it was safe for her to learn grammar, which was taught from texts that would corrupt any young person's mind. The ideal woman for Eirene and Anna was the woman of Proverbs 31, whose role as a good wife included competence in business and the management of the family finances. She was shrewd and astute and wise, and respected by her husband for these qualities. The ideology of Eirene and Anna did not dismiss the virtues of philanthropy and love for the family: it merely added the use of the mind for practical and intellectual purposes.

Anna's political ambitions revealed more about women as Eirene and Anna saw them. Anna wanted the throne for herself and her husband, Bryennios, and Eirene aided her in this mission. To explain Anna's inclusion of Bryennios in her plans as dictated by realistic cynicism is to expect ambition to be exclusively personal. What the succession crisis revealed was that Eirene and Anna considered that politics was a game they could play, and they had no qualms about joining in the 'men's game'. Anthropologists have righted the record about the relative importance of the public and private spheres by emphasising that women consider the private sphere as important as the public one, in which they have little or no dealings. These Byzantine women had a different view of the two spheres; indeed it could be argued that a division of life into two spheres at all is inaccurate for the Komnenian era, where the family circle was nearly identical to the pool of public officials. Since the family was the empire, Eirene and Anna did not see any reason why they should not influence the decision-making at the highest level as they no doubt did at all others. We hear more about women's decisions in politics in this period than in any earlier one precisely because the division between public and private was in abeyance. Their actions do not imply any more of a personal goal than that of the active mother. The smart, level-headed, quick-witted woman still schemed for her family.

In this context it should be remembered that Eirene Doukaina did not approve of the usurpation of a reigning emperor. Once John was on the throne Eirene refused to plot to lever him off it. That would be proclaiming trouble in the family to the world. Attempting to influence the choice of one family member over another while the matter was still in the hands of the undisputed head was a different matter, and she certainly believed in that. The women's ideology saw the whole of life as the legitimate concern of women, therefore they stepped forward to take their part. The dominant ideology clearly considered that sons had a better right to inherit the throne than daughters, but the women's ideology did not. There had of course been female rulers in Byzantium, two of them in their own right and not as regents for young sons. Eirene and Anna considered that Anna's claim as the first-born was better than John's claim as a male. They saw the sexes as equal in importance and ability.

Both Italikos and Tornikes betrayed that the qualities they were praising in Eirene Doukaina and Anna Komnene are not what they expected to find in 'woman', thereby signalling that this ideology is different from the dominant one. The speech and the funeral oration were both written by men, and a certain tension is present in both of them. A measure of historical truth has to be granted in these texts: Anna Komnene really was better educated than many of her contemporaries, and did aim towards being highly learned, and Eirene Doukaina did appear shrewd and clever. The men praised these attributes because they had to, but their casual comments and their categories of comparison reveal their underlying dominant ideology. Such comments on Tornikes's part include the statement that women belong by nature to a delicate and soft sex, and are only wise in weaving and spinning. He developed this theme into a comparison to Anna Komnene who was wise in secular learning. At the end of the speech, he returned to women's work of spinning to say that Anna wove words in the same manner. He praised the way in which she was capable of nursing her parents although she had the delicate body of a woman. The body of a woman had more disadvantages than lack of physical strength; it was a constraint to a clever tongue, allowing it no fitting place for display. He regretted that Anna's history of her parents will not be for public consumption because women stay at home.

Not only the offhand comments, but the methods of comparison show these men's problems with praising these women. Both Italikos and Tornikes had no other way of praising women who displayed the qualities of the mind and the will but to compare them to men. This trend is not confined to the Byzantine empire. Art historians have frequently encountered the same phenomenon where critics of recent centuries can only comment that the woman paints 'like a man'.[2] It may be understandable, but it is an immediate signal that, in the society, man is the Subject and woman is the Other. Italikos attributed the unusual quality of courage to Eirene, as part of his eulogy on the four imperial virtues, all of which she possessed. He said that she surpassed the nature of men in her courage. Tornikes's treatment of Anna was fuller but equally weighted. He finished with an analysis of her character which concluded that she was not a woman at all. Throughout the speech, he compared her to men in her learning, hesitating to say, out of respect for men, that she was better at letters, but able to say that, at least, she was not less bright. Her resistance of the temptations of imperial luxury and her reaching for wisdom was understood as 'manly' virtue. She was far above any famous women before her, like the priestesses and women through whom the oracle spoke, for they were passive victims of the power of the god and did not know what they were saying or what it meant, while Anna was in full control. Her 'manly spirit' allowed her to shake off womanly modesty when needed and nurse her parents. He compared her to a soldier in her singlemindedness. In prudence and wisdom she surpassed the most manly of men. She too had courage and a strong soul which would befit a man, but which was confined inside her soft female body. The whole race of men was impoverished, as much as the race of women had benefited, because Anna was a woman and not a man. To whom could he compare her? Not women, for she surpassed them in brilliance. Not men, for she had defeated them, since she was their equal although a woman. She was unique, both the sun and the moon. In other words, she is not a member of either sex, but something in between. Eirene Doukaina was also not a woman or a man since she had surpassed the nature of men. She, too, was an anomaly in terms of the dominant ideology, by means of which these men had

2. R. Parker and G. Pollock, *Old Mistresses. Women, Art and Ideology* (London, 1981), p. 8.

to try to compare such women against standards they understood. The standard was obviously a man. Eirene and Anna could not be compared to women as women, because women did not embody such qualities. They were not women; their qualities lifted them above women into the realm of the superior sex, that of men.

Anna Komnene and the Alexiad

The texts considered previously were all written by men. The *Alexiad* of Anna Komnene stands in a category of its own, both by its subject-matter and its author. It too reveals the perceptions of its author about how the world works, which is why it merits such attention for students of gender since it is the sole history written by a woman to have survived from Byzantium. As a biography of her father, it is clearly the account of a hero, the perfect emperor. Anna's ideal man can be constructed. But her ideal imperial woman is a harder task. Several factors, such as education, gender and the actual circumstances of production, have to be considered before it is prudent to embark on an analysis of what Anna actually did and did not write.

Anna's education was extensive: the *Alexiad* is written in a high style of Greek which was not spoken by the people in the twelfth century. It abounds in literary allusions and quotes from the famous poets which all educated people read such as Homer and Herodotus. Also, despite Anna's assertion that she never displeased her parents, her funeral oration revealed that Anna took lessons in grammar and poetry secretly from an old eunuch of the court until she was married, after which she was allowed to pursue them openly. Her abiding interest was philosophy, into which she delved after her retirement to Kecharitomene, assembling a circle of scholars from whom she commissioned a set of commentaries on Aristotle. Rules existed for writing in Byzantium, rules which Anna would have learnt. Her work can therefore be compared to that of male historians of the time such as Psellos, Bryennios, Kinnamos and Choniates. When this is done, it becomes clear that they all cover more or less the same subjects: wars, rebellions, religious controversies, political upheavals. Indeed, Anna's concentration on the military aspects of her father's life have caused scholarly doubts as to the authorship of the *Alexiad*.[3] However, the arguments against Anna's authorship

3. J. Howard-Johnston, 'Anna Komnene and the Alexiad', in M.E. Mullett and D.C. Smythe (eds), *Alexios I Komnenos* (Belfast, 1996), pp. 260–301. See above, p. 2.

seem to be influenced mainly by assumptions on what women can or cannot do rather than real questions of access to the raw material. There are other similiarities between all these high-style histories: Anna is present in her text in a way that was against the traditional rules but was becoming a feature of eleventh- and twelfth-century writing. The *Alexiad* is neither straight history nor straight biography as they should be written according to the rules of literature, and neither is Psellos's *Chronographia*. The two are a mixture of styles which in Anna's case contributes to the question of her motive in writing.

The questions of education and gender cannot easily be separated. When the *Alexiad* is compared to the other histories in terms of vocabulary and sentence structure which might reveal a woman's voice there is no difference to be found. Smythe addresses this question, concluding that the display of educated culture could be of more importance than any gender difference.[4] He also makes the point that Anna's nobility may have operated as a boundary, dividing her from other women more effectively than her feminine gender could unite her to ordinary women. Class and race are powerful signifiers and it must never be assumed that a gender divide is in operation until it has been proved. The only difference between the *Alexiad* and the histories of Kinnamos and Choniates is the warm family feeling and descriptions of family life to which the others did not have access. Anna's main interest throughout the *Alexiad* is her father's career in military strategy and the battles in which he fought, to the extent that her authorship has been challenged. Anna Komnene was a member of the family and that was how she defined herself throughout the *Alexiad*.

Smythe raises the question of the presentation of women in the *Alexiad* as outsiders. He concludes that the only outsider in the *Alexiad* is Anna Komnene herself. As a first-born child born in the imperial purple-hung chamber, she would have been the heir had she been male. Therefore gender relegated her to a role she neither chose nor relished. All the other women in the *Alexiad* are presented as insiders. This is true not only of the *Alexiad* but of all the other histories written which related even part of the tale of the Komnenian rise to power. The women were always a vital part of the process.

4. D.C. Smythe, 'Women as outsiders', in L. James (ed.), *Women, Men and Eunuchs: Gender in Byzantium* (London and New York, 1997), pp. 149–67. But compare the comments of J. Nelson, 'Gender and genre in women historians of the early middle ages' in J. Nelson, *The Frankish World, 750–900* (London, 1996), pp. 183–98.

The actual circumstances of production must also be considered. Anna wrote the book in the 1150s during the reign of her nephew Manuel Komnenos. For many years, since 1118, she had been in retirement in Kecharitomene after her failed overthrow of her brother John. The *Alexiad* is full of reminiscences of her past life and complaints of her present treatment. Anna never forgot that she was the first-born child of Alexios and Eirene and that she had been betrothed to the heir to the throne before her brother John's birth in 1087. Anna and her husband Constantine Doukas had been given the imperial acclamations and considered as the next emperor and empress. Anna was eleven years old when John was proclaimed co-emperor in 1092 and her betrothal to Constantine was broken off. She continued to have imperial pretensions all her life. When Alexios died in 1118, Anna attempted to take the throne herself with the help of her mother. When this failed Anna was sent to Kecharitomene in exile.

Anna's motive is a vexed question among Byzantinists. The inconsistencies, omissions and misplacement of events contribute to the debate. For example, Anna never mentions the retirement of her grandmother Anna Dalassene, surely an important milestone in the history of the reign. The rest of Anna's narrative is too sharp to excuse such lapses as a result of her failing memory. A reason must therefore be postulated. Generally, Byzantinists believe that Anna was in full control of her narrative and that all omissions and transpositions were deliberate as part of her attempt to present Alexios as the perfect man and perfect emperor and herself as the obvious heir. Mullett suggests this option through a consideration of the set piece ending to the *Alexiad* which depicts Alexios surrounded by the women of his family, while being neglected by his son John. The *Alexiad* can also be seen as criticism of the reigning emperor of the time, Anna's nephew Manuel, through an idealisation of his grandfather, particularly in relation to Manuel's favouritism of westerners at court. The *Alexiad* should be seen in relation to other Komnenian imperial productions, like the *Muses of Alexios Komnenos*, possibly written by John as a male-to-male legitimation, to which the *Alexiad* is the female legitimation counterpart.[5]

The circumstances of the *Alexiad*'s production add to the difficulties of interpretation. Anna's main character is a man and her women characters fit round that man and his life. Several of her

---

5. See M.E. Mullett and D.C. Smythe (eds), *Alexios I Komnenos*, vol. 2, forthcoming, for discussions of Anna's motives.

comments on the nature of women found in the *Alexiad* have led
to the accusations that Anna acquiesced in and perpetuated the
unfavourable dominant ideology about women. She has been understood as an example of women who agreed with their oppressors,
who blamed women for all the evils of the world, and had as poor
an opinion of them as men had. She has been seen as a victim of
the overpowering patriarchal ideology of Byzantium with no choice
but to denigrate and despise her own sex.[6] The technical word
for this behaviour is collusion. The case against her seems strong.
Anna does describe women in general as tearful and as frightened
when faced with danger, in the same sort of unconscious manner
in which Tornikes made his comments about soft and delicate
natures. She seems as much concerned with physical beauty as any
man, providing descriptions of three out of four of the main women
in her story. Most damaging of all evidence, her highest accolade of
praise is to describe a woman as 'manly': the male is as much her
standard unit of measurement as it is for men. In so far as she does
this, she can be accused of colluding with the dominant ideology.
In Buckler's words; 'to our special writer Woman is emphatically
The Lesser Man'.[7] But the picture of women's life in the *Alexiad* is
also the basis of many of the arguments for the favourable status
of women in Byzantium in comparison to other societies, and contemporary documents bear it out. Buckler is led by the description
of women in the book to state that 'The importance of women in
Anna's day, we may remark, was great enough to compare very
favourably even with our own times, certainly greater than in many
of the intervening centuries'.[8]

We have here an example of the complicated relationship between ideology and reality. The author of the *Alexiad* expresses her
meanings in terms that she understands, like 'manly courage', but
she also portrays what was happening. Some of the stereotypes are
expressed, although they occur infrequently in a book of this length
containing so much information about women, but much more
often Anna contradicts the stereotypes she has stated by recounting
the actions and reactions of the women who appear. For instance,
Anna says that women are inclined to be tearful, but none of the
women in the *Alexiad* cry, unless it is prescribed correct behaviour

6. G. Buckler, *Anna Comnena* (Oxford, 1929), pp. 114–21; A. Laiou, 'The role of
women in Byzantine society', *JÖB* 31/1 (1981), p. 260; Galatariotou, 'Holy women
and witches', pp. 67–8; V. Bullough, *The Subordinate Sex: A History of Attitudes towards
Women* (Chicago, 1973), ch. 6.
7. Buckler, *Anna Comnena*, p. 121.   8. Ibid., p. 121.

such as funeral laments. Context must also be carefully noted.
Women are described as tearful when their menfolk are going off
to war. Such partings, when danger is involved, can be made with
tears as part of the obligation to love the family; it is tears which
hinder action which are condemned. In spite of her declaration
that women are timorous, none of Anna's women display anything
but courage, although they are often faced with distressing circumstances. It has been suggested by Buckler that Anna repeated the
stereotypes about women unconsciously to exalt herself in comparison, and this suggestion could be extended to cover her treatment
of her family. No doubt Anna was a snob, and thought that her
family was second to none, but the result of her book is to present
women in all their glory, not to perpetuate misogyny. For it is not
only her own female family members who are praised. The Lombard
Gaita, the wife of Robert Guiscard, is also shown in a positive light,
although Anna is careful to differentiate what constitutes virtue in a
barbarian woman from that operating for her own civilised family.[9]
As far as physical beauty is concerned, Anna no doubt held that
inner character was reflected in outer characteristics, but she also
understood the power of female beauty over men, and the clearest
statement of its power is made by her in her statement that her
grandmother Maria of Bulgaria was so beautiful that all men were
concerned about her safety.

Anna seems unaware of the contradiction between her small
but revealing comments on the nature of women, and the actual
nature of women which is painted by the bulk of her recital. This
contradiction raises the question of Anna's attitude to women and
what label to use to categorise her. The most useful is still 'feminist', for although Anna did not analyse and criticise her society in
the manner of feminists of modern times, she did value women as
women. The only available term for such a woman is feminist. Anna
did not take the crucial consciousness-raising step of asking why
women were perhaps fearful when exposed to the reality of battle
and whether it was a good idea. Today, we would be more likely
to say that everyone should be. Her failure to stand out from her
society rather than work inside it does not mean that she agreed
with the ideology which understood women as weaker characters
than men. Her own life illustrates a reality different from the stereotypes: she was educated to a very high level and she deceived her

9. See my 'Actions speak louder than words: Anna Komnene's attempted usurpation', forthcoming.

family to start that education; she ended her life in a monastery out of favour with both brother and nephew. She does not seem to feel that her life was unusual. She ranks herself inside the category 'woman' and merely expands the term to include what she herself was and stood for. It can be said that in so far as collusion equals a failure to challenge stereotypes actively, Anna Komnene did collude in her oppression. But that is not the whole story.

Some of modern feminists' problems with the *Alexiad* stem from their own ideology. Anna, in a departure from the norm for her time, paints a picture of women with self-control, the eminent point of virtue. Women were usually accused of emotionalism, an inability to distinguish right from wrong because of a nature which could not reason. Anna's women on the contrary were firmly in control of themselves and of whatever circumstances surrounded them: for Maria of Alania, this was the succession crisis of 1081; for Anna's grandmother, Anna Dalassene, this was government; for Eirene Doukaina, this was home and husband, which included accompanying him to dangerous places and hiding her fear for his safety.

Anna's admiration of her grandmother is easily understood, because Anna Dalassene was taking part in public life, but Anna's praise of Eirene confuses us because she is solely concerned with her husband and family. But to demand that Anna consider political life as the most important sphere of power is to remain a victim of current ideology, which proclaims that political life is most important, and to push women back into the vacuum. Anthropology has begun the quest to see individual societies as they are rather than with our assumptions about spheres of power and their relative importance imposed upon them; it is time historians did so too. We must always beware that our own categories are not clouding interpretation. This is doubly important when faced with a historical society. To Anna Komnene, the family life and Eirene's position next to her husband was as important and as powerful in a public sense as Anna Dalassene's control of the civil government. Both Anna Dalassene and Eirene Doukaina were Anna's heroines, although they exercised power in different ways. Anna saw the roots of power in her own time as clearly as she understood the power of beauty. Government stemmed from family power, and a place next to the emperor in both a physical and metaphorical sense was the most powerful position there was. The *Alexiad* is an illustration of the care which must be taken when attempting to decipher any one person's ideology, and accusing Anna of collusion is a dead end as far as analysis is concerned.

It is clear, however, that Anna was on the defensive regarding both her grandmother and her mother. She was afraid that her readers might criticise Alexios for putting so much power into his mother's hands that it could be said that she drove the chariot of state and he ran beside it. Perhaps such comments were whispered around the court, and Anna remembers hearing them, or she was aware from her understanding of her society that such power in the hands of a female exposed to slander the male who delegated it. (As far as Anna Dalassene was concerned, these slurs rebounded on Alexios, not Anna herself.) What it does not mean is that Anna Komnene believed that power in the hands of a female was an unnatural thing. It is obvious from a reading of Anna's account of her grandmother that she admired her conduct. Had she dis-approved of her position as head of the civil administration, she could have omitted her from the history and concentrated on her father's career on the battlefield. Far from excluding her grandmother, Anna made no attempt even to minimise her power. Alexios's sub-ordinate position was stressed. Anna did not feel that he was weak because he used his mother as a political ally, but she was aware that men, probably the main bulk of her readership, could perceive it that way. This feeling may have been particularly acute at the time she was writing, when her nephew Manuel was busy restoring the personal and aloof prestige of the emperor to new heights.

Anna therefore used four methods to remove her grandmother from the ranks of women. First, she was always presented as the mother of the emperor rather than as a woman holding power. At the very beginning of our acquaintance with Anna Dalassene she was merely the unnamed mother of Alexios, mourning her lost eldest son. Every reference to her thereafter, even those where she was called empress, referred to her as the mother of the emperor. She was endowed with such a strong desire to enter a monastery that Alexios had to keep his intentions secret from her; only her overriding love of her son and her wish to do her duty as a mother kept her at his side, for she set little store by secular matters.

Second, Anna Komnene's deliberate omission of a physical description of her grandmother also helps to keep her sex vague in the reader's mind. As we noted earlier, beauty was not one of the necessary qualities of the ideal mother, and Anna Komnene did not take the chance of diluting her portrait of a mother first and foremost by painting a physical picture. All other major women in the account were given physical descriptions, including her maternal grandmother, whose beauty Anna herself could not have remembered. None of these women required the special pleading which was the reason Anna excluded her paternal grandmother from her usual practice. Given the duty of the mother as head of the family to protect her offspring, Anna Komnene could stress her devotion to duty rather than reveal a taste for power.

Third, Anna Dalassene was set outside the usual category of woman by her granddaughter, and so was not subject to the normal responses of women: she felt no need to cry when she saw her family march off to war. On the contrary, she proved herself a tower of strength and a highly competant administrator. Her son Isaac who had been left behind to comfort the women and counteract the bad effects of enemy propaganda could be of no use to his mother on either count, for she could see through the wiles of the enemy as well as he could. Anna was explicitly compared to the other unnamed women in her possession of courage and intelligence. Anna set Anna Dalassene outside womanhood in the same way that Tornikes set both Eirene Doukaina and Anna herself outside it in his funeral oration on Anna Komnene. To make her point plain, in case her reader should have missed it, Anna Komnene judged Anna Dalassene a credit to the whole human race, to men as well as women.

As a final and most potent defence, Anna elevated her grandmother to the ranks of the saints. Anna Dalassene's rigorous religious observance which she imposed on the whole palace was detailed, and her saintly qualities described. To make her meaning clear, Anna said that her grandmother when young was considered to have an old head on young shoulders. The Byzantine reader would have understood this reference, which was typically used in saint's lives. The attribution of a divine character to humans who act outside the normal parameters of behaviour expected of them is not unusual. For independent women, the accusation is often of witchcraft. Anna Dalassene never stepped far enough over the boundaries to be accused of witchcraft, but her demise is shrouded in obscurity and a possible rumour of heresy, which is at least a relative of witchcraft. At this point her impeccable political sense told her it was time to go, so that she spent her last years in majestic retirement instead of being forced out with all the nasty weapons at the emperor's disposal with her reputation in tatters. Part of the reason she survived whatever scandal she was involved in was her very successful presentation of herself as a mother.

Anna was also on the defensive regarding her own mother's role. This time it was Eirene Doukaina herself who was criticised, not Alexios. Once again, it is clear that Anna admired her mother, but she clearly felt it necessary to explain her presence on campaign with Alexios; Zonaras for one was scornful of Alexios's habit of travelling with the women's quarters in tow. Before outlining the specific reasons why Eirene should accompany Alexios, Anna presented an image of Eirene to the reader. The main ingredient in this image was modesty. Eirene by her own inclination would never have left the palace; she did not even wish her voice to be heard. This picture contrasts markedly to the one painted by Zonaras who noted that Eirene displayed her autocratic style and used her voice to good effect on those who attempted to approach the emperor.

Anna's description of Eirene's spiritual courage as opposed to the sort of male courage which the men in the book display was also part of the picture she was trying to draw. Eirene was armed with faith and perseverence, not weapons. She did not take part in battles, unlike the barbarian Gaita, but was as peaceable as her name. Anna was trying to impose an image in the reader's mind. As in the case of Anna Dalassene, Eirene had a very strong sense of duty and it was this that prompted her to leave her home, rather than a wish to interfere in male games. Because duty was her motivation, Eirene could maintain her modesty despite appearing in public places and conversing with all sorts of people in the middle of the ultimate male playground, the army camp. Once her portrait was complete, Anna described the roles of nurse and guard dog that her mother played on campaign with her father. These consisted of treatment for gout, and protection from plots against his life through poison and assassins. Eirene also took the opportunity to dispense alms and advice to the poor and needy when on campaign, the travelling enabling her to spread her largesse over a far wider area than was possible from Constantinople. For all these reasons, Anna believed that Eirene's place was with her husband, despite criticism from the military.

Anna also confided that she herself and her sisters travelled with their parents on campaign. Her scorn was reserved for those who had led a sheltered or pampered existence, which to Anna meant one which revolved around the home. She obviously regarded her lifestyle as the ideal one, despite the fact that it was unusual. She justified the conduct of her mother in terms that the men around her understood, but this did not mean that she herself agreed with them. The very fact that she was defensive betrays the tension between the ideology she saw and that which she herself held. If she disapproved of Eirene's actions, why recount the incidents at all so long after the events?

If we are to turn traditional history on end and understand women as actors instead of victims, it is not sufficient to stand with the critics of women's behaviour and shout 'collusion'! It is necessary to assume that women had goals which they attempted to reach, and to search for their strategies to that end. The perceptions of any particular woman about her situation must be addressed for those perceptions influenced the choices that she made. In this particular case, Anna Komnene chose the family way of life in a society influenced by the ideology that the man was the head of the wife. She clearly expected to be married to a highly born man; disappointment over the death of her betrothed co-emperor Constantine is stressed in her book. She did not visualise either the single life or a denial of relationships as a source of power, but instead perceived marriage as the surer road to her goals. In her testament she insisted that she had wanted to pursue the pure life without marriage, but this sounds hollow in the face of her unquestioning acceptance of marriage in the *Alexiad*, and is no more than a device to prove her extraordinary devotion to her parents, whom she insists she never disobeyed. Interestingly, she does not mention her children in the *Alexiad*, and in her testament they figure only in a marginal way. Anna saw the fruits of conformity to the ideal and had no intention of looking for any others. She believed in a caring role, exemplified by her mother, and she understood that role as compatible with influence in the public life. A career like her mother's would have satisfied her ambition, but this route was closed once by the death of Constantine and then by the attitude of her husband. Anna wished then, according to rumour, that she had been a man and Bryennios the woman, not because she was disgusted with her own sex, but because she would have exploited the readiness of their supporters to fight, while Bryennios would not.[10] Her choice of the family life should not condemn her as a passive colluder, for the rewards of conformity were so high that any woman in her position would have made the same choice. Not only did that role hold the promise of power in varied spheres, but it was also highly valued by the society, thereby conferring a great sense of worth on the woman. It is no wonder that her choice was for the ideal role of wife and mother. That choice should be seen as a strategy for life, not as a failure to live up to a twentieth-century ideal.

10. See my 'Actions speak louder than words: Anna Komnene's attempted usurpation', forthcoming.

Even outright collusion where it occurs is not the whole story. Anthropologists have found that in situations where women have colluded with oppressive regimes, they have created counter-cultures by their links with other women.[11] These groups or networks confer power because they break down the isolation which dehabilitates women by offering support and encouragement. In this context, it should be remembered that the women of the family lived very much together, even when in the palace, and that after retirement to Kecharitomene, a whole world of women was built up. The men of the family were frequently on the frontiers fighting the enemies of the empire, and the women of the family concentrated in Constantinople must have been in control of their own daily lives. Unfortunately, there is little evidence of the nature of these links or of the qualities that the women valued, but their piety, devotion to family and intellectual rigour shine forth from Anna's book and the oration by Tornikes.

What has been gained in understanding about power from this study of ideology? This chapter has demonstrated that in addition to the dominant ideology which is one held by men, there is also a muted ideology of women, which can only be glimpsed when there are no powerful men to please. This ideology included the virtues of philanthropy and devotion to family, but presented women as creatures with minds, able to reason and take equal part in intellectual activities. Women who held this ideology saw the public and private spheres of the empire as equivalent and did not regard themselves as barred from participating in both. Therefore they attempted to influence political choices when their interests demanded it. It is therefore not surprising to find women of the Komnenian era involved with the exercise of public power. To understand fully the muted ideology of women and the value of the alternative centres they set up, we need more evidence from the women themselves. Unfortunately, this is not available for Byzantium.

---

11. G. Greene and C. Kahn, 'Feminist scholarship and the social construction of women', in G. Greene and C. Kahn (eds), *Making a Difference: Feminist Literary Criticism* (London, 1985), p. 21; N.B. Leis, 'Women in groups: Ijaw women's associations', in M. Rosaldo and L. Lamphere (eds), *Women, Culture and Society* (Stanford, 1973), pp. 223–42; R. Kennedy, 'Women's friendships on Crete: a psychological perspective', in J. Dubisch (ed.), *Gender and Power in Rural Greece* (Princeton, 1986), pp. 121–38. See A. Fine, 'A consideration of the trousseau: a feminine culture?', in M. Perrot (ed.), *Writing Women's History* (French ed. 1984, tr. F. Pleasant, Oxford, 1992), pp. 118–45, for women's feelings towards a specifically female practice which is both a constraint and a marker of status. Most recently, see R. Webb, 'Salome's sisters: the rhetoric and realities of dance in late antiquity and Byzantium', in L. James (ed.), *Women, Men and Eunuchs* (London, 1997), p. 138.

Their ideology, however, was not in total conflict with the dominant one, but added to it the values that enabled women to express themselves with confidence: good sense, judgement, and shrewdness. Although in some ways women did collude with the dominant ideology, particularly in the desirable qualities that they considered as masculine, they also created their own power group by their links with other women, which were a source of strength for them, where they could develop their own ideology without the interference of an authoritarian male.

CHAPTER EIGHT

The collapse of the Komnenian system

The only question left is historical: how much power did ideology of itself give women in Byzantium between 1080 and 1180? The answer depends on the strength of the emperor. Byzantium was an autocratic society, where the figure of ultimate importance was the autocrat. In the fifty-three years before the accession of Alexios Komnenos, three women had held supreme power, two of them in their own right and one as regent for her sons. After his accession, until the end of the empire, there were none at all. This was a consequence of the system that Alexios set up with its spawning of numerous heirs and privileging of the male. Alexios has been accused of being under the thumb of his mother and his wife,[1] but it is a fact that women never played the same part after his reign. In fact he restored the male stranglehold on power. In times of crisis the latent structures are more clearly seen, but the most revealing moment is when the danger has passed and the mopping up opera-tion begins, because victory is followed by repression.

Alexios Komnenos is already famous for repressing so-called progressive elements in the state, like the guilds which could have become the upwardly-mobile middle class. His reign marks the dis-solution of a mother's power of legitimacy which had not only been the secret of his success, but the dynamic of the crisis years between 1067 and 1080, but which failed at the other end of his reign. The crisis for Alexios was not over when he gained the throne, indeed his most dangerous years were upon him. And so he put power firmly on the shoulders of his male kinsmen, building a hierarchy

---

1. P. Lemerle, *Cinq études sur le XIe siècle byzantin* (Paris, 1977), p. 98. But see B. Hill, 'Alexios I Komnenos and the imperial women', in M.E. Mullett and D.C. Smythe (eds), *Alexios I Komnenos* (Belfast, 1996).

where males ranked above females by virtue of their sex. His mother, powerful though she was, had to leave gracefully (for Anna Dalassene had a great sense of timing and was no fool) when he decided that he could do without her, and the details of her final fate are unknown. Was Alexios repressing mothers as well as guilds? His wife only gained power with Alexios's failing health, and even then, his decision-making was the object of her pressure. Anna needed her father's consent to succeed. That Eirene believed that Alexios's decision was all-powerful reveals the extent to which Alexios had regenerated the authority of the emperor. The family virtues were all-important in the 1080s, but the male-only ideology gained ground after that, with the vigorous militarism of Alexios and his sons. In 1160, Basil of Ochrid was still stressing what a good thing family was in and of itself, but it was moral high ground and not practical responsibility to which he referred.

Once the crisis years were over Alexios started to consolidate his gains, and mothers, whose underlying power had been thrust to the surface during them, once again took a back seat, with power being firmly handed on from father to son. Not all the ideology of the power of the mother could confer power if the emperor was in control. The system set up by Alexios required a strong hand to run it: this was only too clearly demonstrated when that strong hand was removed. In the last crisis of 1180, with the death of Manuel and the accession of a minor, the mother was back in control, but there were so many other potential contenders for the throne that keeping that control until the emperor grew up proved beyond her. Alexios had such a strong hand himself, repairing the holes in the dominant ideology, reinstating the emperor as the head of the system, and relegating women to a position of secondary importance within the family, by gathering a wide circle of his male relatives around him as his advisors who were in Magdalino's words 'partakers in, rather than executives of, imperial authority'.[2] The system developed with time of course, but Alexios created it and he must bear most of the responsibility for removing the power that women had and restoring the authority of the male at the pinnacle of society. Women retained their powers of philanthropy, but, since these were unacknowleged, as far as the dominant ideology was concerned women's power did not exist. Despite this fact, we can glimpse that women, by means of their own associations and values, were able to

2. P. Magdalino, *The Empire of Manuel Komnenos, 1143–1180* (Cambridge, 1993), p. 182.

retain a sense of self-worth. We can only wish that they had left more evidence of it behind them.

The preceding chapters have described a system of government and the place of women within it. In all the areas examined it has become clear that the role and political importance of women declined over the period from 1080–1180. The reason for this decline is to be found in the strengthening position of the individual emperor, who was given the chance to re-establish his superiority by the stable system set up by Alexios I Komnenos. The importance of the personality of that individual is demonstrated amply by the events of the years 1180–1204. 1204 was of course the date of the most cataclysmic disaster to befall the empire in its 900-year history, the capture of the city by the soldiers of the Fourth Crusade and the onset of fifty years of Latin rule. In twenty-four years the empire lost its way from the highly prestigious government of Manuel Komnenos. These years perhaps demonstrate most clearly the nature of Komnenian rule and what it meant for women.

The events of these years are narrated by two main sources, one contemporary and one writing after 1204. The contemporary and more balanced source is the history of the fall of the city of Thessalonica in 1187 by its bishop, Eustathios. The other is the history of Niketas Choniates, who was quite openly searching to discover the causes of the disaster of 1204 in the reigns of the emperors preceding it. His attitude to women is very clear throughout the history. Women should love their husbands and never try to do anything for themselves if they wish to be approved by Choniates. Women who were able to exercise power for whatever reason were therefore criticised by Choniates with varying degrees of savagery.

Maria of Antioch

The fate of Maria of Antioch is salutary and indicative of the assumptions held by Byzantine men after one hundred years of Komnenian rule when they encountered a woman with power. Maria was Manuel Komnenos' second wife, a Latin from the crusader state of Antioch and therefore without family or kin inside the empire itself. She was also young and by all accounts very beautiful. When Manuel died she was left as regent for their underage son, Alexios, who was married to Agnes of France. This was a traditional role for widowed mothers, as has already been explained in Chapter 3. It conferred both power and respect, but could be easily squandered.

The situation was particularly difficult for Maria, for the proliferation of the family during the Komnenian era had created many men with a viable claim to the throne. Unlike the earlier successful regency of Eirene of Athens, when her husband's brothers had all been blinded to make them ineligible for the supreme post, or the position of Maria of Alania, when no one man was powerful enough to oust her son without Maria's active help in legitimising him, Maria of Antioch was surrounded by healthy men inside a huge family accustomed to holding power. Both Eirene of Athens and Maria of Alania were foreigners, like Maria of Antioch without a kin group, but they did not have to confront a huge imperial family. The history of the eleventh century had shown Maria of Antioch that marrying to create a protector for a son was not an option, since the new emperor merely took control. Her own solution was no more successful.

The rot set in almost immediately after Manuel's death in 1180 because what the system needed above all to survive was a strong hand and personality at the helm. Alexios, John and Manuel Komnenos had all succeeded when they were grown men, surrounded by a network of support which was more or less unanimous. There was some dispute within the family on each succession, some challenge from siblings, but basically there was always a male Komnenos with the resources to triumph in a short time. In 1180 the case was entirely different. Maria of Antioch took a lover, her husband's nephew, Alexios the *protosebastos*, to help her keep the throne for her son. This action sparked off a competition for her favour which issued in a period of chaos and faction. Her activities were far from those of the chaste regents of the past and exposed her to devastating criticism and eventually rebellions. The first of these was led by Manuel's daughter by his first wife, another Maria, with her husband Renier, with at least the tacit support of the patriarch, and a sprinkling of imperial relatives. This Maria is described by Choniates as very masculine, a necessary point of view for him to hold since she was participating in areas which Choniates did not deem usual for women. In the event, Maria and Renier were barricaded inside Hagia Sophia and their soldiers cut to pieces outside. Maria of Antioch survived that revolt but was overthrown by the next one, led by Manuel's cousin Andronikos Komnenos.

Part of Andronikos's strength was that he was able to argue that he was protecting the real emperor from the designs of the *protosebastos* Alexios, and that he was going to restore order as a legitimate male relation. In this way, Maria played into his hands by her conduct. Removed from the protection which the maintenance of her chastity would have afforded her, she left herself open to Andronikos's plans. In the smoothest way possible, Andronikos assumed power, first imprisoned and then murdered Maria and finally managed to murder the young emperor Alexios. He had the support of the mob of Constantinople, which stood him in good stead, for although other male members of the family would have been pleased to see Alexios the *protosebastos* removed, they were probably not keen on Andronikos's assumption of complete control. In order to render himself legitimate, Andronikos married Alexios's young wife, Agnes of France. This was seen as a hideous act by all sides, for Andronikos was old enough to be her father and had led a life of debauchery. This is one example of the horrible fate that could overtake a young princess in the matrimonial strategies of the time. Agnes had been sent to Constantinople on her marriage to Alexios, but at least he was young too. Nothing is known of her life after her marriage to Andronikos or her fate after his death. Andronikos's rule was short: two years after his bloody coup the same mob which had raised him to power cut him to pieces in the Hippodrome, bringing to an end a reign which was degenerating into a regime of terror as Andronikos became more and more paranoid.

Maria's fate highlights several characteristics of the Byzantine mind at the time. First, the Byzantine was not prepared to countenance a lack of morals in a woman, although it had had to accommodate a certain looseness in Manuel's behaviour. Perhaps more accurately, an immoral lifestyle was more dangerous for a woman to pursue. Manuel's affairs had not been popular either, but there was little that people could do against an emperor so firmly established. Maria, on the other hand, was isolated. In her case, as in Zoe's, the personal was ultimately political in a way that it was not for a man. In Manuel's case, his personal life and his political position could be kept separate, but for a woman in power the two coalesced with disastrous results. Only a lifestyle of total chastity could keep a Byzantine woman secure in power. Eirene the Athenian managed it, but other regents did not, like Theophano in the tenth century who was known to be the mistress of the general thirsting for the throne; the patriarch made her dismissal the price of the general's coronation. Eudokia Makrembolitissa, so clever and competent, was displaced with the threat of violence when the man she had married was toppled by his enemies. Anna Dalassene managed to rule for years because of her spotless reputation. Maria of Antioch was a mother, but could not survive the press of competition for the throne long enough to see her son succeed.

Between 1185 and 1204 four members of the Angelos family ruled, although only two of those reigns lasted longer than a year. Isaac II, who succeeded Andronikos Komnenos, was married to Maria of Hungary but nothing is known about her. He was deposed by his older brother Alexios III Angelos, who was married to Euphrosyne Doukaina. Euphrosyne, a member of a prominent Byzantine family, had important connections and a family to protect her. Her career signifies the breakdown of the Komnenian system. Choniates exercised all his powers of denunciation against Euphrosyne, for she was exactly that type of woman which he hated.

Euphrosyne Doukaina

It is always difficult to extract historical truth from the writings of a historian with an axe to grind, as has already been proved in the reconstruction of Zoe's life. Choniates includes a wealth of detail on Euphrosyne's career accompanied by criticism of her. But from his rumblings it is clear that she really did hold the reins of power in her very capable hands. Euphrosyne was a woman who would have been admired by the twentieth century but was reviled by the twelfth. The very fact that evidence survived about her already demonstrates that the powerful Komnenian system was breaking down. When men like Manuel Komnenos were in control, their wives were not important enough to merit attention from the chroniclers. The instability which Alexios I had banished had returned in full measure, and in such situations women can take control.

Alexios Angelos had the ambition to be emperor but no idea how to achieve or hold that position. Euphrosyne must be credited with arranging his safe and successful entry into the Great Palace on the heels of the deposition of his brother. Some of the Senate and the state officials were content that he should reign. The members of the distinguished families who had accompanied Euphrosyne to the palace, the Doukai among them no doubt, made short work of the supporters of Alexios Kontostephanos, who had persuaded some to rally to him. Once calm was restored, Euphrosyne bribed the rest to conform, even managing to induce the patriarch to yield. In Choniates's words, 'all came to the palace and deserted to the empress as if they were slaves'. His description of their fawning behaviour is no doubt informed by disapproval of the procedure but through it comes the impression that Euphrosyne was in control.

Using her sophistic gifts, the wily empress reassured them all, pleasing them so much that they forgot to be angry about the deposition of Isaac. Alexios was able to enter the palace without bloodshed or confiscation of property.

Once settled on the throne, Alexios did not pursue rulership with any diligence, but relaxed, spending money recklessly. In the face of his *de facto* neglect of responsibilities, Euphrosyne, who could not be accused of apathy, stepped forward to direct the empire. Although he cannot deny her abilities, her appearance on the public scene provoked from Choniates his most fevered and wide-ranging denunciation of a woman. Bringing into play every possible accusation which had ever been levelled against woman, Choniates described Euphrosyne as innovative, extravagant, manipulative, immodest, persuasive and immoral. Her actions brought reproach to her husband. No worse catalogue could exist. Choniates raved that all these traits were improper for women, which included empresses. Euphrosyne's contempt of the time-honoured conventions divided the empire, creating two courts where courtiers fawned and ministers appeared. Offices were sold to the highest bidder, the affairs of state became the playthings of the women's chamber (shades of Psellos's judgement on affairs under Zoe and Theodora) and the emperor's blood relations, and meanwhile the emperor knew nothing and cared nothing, for which he was denounced by all sides.

Under these circumstances, Euphrosyne took control, appointing Constantine Mesopotomites as her minister to administer public affairs. Choniates situated her motive in her jealousy that no money should escape her grasping hands, but the fact that Mesopotomites had been chief of affairs under Isaac Angelos argues that he had the experience to handle government effectively. Since he had disapproved of Alexios Angelos's usurpation on the grounds that it brought chaos to the empire and disrupted even government, Euphrosyne must have impressed him with her superior sense in managing to get him back on board. His promotion and consequent domination of government provoked blood relations of the empress to attempt to get rid of him in their own interests. Their most effective weapon was the weak-minded emperor and they convinced him that Euphrosyne had been unfaithful to him and had made him a laughing stock. Alexios, won over by their words, expelled her from the palace after torturing some of her attendants. Like Zoe and Eudokia Makrembolitissa before her, she left the palace by a little-known passageway, divested of imperial dress, and entered a monastery.

In common with other banishments to monasteries, that of
Euphrosyne did not last nor curtail her power. It also awakened
sympathy for the exile. When Zoe was expelled from the palace,
both Psellos and Skylitzes began to question the propriety of that
expulsion. When Eudokia was exiled, she found the opportunity to
communicate with Nikephoros Botaneiates, nearly succeeding in
accomplishing a third marriage and a return to power as empress.
Likewise, even Choniates cannot approve of Euphrosyne's banishment, relating that most of the people of the court had sympathy
with her and were counselling the emperor to weigh his actions
very carefully before he committed himself. After the fact, even the
conspirators were uncomfortable: they were after all her own relations and such actions towards kin were not approved of in the
highly kin-oriented world of twelfth-century Byzantium. They were
reproached and taunted by the populace because they had brought
shame on their own family. After six months, the conspirators found
the general public condemnation of their actions too much to bear
and sought a means of restoration for Euphrosyne. While such
respect for family was indeed a feature of the Komnenian empire,
it is also probably relevant that the conspirators found that they
could still not topple Mesopotamites from his perch even with
Euphrosyne gone. Once she was reinstated, Mesopotomites became
more powerful than ever, and Euphrosyne herself, controlling her
anger against those who had brought her down, wheedled the
emperor into allowing her free rein again.

In 1199, Alexios became ill. Euphrosyne was concerned for the
future of the empire, for they had no sons and both their daughters
were recently widowed. Choniates once again found an opportunity to slander her, for in the event of Alexios's illness Euphrosyne
would have been even more to the fore than she was in normal
circumstances. According to Choniates, the empress resorted to witchcraft to tell the future, committing 'unspeakable rituals and divina-
tions' and practising 'many abominable rites'. Alexios recovered,
but he abandoned the city and his family because of the proximity
of the Latin crusaders. During the resulting confusion in the city,
Alexios's older brother Isaac was proclaimed emperor once again
and he seized Euphrosyne and imprisoned her to prevent her from
forming her own faction. Isaac could not save the city from the
crusaders and Euphrosyne was only saved by Alexios Doukas, her
relation, who went into the Great Palace before the Latins reached
it and put her and her daughters on a fishing boat. After the Latin
occupation was complete, Alexios came before the new rulers and

was granted a ration of bread and an allowance of wine in exchange for the imperial insignia. He was sent, with Euphrosyne, to the ruler of the Germans.

Euphrosyne was able to exercise overt authority because Alexios Angelos was weak and she had ability. The highly personal foundations of Komnenian rule were revealed by his weakness, foundations which would crumble when the emperor was not effective enough to hold the reins firmly. In a remarkably short time, the empire fell apart. Once again, a woman with the talent was able to rule with such authority that all recognised that she was the real power. No backstairs influence in this case, but the visible exercise of a power to which she had no right by any ideology. The ideal wife was not a dictator of policy in the dominant ideology but a gentle helpmeet. Euphrosyne Doukaina more nearly resembled the evil witch of the monks' ideology, which was of course why Choniates criticised her so harshly. It can be seen that Euphrosyne fulfilled all the requirements laid out by the women's ideology of shrewd, intelligent, competent action to safeguard that which belonged to her family. The empire was still a family run concern and Euphrosyne was a native Byzantine, accustomed to the ways of her homeland. Although her kin were of more hindrance than help to her, the fact that she was not a foreigner must have had an effect on her potential for holding power. The foreign-born consorts of the Komnenian emperors before her had not been visible, perhaps hampered by lack of ability but also isolated in a new country.

In the short space of twenty-four years, the seemingly secure empire of Manuel Komnenos collapsed and was taken over by the hated Latins. Inside this time there were two very visible, very active women. Once again, during the period of crisis, the women came forward to save what they could from the instability surrounding them. Once again, they earned criticism for their actions, particularly when acting without the justification of the mother's role. Alexios Komnenos's structure had crumbled, leaving the empire at a loss and allowing women to became visible, demonstrating once again the magnitude of his achievement in restricting their role during the years in which the empire functioned as he had intended.

CHAPTER NINE

Conclusion

This book has focused as far as is possible on women's choices, on women as actors, on women's power. The question which has been waiting in the background concerns the nature of the constraints on their power, which could be characterised as patriarchy. But patriarchy as a concept is ahistorical, and has been rejected in this book for that reason as an explanation of women's power or lack thereof. A more useful statement is that Byzantium was a male-dominated society, for male dominance is a description, not a value-judgement. Male dominance is beyond doubt, and a woman-centred viewpoint cannot alter it. A glance at an emperor list reveals the truth: only two women over the whole of Byzantine history held supreme power in their own right. This fact does not mean that women could not rule: many women were regent for their sons for many years and would have taken decisions as an autocrat. But it does mean that women could not be seen to rule, that Byzantium could not easily conceive of supreme power in the hands of a member of the female sex. There were two reasons for this. At the level of ultimate political legitimisation, the Byzantines' religious ideology that the emperor was the representative of Christ on earth defined power-holding as male. This view upheld the strain of misogyny which prevailed in certain segments of the population. Then, the Byzantine attitude that women could not lead armies[1] meant that women would always be at a disadvantage in a military

---

1. For example note Psellos's assumption that the military needs of the empire required a man's strong hand which excused Eudokia's second marriage in his eyes. *Chronographia*, trans. E. Sewter, *Fourteen Byzantine Rulers* (Harmondsworth, 1966), p. 348.

society, where military success was of overriding practical importance because of the need to maintain the borders of the empire against the incursions of many varied barbarians. Ideologically, the courage which was the supreme imperial virtue was given its purest expression on the battlefield. These two precepts held good over the whole of Byzantine history and are central to an understanding of it. They could indeed be classed as patriarchal. But the eleventh and twelfth centuries must be considered as a whole and together to advance knowledge of the nuances of Byzantine history, and to avoid ahistoricity.

Over the two centuries under consideration, we witness a pattern in the exercise of women's power. From 1025 to 1118 women were visible in the histories, taking part in the unfolding of events, ruling alone, regulating the succession to the empire. Zoe, Theodora, Eudokia Makrembolitissa and Anna Dalassene were the most in evidence. Certainly from 1118 and perhaps even before that date, women's visibility declined, to become manifest again in 1195 when the determined and politically astute Euphrosyne Doukaina masterminded her husband's succession. This pattern relates to the parallel pattern of instability in the reigns of emperors through tight control by the emperor to loss of control once again.

The most interesting figure of these centuries for a historian of women is Anna Dalassene. Unfortunately, Anna did not leave behind any other writings besides her official documents which might express her own awareness of herself and her role, but she appears in every history written of the time. Her stature is beyond doubt. Her power derived from her status as a mother and she was aware of that. In the official documents which do bear her name she presented herself always as the mother of the emperor and used that designation almost like another title. Anna knew her power was delegated to her by her son and she was content to remain the mother of the emperor. Indeed, because of her intense belief in the advancement of the family, attempting to gain sole rule for herself apart from Alexios would not have made sense to her as an option. She was legitimised by the emperor, not the other way round. Anna's realisation of the basis of her authority governed even her retirement. In Zonaras's account, Alexios came to resent the powerful position into which he had put her, and Anna, with unparalleled political insight, retired of her own accord in honour to her monastery of Pantepoptes. Anna Komnene made no reference whatever to her grandmother's retirement, which is suspicious given her earlier detailed treatment of her. From other sources comes a rumour of heresy surrounding Anna Dalassene.[2] Whether this was the cause or the excuse for her withdrawal we are unable to discover, but she certainly disappeared from the political scene in the early years of the twelfth century.

Her activities have been explored in the previous chapters. In each case, it was obvious that she was the most visible of the women examined, whether through titulature, marriage brokery or patronage. An important point must be made concerning her position, which is significant from two points of discussion. Historically speaking, Alexios's choice of solution to his pressing problems was one option in a range of options. The fact that he chose to elevate his mother was one man's choice at one historical moment and must not be enlarged into a general theory that this was now the pattern. That conclusion would be a distortion which would lead to an erroneous view of the empire. However, from a theoretical point of view, Anna Dalassene's position is a marker in the possible range of roles for women. The fact that she was able to exercise such authority, and be praised for it, does stretch the role of 'woman' further than had previously been the case. In any discussion of the place of women in Byzantium, her activities must affect a judgement about what was possible.

The empire must also be understood on the same two levels. Historically speaking, the Komnenian re-establishment of male authority regulated the power of women in a particular manner. Between 1080 and 1180 we witness the implementation and consolidation of a system. That system continued to be the basis for imperial society until the end of the empire, despite the disruption of 1204. It was undoubtedly of benefit to the empire, but its effects on women were more questionable.[3] In order to understand its dual effect it is necessary to examine the circumstances in which it was born and weaned. The eleventh century may not have been a crisis

2. S. Runciman, 'The end of Anna Dalassena', *Melanges H. Gregoire: Annuaire de l'institute de philologie et d'histoire orientale et slave*, 9 (1949), pp. 517–24.

3. It has been noticed by feminists that in periods when what is termed 'society' experiences rapid development, women as a sex generally suffer losses. Some feminists contend that society only develops on the basis of women's loss. See L. Dube, Introduction, xxx; section 3 'Women and Development' in L. Dube, E. Leacock and S. Ardener, eds, *Visibility and Power* (Oxford, 1986). For a view of the Renaissance along these lines, see J. Kelly-Gadol, 'Did women have a Renaissance?', in R. Bridenthal and C. Koonz (eds), *Becoming Visible: Women in European History* (London, 1977), pp. 137–64.

in the traditional economic[4] and political sense, but it was certainly a crisis for male authority. It was the century in which two women ruled as empress in their own right, in which men had to justify their actions in relation to these women. Zoe and Theodora themselves may have had little control over the rise and fall of men during their reigns, but men rose and fell because they won or lost the support of a woman. Authority was defined as female, and the tension that caused in the minds of men can be felt in Psellos's account of their reigns. He is on surer ground with Eudokia Makrembolitissa who was fulfilling a much more circumscribed role, even if in a very decisive way. The authority of the male was undermined to the extent that the prestige of the emperor when there was one was not sufficient to protect him from attack. Emperors had always been in danger of overthrow, but the swift changes and numerous usurpations of the eleventh century proclaim the low level of respect for the person who occupied the imperial throne. The emperor's decision was not final, even, and especially, about succession. When Botaneiates tried to nominate a successor against the wishes of Maria of Alania, she did not waste her breath arguing with him, but circumvented him, building her own power-base by throwing her support firmly to the Komnenoi. At times of crisis in male authority, females appear on the scene. This is such a well-known phenomenon that women are accused of causing the crises which show their power. Women at such times leave traces of their activity which can be picked up by historians centuries later. At these times, they can be seen even on the most public stage. The patterned, expected, but invisible influence that women always have becomes visible and overt. This was the situation before the Komnenian coup. It explains why the activities of Eudokia Makrembolitissa, Maria of Bulgaria, Maria of Alania and Anna Dalassene are sufficiently visible to be investigated by twentieth-century historians. And these four were competent arbiters of the empire's destiny. The hapless John Doukas, engaged on the same front, was out-manoeuvred by all these women: Eudokia out-generalled him to marry again against his brother's expressed wishes which took the throne away from the Doukas family; he had to be shown the route to follow by Maria of Bulgaria, his daughter-in-law; he played into Maria of Alania's hands at another

---

4. M. Hendy, 'Byzantium, 1081–1204: the economy revisited: twenty years on', *The Economy, Fiscal Administration and the Coinage of Byzantium*, III (Aldershot, 1989), and A. Harvey, *Economic Expansion in the Byzantine Empire 900–1200* (Cambridge, 1989) present a scenario of expansion rather than decline.

stage; he was out-manoeuvred constantly by Anna Dalassene, who set up such an alliance of families that the only chance the Doukai had of surviving was to join in: the Caesar couldn't even hold his nephew's loyalty against her. Angold searches for a more sympathetic understanding of the Caesar, but the explanation he finds, that John was interested in his family and not in power *per se*, does not explain why he retired to his estates when his family most needed him. The Caesar was simply not as good at the game as the four women.[5]

Alexios's reign is perhaps the turning point. Still seeking to control an unstable situation for at least the first decade of his reign, he put great power into the hands of his mother, who, like Eudokia Makrembolitissa, was fulfilling a recognised role, even if in a rather unusual way. Anna's power was unparalleled in that it was visible and official, for she was the only one to exercise this type of power. All the family had to pull together in those first years to ensure their survival as a whole. The younger members were not quite so aware of this fact as the older ones: Alexios's nephew, John, was unwise enough to consider treachery, but in general most trouble came from scions of imperial families superseded by the Komnenoi, like the Diogenes brothers. Alexios succeeded in re-establishing male authority: by the end of his reign the female method of legitimisation no longer worked. This is clearly demonstrated by the succession crisis in 1118. Eirene Doukaina for whatever reason preferred her daughter and son-in-law to her son, and made an effort to ensure their succession. But in contrast to Maria of Alania she did not circumvent Alexios, but argued with him continually, attempting to change his decision. Her other strategies included broadcasting her bad opinion of John and turning over the administration of justice to Bryennios when she was empowered by Alexios to 'manage affairs' in Zonaras's words, but it was John who canvassed the nobles who had sworn allegiance to him to build up an alternative base of support. Eirene's conviction that the way to victory lay through Alexios's decision represented a complete turn around from the situation at the beginning of his reign.

Women's visibility in politics declined after Alexios's reign, although their activity as patrons continued, a public role which conferred more power in Byzantium than modern commentators initially understand. As well as displaying *philanthropia*, they continued

5. Michael Angold, *The Byzantine Empire 1025–1204: A Political History*, 2nd edn (London, 1997), p. 127.

to display mercy by pleading against the decisions of justice, thereby exercising great, although totally unacknowledged, power. There is no single clear reason for this change. Firstly the nature of the change is questionable. Eirene Doukaina's high reputation for interfering comes partly from the visibility accorded her by the *Alexiad*; if we had an *Alexiad* for the reigns of John and Manuel no doubt their wives would appear in the same sort of light. But Zonaras's story that Eirene threw her son-in-law out of the palace and had him tonsured for failing to treat her daughter with the necessary respect reinforces the picture drawn in the *Alexiad*. This is a unique action which has raised her profile. And of course she did manage affairs and interfere in the succession. But during the years of Alexios's health she did not arrange marriages in any public sense, although no doubt she influenced them. But influence is not in question for it is not quantifiable: it is acknowledged influence that is under consideration. Zonaras states that Alexios arranged the marriages of his children and his brother's children. Alexios never delegated the management of the administration to Eirene in his absence as he had to his mother; Anna states that he appointed servants to take control.[6] Sometimes he took Eirene with him on campaign, and it is interesting that this became the pattern after Anna Dalassene retired. But it should be noted that Manuel did the same thing at least once. Eirene's political importance has been magnified in proportion to the argument about Alexios's weakness. John and Manuel's wives cannot be seen arranging marriages, and there are two reasons which may be responsible, between which it is impossible to choose in the absence of information about the women in question.

Firstly, these women were all foreign. The argument for the importance of a kin network has been addressed already in Chapter 5. The other reason may be the consolidation of the system. Alexios reinstated male authority by the system he set up: by John and Manuel's reigns the system was up and running, with males firmly back in control, and the period of crisis had passed. Females therefore slid back into the background. Eirene Doukaina did not exercise the same sort of power as a mother that Anna Dalassene had, and Manuel's mother was dead before he ascended the throne. Male reinstatement was not the only effect of Alexios's system and his successors who inherited it had to deal with all the consequences.

---

6. Anna Komnene, *Alexiad*, trans. E. Sewter, *The Alexiad of Anna Comnena* (Harmondsworth, 1969), p. 395.

One of these, as Magdalino has noted, was the proliferation of near kin all of whom perceived that they had a valid claim to the throne. The problems within the family were only beginning with Anna and John's rivalry. From that time on the emperor was under pressure again, not from outsiders but from his family.[7] Magdalino has convincingly interpreted Manuel's policies as an attempt to raise the prestige of the individual emperor above the mass of the family in various ways. One was to take all arranging of marriages into his own hands.[8] Another was to stamp out the foundation of monasteries by his relatives, because even if they were not hot-beds of dissension, they generated too much prestige for his peace of mind.[9] When the emperor appropriated these functions, he not only arrogated two of the occupations of the empress, but curtailed the activities of his male kin as well. Women were less visible under John and Manuel because the emperor was concerned to raise his own prestige at the expense of his kin, which included women.

One incident survives from Manuel's reign which demonstrates the altered role of the emperor. When Manuel decided to marry off the daughter of the *sebastokratorissa* Eirene to Henry of Austria, Eirene protested, but her objections were not heeded: Manuel proceeded to do what he wished. The influence of kin in marriage alliances no longer prevailed. The tight family atmosphere continued, but in a very different way from Anna Komnene's portrayal. Family had been a good thing in the early years of implementation of the system, but the problems attendant on its growth isolated the emperor and encouraged him to turn to servants and outsiders rather than to his kin. Women and men of the family lost some of their influence, but even if the system had not run into those particular problems, the position of women would probably have taken a downturn because, for better or for worse, male control was again established.

Other factors, like the importance of marriage and family, are less significant for an understanding of women's place in the Komnenian system, because they were not gender-related. Arranged marriages are usually understood as oppressive to women, but in the imperial Komnenian context they were not. Imperial daughters did not leave their natal family; instead their spouses moved in.

7. P. Magdalino, *The Empire of Manuel Komnenos, 1143–1180* (Cambridge, 1993), pp. 190–4.

8. Ibid., p. 205.

9. P. Magdalino, 'The Byzantine holy man in the twelfth century', in S. Hackel (ed.), *The Byzantine Saint* (London, 1981), pp. 51–66.

The daughters were still at the heart of the family, with the protection of their family all around them. Love and affection were presupposed in marriage by women. This does not of course guarantee equality, but it is more equitable than a culture in which harsh treatment of wives and daughters is taken for granted and accorded cultural legitimisation. Families were supposed to love and esteem each member; Anna's family portrait gives this impression,[10] Zonaras is certainly critical of Alexios's extra-marital adventures which prevented him from loving his wife,[11] and Choniates describes Bertha-Eirene as wronged by Manuel's practice of copulating with many women.[12] Men in the Komnenian system were also intended for marriage and family, and there was no place for an unmarried man. Celibacy was no more of an option for men than it was for women. Power was to be found in dancing to the emperor's tune concerning marriage for men as well as women, in contradiction to other centuries where monasticism and withdrawal from the world represented power.[13] Imperial men could of course become monks, as women became nuns, but these were all married men who had lost their spouses or were in retirement for political reasons. The theoretical authority of the emperor over men was as absolute as over women and exercised just as often.

Physical proximity to the ruler was the source of power for men as for women. The similarities between men and women's place in Byzantium were greater than the differences. The differences are, however, important. There were roles for men which did not imply the existence of a family, like warrior or ambassador, and most of the imperial men spent their lives fighting on the battlefield or going as envoys to enemies. Their lives were spent largely in male company, with little reference to the women in their lives.

Byzantium was not like the contemporary west with its model of courtly love, which has been understood as restoring to women some of the personhood though power which feudal marriage took away.[14] There was no model of courtly love in Byzantium because the family was expected to find its satisfaction in itself. In marriage,

10. *Alexiad*, Sewter: for family meals p. 178; for Alexios telling stories p. 226; for daughters on campaign to look after father p. 376; for loyalty at death-bed scene pp. 506–15.

11. Zonaras, XVIII, 24, ed. T. Büttner-Wobst, 3 vols (Bonn, 1897), III, p. 747.

12. Niketas Choniates, *Historia*, trans. H. Magoulias, *O City of Byzantium* (Detroit, 1984), p. 32.

13. See Chapter 5, The method of marriage.

14. E. Janeway, *Man's World, Women's Place* (Harmondsworth, 1977), p. 227; E. Power, *Medieval Women* (Cambridge, 1975), ch. 2.

the feudal wife herself became a possession.[15] In Byzantium, a wife remained a person in economic terms, and the land was in trust for her children. Although this system was still far from liberated, it placed women in Byzantium in a better position in economic terms than women in western Europe. In ideological terms, court sources like speeches and orations did not repeat the unfavourable opinions of the church fathers, even if isolated monks on the peripheries of the empire did.[16] Instead, imperial women were described with respect, although this respect could be criticised by a twentieth-century feminist for its content and assumptions. Theoretically speaking, the empire deserves to be seen as a civilisation in which women could hold the highest positions, even if the corridor of opportunity was narrow.

This book has attempted to put imperial women out in front, searching for the goals which they were working to achieve. It has also worked within the feminist assumption that women do choose, that they are actors, and that the choices are worth considering even when they are constrained. In this book women have appeared as absolute rulers and arbiters of the succession. They have featured as the most skilled creators and manipulators of kinship alliances which set up the power groups in competition for the throne. They were also active patrons, bolstering the careers of those who were close to them, and participating in the cultural activities of their day, whether the foundation of monasteries or literary circles. An attempt has been made to pierce the silence around them to learn how they perceived their world, with the aid of orations specifically addressed to them and the *Alexiad*. The result suggests that women did not concur with the dominant ideology of women's nature, but considered that they possessed minds which they were at liberty to use. In Alexios's reign they realised that the family represented the public arena of power, and interfered in that arena with impunity. In Manuel's reign at least one imperial woman, the *sebastokratorissa* Eirene, took issue with the emperor over the marriage of her daughter Theodora to Henry of Austria. She achieved nothing, but her protest is evidence of courage. Anna Komnene's choice of marriage and family is an indication that that was how she believed power was achieved and exercised. The system allocated power to women

15. Power, *Medieval Women*, ch. 1; A.M. Lucas, *Women in the Middle Ages* (Brighton, 1983), pp. 61–105.
16. C. Galatariotou, 'Holy women and witches: aspects of Byzantine conceptions of gender', *BMGS* 9 (1984/5), pp. 55–94.

and expected that they would exercise it; but in so far as it did not acknowledge that power, except in the sphere of motherhood, women were oppressed by the system. We could describe Byzantium in the eleventh and twelfth centuries as patriarchal, but a more valuable historical conclusion is that the Komnenian period saw a decline in women's power due to the consolidation of a male-dominated system of prestige, which denied to women the prominent and visible role they had held in the years before the revolt of 1081 and after the death of Manuel in 1180.

Chronology

1025	death of Basil II, accession of Constantine VIII
1028	marriage of Zoe and Romanos Argyros; death of Constantine VIII, accession of Romanos III Argyros
1034	death of Romanos; marriage of Zoe and Michael IV
1040	marriage of John Komnenos and Anna Dalassene
1041	adoption of Michael by Zoe; death of Michael IV, accession of Michael V
1042	exile of Zoe; riot by populace of Constantinople; deposition and blinding of Michael V, joint rule of Zoe and Theodora
1042	marriage of Zoe and Constantine IX Monomachos; end of reign of Zoe and Theodora
1050	death of Zoe
1055	death of Constantine IX, accession of Theodora
1056	death of Theodora, accession of Michael VI
1057	accession of Isaac I Komnenos
1059	abdication of Isaac I, accession of Constantine X Doukas
1066	marriage of Maria of Bulgaria to Andronikos Doukas
1067	death of Constantine X, regency of Eudokia Makrembolitissa
1067	marriage of Eudokia to Romanos IV Diogenes
1068	Accession of Romanos
1071	defeat of Byzantine army at Manzikert; deposition of Romanos IV; exile of Eudokia Makrembolitissa, accession of Michael VII
1073	marriage of Michael VII to Maria of Alania
1074	birth of Constantine Doukas, son of Michael VII and Maria of Alania
1078	abdication of Michael VII, accession of Nikephoros Botaneiates; marriage of Maria of Alania to Nikephoros
1078	marriage of Alexios Komnenos and Eirene Doukaina

218

1081	revolt of Alexios Komnenos; deposition of Nikephoros Botaneiates, accession of Alexios I Komnenos
1081–*c*.1110	Anna Dalassene at head of civil government
1083	birth of Anna Komnene, betrothal of Anna to Constantine Doukas
1087	birth of John Komnenos
1096	marriage of Anna Komnene to Nikephoros Bryennios
1104	marriage of John Komnenos to Eirene of Hungary
1118	death of Alexios I Komnenos; revolt of Anna Komnene, accession of John II Komnenos
1124	marriage of Andronikos Komnenos, *sebastokrator*, to Eirene, *sebastokratorissa*
1133/38	death of Eirene Doukaina
1136	death of Eirene Piroska of Hungary
1142	death of Andronikos Komnenos
1142	arrival of Bertha-Eirene of Sulzbach in Constantinople
1143	death of John II Komnenos, accession of Manuel Komnenos
1146	marriage of Manuel I Komnenos to Bertha-Eirene
1148	death of Anna Komnene
1152	birth of Maria
1155	death of Eirene the *sebastokratorissa*
1160	death of Bertha-Eirene
1161	marriage of Manuel I Komnenos to Maria of Antioch
1168/9	birth of Alexios Komnenos
1180	marriage of Alexios Komnenos to Agnes of France
1180	death of Manuel I Komnenos, accession of Alexios II Komnenos; regency of Maria of Antioch
1183	revolt of Andronikos Komnenos; deposition and blinding of Alexios II Komnenos; murder of Maria of Antioch
1185	deposition of Andronikos I Komnenos, accession of Isaac II Angelos; marriage of Isaac to Maria of Hungary
1195	deposition of Isaac Angelos, accession of Alexios III Angelos and Euphrosyne Doukaina
1203	deposition of Alexios III Angelos; exile of Alexios and Euphrosyne Doukaina, return of Isaac and accession of Alexios IV Angelos
1204	fall of Constantinople to the Fourth Crusaders

Appendix: Family trees

1. The end of the House of Macedon

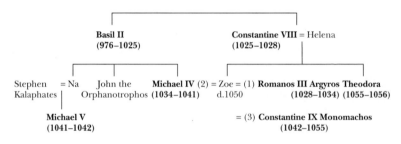

```
                    ┌─────────────────────────────┴──────────────────────────────┐
              Basil II                                            Constantine VIII = Helena
              (976–1025)                                          (1025–1028)
    ┌──────────────┼──────────────┐              ┌───────────────────────┴───────────────────┐
Stephen   = Na   John the     Michael IV (2) = Zoe = (1) Romanos III Argyros   Theodora
Kalaphates  │    Orphanotrophos (1034–1041)   d.1050       (1028–1034)        (1055–1056)
        Michael V                                       = (3) Constantine IX Monomachos
        (1041–1042)                                             (1042–1055)
```

2. The House of Doukas

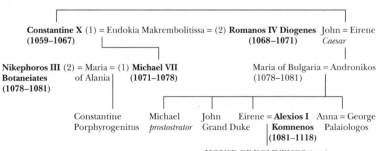

```
        ┌────────────────────────────────────────────────────────────────────┐
   Constantine X (1) = Eudokia Makrembolitissa = (2) Romanos IV Diogenes  John = Eirene
   (1059–1067)        │                                 (1068–1071)       Caesar
                                                                             │
Nikephoros III (2) = Maria = (1) Michael VII              Maria of Bulgaria = Andronikos
Botaneiates        of Alania│     (1071–1078)             (1078–1081)
(1078–1081)                │                                              │
              ┌────────────┼──────────────┬───────────────┐              │
        Constantine     Michael        John        Eirene = Alexios I   Anna = George
        Porphyrogenitus prostostrator  Grand Duke       │   Komnenos     Palaiologos
                                                         │  (1081–1118)

              HOUSE OF KOMNENOS (q.v.)
```

3. The House of Komnenos

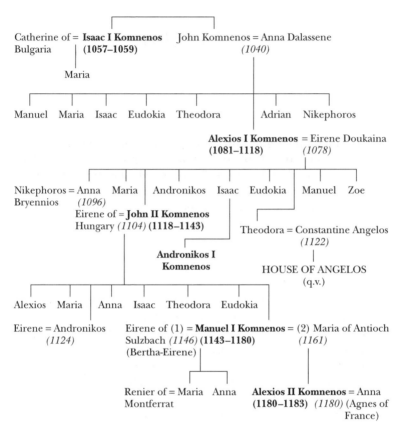

Dates in italic: marriages
Dates in bold: reigns

4. The House of Angelos

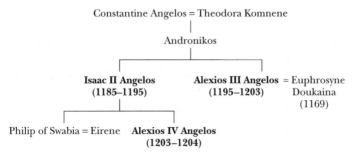

Bibliography

The bibliography begins with primary sources which are referred to in all chapters (details of translations are given where available). Then the secondary literature is presented, starting with general Byzantine and medieval works. Books and articles dealing with Byzantine women are next, followed by feminist theory. Then the remaining sections deepen the themes of Chapter 2 onwards.

Primary sources

Actes de Docheiariou, ed. N. Oikonomides (Paris, 1984).

Athanasios of Constantinople, letters, ed. A-M. Talbot, *The Correspondence of Athanasios, Patriarch of Constantinople* (Washington, 1975).

Attaleiates, *Historia*, ed. I. Bekker (Bonn, 1853).

Basil of Ochrid, '*Τοῦ γεγονότος Θεσσαλονίκης κῦρ Βασιλείου τοῦ Ἀβριδηνοῦ λόγος ἐπιτάφιος ἐπὶ τῇ ἐξ Ἀλαμανῶν δεσποίνῃ*, ed. W. Regel, *Fontes Rerum Byzantinarum* (Leipzig, 1982).

Synod list of Blachernae synod, ed. P. Gautier, 'Le synode de Blachernes (fin 1094). Étude prosopographique', *REB* 29 (1971), pp. 213–84.

Nikephoros Bryennios, ed. P. Gautier, *Nicéphore Bryennios, Histoire* (Brussels, 1975).

Niketas Choniates, *Historia*, ed. J.A. van Dieten, *Nicetae Choniatae Historia* (Berlin, 1975), tr. H. Magoulias, *O City of Byzantium* (Detroit, 1984).

Dölger, F., *Regesten der Kaiserurkunden des Oströmischen Reiches von 565–1453* (Berlin, 1976).

Ecloga: Ecloga, das Gesetzbuch Leons III und Konstantinos V, ed. L. Burgmann (Frankfurt, 1983); English translation in E.H. Freshfield, *A Manual of Roman Law: the Ecloga*.

Eustathios of Thessalonike, ed. T.L.F. Tafel, *Eustathius Opuscula* (Amsterdam, 1964).

Gregory the Oxite, letters, ed. P. Gautier, 'Les lettres de Grégoire d'Oxia', *REB* 31 (1973), pp. 221–5.

Grumel, V., *Regestes des Actes du Patriarchate de Constantinople* (Paris, 1932–47).

Institutes of Justinian, tr. P. Birks and G. McLeod, *Justinian's Institutes* (London, 1987).

Michael Italikos, letters and orations, ed. P. Gautier, *Michel Italikos. Lettres et discours* (Paris, 1972).

John the Oxite, orations, ed. P. Gautier, 'Diatribes de Jean l'Oxite contre Alexis Ier Comnène', *REB* 28 (1970), pp. 5–55.

Jus graecoromanum, ed. I. and P. Zepos, 8 vols (Athens, 1931; repr. Aalen, 1962).

Nicholas Kallikles, ed. R. Romano, *Nicola Callicle Carmi* (Naples, 1980).

Kecharitomene *typikon*, ed. P. Gautier, 'Le typikon de la Théotokos Kécharitôménè', *REB* 43 (1985), pp. 5–166.

John Kinnamos, *History*, ed. A. Meineke, *Historia* (Bonn, 1836), tr. C. Brand, *The Deeds of John and Manuel Comnenus* (New York, 1976).

Anna Komnene, *Alexiad*, ed. B. Leib, *Alexiade*, 3 vols (Paris, 1937–45), tr. E. Sewter, *The Alexiad of Anna Comnena* (Harmondsworth, 1969).

Kosmosoteira *typikon*, ed. L. Petit, 'Typikon du monastère de la Kosmosotira près d'Aenos (1152)', *IRAIK* 6 (1900), pp. 1–153.

Constantine Manasses, *Synopsis Historike*, ed. I. Bekker (Bonn, 1837).

Constantine Manasses, Astrological poem, ed. S. Lampros, *NE* 16 (1922), pp. 22ff.

Markianos Codex 524, ed. S. Lampros, 'Ὁ Μαρκιανὸς κώδιξ 524', *NE* 8 (1911), pp. 1–59, 123–92.

Menander Rhetor, ed. with tr. D.A. Russell and N.G. Wilson, *Menander Rhetor* (Oxford, 1981).

Miklosich, F. and Müller, J., *Acta et Diplomata Graeca Medii Aevi Sacra et Profana*, 6 vols (Vienna, 1866–90).

Pantokrator *typikon*, ed. P. Gautier, 'Le typikon du Christ Sauveur Pantocrator', *REB* 32 (1974), pp. 1–145.

Procheiros Nomos: E.H. Freshfield, *A Manual of East Roman Law (the Procheiros Nomos)* (Cambridge, 1928).

Theodore Prodromos, Ἐπιτάφιοι τῇ γυναικὶ τοῦ υἱοῦ τοῦ πανευτυλεστάτου καίσαρος κυροῦ Νικηφόρου τοῦ Βρυεννίου, κυρὰ Θεοδώρα, Gautier, *Nicéphore Bryennios, Histoire*, pp. 354–67.

Theodore Prodromos, Ἐπιθάλμους τοῖς τοῦ εὐτυχεστάτου καίσαρος υἱοῖς, Gautier, *Nicéphore Bryennios, Histoire*, pp. 340–54.

Theodore Prodromos, Historical Poems, ed. W. Hörandner, *Theodoros Prodromos. Historische Gedichte* (Vienna, 1974).

Theodore Prodromos, Monody to Gregory Kamateros, ed. A. Majuri, 'Anecdota Prodromea dal Vat.gr. 305', *Rendiconti della Reale Accademia dei Lincei. Classe di scienze morali, storiche e filologiche*, series v, 17 (1908), pp. 518–54.

Theodore Prodromos, Τοῦ φιλοσόφου τοῦ Προρόμου στίχοι δεητήριοι, A. Majuri, 'Una nuova poesia di Teodoro Prodromo in greco volgare', *BZ* 23 (1914/19), pp. 397–407.

Theodore Prodromos, Astrological poem, ed. E. Miller, *Notices et extraits des manuscripts de la Bibliothèque Nationale et d'autres bibliothèques*, 23 (1872), pp. 2, 8–39.

Theodore Prodromos, Unedited poems, ed. E. Miller, 'Poésies inedits de Théodore Prodrome', *Annuaire de l'Association pour l'encouragement des études grecques en France* 17 (1883), pp. 18–64.

Theodore Prodromos, Codex Markianos graecus XI.22, ed. S. Papademetriou, 'Ὁ Πρόδρομος τοῦ Μαρκιανοῦ κώδικος XI.22', *VV* 10 (1903), pp. 102–63.

Michael Psellos, *Chronographia*, ed. E. Renauld, 2 vols (Paris, 1926–28), tr. E. Sewter, *Fourteen Byzantine Rulers* (Harmondsworth, 1966).

Abbot of St George of the Mangana, letter, ed. G. Mercati, 'Gli aneddoti d'un codice Bolognese', *BZ* 6 (1897), pp. 138–9.

Schlumberger, G., *Sigillographie de l'empire Byzantin* (Paris, 1884).

Manuel Straboromanos, orations, ed. P. Gautier, 'Le dossier d'un haut fonctionnaire d'Alexis Ier Comnène, Manuel Straboromanos', *REB* 23 (1965), pp. 168–204.

Theophylact of Ochrid, letters, ed. P. Gautier, *Théophylacte d'Achrida: Lettres* (Thessalonike, 1986).

Theophylact of Ochrid, orations, ed. P. Gautier, *Théophylacte d'Achrida: Discours, traités, poésies* (Thessalonike, 1980).

George Tornikes, letters and orations, ed. J. Darrouzès, *Georges et Démétrios Tornikès. Lettres et discours* (Paris, 1970).

John Tzetzes, *Theogony*, ed. I. Bekker (Berlin, 1840), pp. 147–69.

John Tzetzes, *Iliad Allegories*, ed. J.F. Boissonade (Paris, 1951).

John Tzetzes, ed. Hart, 'De Tzetzarum nomine vitas scriptas', *Jahrbücher für Klassisch. Philologie*, 12, Supplementband (1881).

John Tzetzes, *Historiae*, ed. P.A.M. Leone (Naples, 1968).

John Tzetzes, *Epistulae*, ed. P.A.M. Leone (Leipzig, 1972).

Vita Christodoulos, ed. I. Sakkelion and K. Voines, Ἀκολουθία τοῦ ὁσίου και θεοφόρου πατρὸς ἡμῶν Χριστοδούλου (Athens, 1884), pp. 109–33.

Vita Cyril, ed. E. Sargologos, *Vie de St Cyrille de Philéote par Nicholas Katasképenos* (Brussels, 1964).

Zacos, G. and Veglery, A., *Byzantine Lead Seals*, I (Basle, 1972).

John Zonaras, *Epitome Historiarum*, ed. T. Büttner-Wobst (Bonn, 1897).

General reading: Byzantium and medieval culture

Angold, M. (ed.), *The Byzantine Aristocracy, IX–XIII Centuries* (Oxford, 1984).

—— *The Byzantine Empire, 1025–1204. A Political History* (2nd ed. London, 1997).

—— *Church and Society in Byzantium under the Comneni* (Cambridge, 1995).

Ariès, P. (ed.) *A History of Private Life*, I, *From Pagan Rome to Byzantium* (London, 1987).

Baldwin, B., 'Physical descriptions of Byzantine emperors', *B* 51 (1981), pp. 8–21.

Barzos, C., *Ἡ Γενεαλογία τῶν Κομνηνῶν*, 2 vols (Thessalonica, 1984).

Benson, R., 'Political *renovatio*: two models from Roman antiquity', in R. Benson and G. Constable (eds), *Renaissance and Renewal in the Twelfth Century* (Cambridge, Mass., 1982), pp. 339–86.

Brooke, C., *The Medieval Idea of Marriage* (Oxford, 1989).

Brown, P., *The Body and Society: Men, Women and Sexual Renunciation in Early Christianity* (New York, 1988).

Bullough, V., *The Subordinate Sex: A History of Attitudes towards Women* (Chicago, 1973).

Bynum, C., *Holy Feast and Holy Fast* (London, 1987).

Chalandon, F., *Les Comnène I: Essai sur le règne d' Alexis Comnène* (Paris, 1900).

—— *Les Comnène II: Jean II Comnène et Manuel I Comnène*, 2 vols (Paris, 1912).

Cheynet, J-P., *Pouvoir et contestations à Byzance (963–1210)* (Paris, 1990).

Cormack, R., 'Interpreting the mosaics of S Sophia at Istanbul', *Art History* 4 (1981), pp. 131–49.

—— *Writing In Gold* (London, 1985).

Diehl, C., *Figures byzantines* (Paris, 1903).

Franses, H., *Symbols, Meaning, Belief: Donor Portraits in Byzantine Art* (Unpub. PhD thesis, Courtauld Institute of Art, 1991).

Grierson, P., *Byzantine Coins* (London, 1982).

Harvey, A., *Economic Expansion in the Byzantine Empire, 900–1200* (Cambridge, 1989).

Hendy, M., *Studies in Byzantine Monetary Economy c.300–1450* (Cambridge, 1985).

—— 'Byzantium, 1081–1204: an economic reappraisal', *TRHS* 20 (1970), pp. 31–52, repr. *The Economy, Fiscal Administration and Coinage of Byzantium*, II (Aldershot, 1989).

—— 'Byzantium, 1081–1204: the economy revisited, twenty years on', *The Economy, Fiscal Administration and Coinage of Byzantium*, III (Aldershot, 1989).

Herrin, J., *The Formation of Christendom* (London, 1987).

Jenkins, R.J.H., *Byzantium: The Imperial Centuries* (London, 1966).

Kazhdan, A. and Constable, G., *People and Power in Byzantium: An Introduction to Modern Byzantine Studies* (Washington, 1982).

—— 'Certain traits of imperial propaganda in the Byzantine empire from the eighth century to the fifteenth century', *Prédication et Propagande au Moyen Âge, Islam, Byzance, Occident*, ed. G. Makdisi (Paris, 1983), pp. 13–28.

Kazhdan, A. and Franklin, S., *Studies in Byzantine Literature of the Eleventh and Twelfth Centuries* (Cambridge, 1984).

Kazhdan, A. and Epstein, A., *Change in Byzantine Culture in the Eleventh and Twelfth Centuries* (Los Angeles, 1985).

Kazhdan, A., 'Byzantine hagiography and sex in the fifth to twelfth centuries', *DOP* 44 (1990), pp. 131–43.

—— (ed.), *The Oxford Dictionary of Byzantium*, 3 vols (New York and Oxford, 1991).

Loverance, R., *Byzantium* (London, 1988).

Lowden, J., 'Observations on Byzantine illuminated psalters', *Art Bulletin* 70 (1988), pp. 242–60.

MacCormack, S., *Art and Ceremony in Late Antiquity* (London, 1981).

Magdalino, P., *The Empire of Manuel Komnenos, 1143–1180* (Cambridge, 1993).

—— 'Byzantine snobbery', in M. Angold (ed.), *The Byzantine Aristocracy, IX–XIII Centuries* (Oxford, 1984), pp. 58–78; reprinted in *Tradition and Transformation in Medieval Byzantium, I* (Aldershot, 1991).

—— 'The Byzantine holy man in the twelfth century', in S. Hackel (ed.), *The Byzantine Saint* (London, 1981), pp. 51–66; reprinted in *Tradition and Transformation in Medieval Byzantium*, VII (Aldershot, 1991).

—— 'The phenomenon of Manuel Komnenos', in J. Howard-Johnston (ed.), *Byzantium and the West c.850–1200* (Amsterdam, 1988); *BF* 13 (1988), pp. 173–99; reprinted in *Tradition and Transformation in Medieval Byzantium*, IV (Aldershot, 1991).

—— 'Innovations in government', in M.E. Mullett and D.C. Smythe (eds), *Alexios I Komnenos* (Belfast, 1996), pp. 146–66.

—— 'The reform edict of 1107', in Mullett and Smythe, *Alexios I Komnenos*, pp. 199–218.

—— 'Aspects of twelfth-century *Kaiserkritik*', *Speculum*, 58 (1983), pp. 326–46; reprinted in *Tradition and Transformation in Medieval Byzantium*, VIII (Aldershot, 1991).

Mango, C., *Byzantium, The Empire of New Rome* (London, 1980).

—— 'Daily life in Byzantium', *JÖB* 31/1 (1981), pp. 337–53.

Oikonomides, N., *Dated Byzantine Lead Seals* (Washington, 1986).

Ostrogorsky, G., *A History of the Byzantine State* (Oxford, 1968).

Patlagean, E., 'Byzantium in the tenth and eleventh centuries', in P. Veyne (ed.), *A History of Private Life*, I (Cambridge, Mass. and London, 1987), pp. 553–641.

Rousselle, A., *Porneia: On Desire and the Body in Antiquity* (Oxford, 1988).

Runciman, S., *The Emperor Romanus Lecapenus and his Reign* (Cambridge, 1963).

Schlumberger, *Sigillographie*.

Spatharakis, I., *The Portrait in Byzantine Illuminated Manuscripts* (Leiden, 1976).

Talbot, A-M., 'Old age in Byzantium', *BZ* 77 (1984), pp. 267–78.

Wessel, K., *Byzantine Enamels* (Shannon, 1969).

Whitting, P., *Byzantine Coins* (London, 1973).

Wroth, W., *Catalogue of the Imperial Byzantine Coins in the British Museum*, 2 vols (London, 1908).

Zacos and Veglery, *Byzantine Lead Seals.*

Byzantine women and their predecessors

Abrahamse, D., 'Women's monasticism in the middle Byzantine period: some problems and prospects', *BF* 9 (1985), pp. 35–58.

Adams, P., *Princesses byzantines* (Paris, 1893).

Albani, J., 'Female burials of the late Byzantine period in monasteries', in J. Perreault (ed.), *Les femmes et le monachisme byzantin* (Athens, 1991), pp. 111–17.

Basilikopoulou, A., 'Monachisme: l'egalité totale des sexes', in Perreault, *Le monachisme byzantin*, pp. 99–110.

Beard, M., 'The sexual status of Vestal Virgins', *JRS* 70 (1980), pp. 12–27.

Beaucamp, J., 'La situation juridique de la femme à Byzance', *Cahiers de civilisation médiévale* 20 (1977), pp. 145–76.

—— *Le statut de la femme à Byzance (4e–7e siècle)*, I, *Le droit impérial* (Paris, 1990).

Browning, R., 'An unpublished funeral oration on Anna Comnena', *Proceedings of the Cambridge Philosophical Society*, 188 (ns 8) (Cambridge, 1962), pp. 1–12.

Buckler, G., *Anna Comnena* (Oxford, 1929).

—— 'Women in Byzantine law around 1100AD', *B* 11 (1936), pp. 391–416.

Cameron, A., 'The empress Sophia', *B* 45 (1975), pp. 5–21, repr. *Change and Continuity in Sixth-Century Byzantium*, XI (London, 1981).

—— 'Virginity as metaphor: women and the rhetoric of early Christianity', in A. Cameron (ed.), *History as Text* (London, 1989), pp. 181–205.

Clark, E., 'Authority and humility: a conflict of values in fourth-century female monasticism', *BF* 9 (1985), pp. 17–34.

Diehl, C., *Impératrices de Byzance* (Paris, 1959).

Fledelius, K., 'Women's position and possibilities in Byzantine society with particular reference to the novels of Leo VI', *JÖB* 32/2 (1982), pp. 425–532.

Galatariotou, C., 'Holy women and witches: aspects of Byzantine conceptions of gender', *BMGS* 9 (1984/5), pp. 55–94.

—— 'Byzantine women's monastic communities: the evidence of the *typika*', *JÖB* 38 (1988), pp. 263–90.

Garland, L., *Byzantine Empresses: Women and Power in Byzantium AD527–1204* (London, 1998).

—— 'The life and ideology of Byzantine women: a further note on conventions of behaviour and social reality as reflected in eleventh- and twelfth-century historical sources', *B* 58 (1988), pp. 361–93.

Gill, J., 'Matrons and brides of fourteenth-century Byzantium', *BF* 10 (1985), pp. 39–56.

Grosdidier de Matons, J., 'La femme dans l'empire byzantin', *Histoire mondiale de la femme*, III (Paris, 1967), pp. 11–43.

Herrin, J., 'In search of Byzantine women: three avenues of approach', in A. Cameron and A. Kuhrt (eds), *Images of Women in Antiquity* (London, 1983), pp. 167–89.

Herrin, J., 'Women and the church in Byzantium', *Bulletin of the British Association of Orientalists* 11 (1979–80), pp. 8–14.

—— ' "*Femina byzantina*": The council of Trullo on women', *DOP* 46 (1992), pp. 97–106.

Hill, B., James, L. and Smythe, D.C., 'Zoe and the rhythm method of imperial renewal', in P. Magdalino (ed.), *New Constantines: The Rhythm of Imperial Renewal in Byzantium, 4th–13th Centuries* (Aldershot, 1994), pp. 215–29.

Hill, B., 'Alexios I Komnenos and the imperial women', in Mullett and Smythe, *Alexios I Komnenos*, pp. 37–54.

—— 'The ideal imperial Komnenian woman', *BF* 23 (1996), pp. 7–18.

—— 'A vindication of the rights of women to power by Anna Komnene', *BF* 23 (1996), pp. 45–54.

—— 'Imperial women and the ideology of womanhood in the eleventh and twelfth centuries', in James, *Women, Men and Eunuchs*, pp. 76–99.

Holum, K., *Theodosian Empresses* (London, 1982).

Hunt, L-A., 'A woman's prayer to St Sergios in Latin Syria: interpreting an eleventh-century icon at Mt Sinai', *BMGS* 15 (1991), pp. 96–145.

James, L. (ed.), *Women, Men and Eunuchs: Gender in Byzantium* (London, 1997).

Kalavrezou-Maxeiner, I., 'Eudocia Makrembolitissa and the Romanos Ivory', *DOP* 31 (1977), pp. 305–28.

Koubena, E., 'A survey of aristocratic women founders in Konstantinople between the eleventh and the fifteenth centuries', in Perreault, *Le monachisme byzantin*, pp. 1–13.

Laiou, A., 'The festival of Agathe: comments on the life of Constantinopolitan women', *Byzantium, Tribute to Andreas Stratos* (Athens, 1980), I, pp. 111–22; reprinted in *Gender, Society and Economic Life in Byzantium*, III (London, 1992).

—— 'The role of women in Byzantine society', *JÖB* 31/1 (1981), pp. 233–60.

—— 'Addendum to the report on the role of women in Byzantine society', *JÖB* 32/1 (1982), pp. 198–204.

—— 'Observations on the life and ideology of Byzantine women', *BF* 9 (1985), pp. 59–102.

—— ' "Consensus facit nuptias – et non": Pope Nicholas I's response to the Bulgarians as a source for Byzantine marriage customs', *Rechtshistorisches Journal* 4 (1985), pp. 189–201; reprinted in *Gender, Society and Economic Life in Byzantium*, IV (London, 1992).

Lefkowitz, M., 'Influential women', in Cameron and Kuhrt, *Images of Women in Antiquity*, pp. 49–64.

Leib, B., 'Nicéphore III Botaniatès (1078–1081) et Marie d'Alania', *Actes de VIe congrès international d'études byzantines* (Paris, 1948), I, pp. 129–40.

—— 'La role des femmes dans la révolution des Comnènes à Byzance', *OCA* 204 (1977), pp. 1–15.

Lucas, A.M., *Women in the Middle Ages* (Brighton, 1983), pp. 61–105.

McCabe, J., *Empresses of Constantinople* (London, 1913).

Mullett, M.E., 'The "disgrace" of the ex-Basilissa Maria', *BS* 45 (1984), pp. 202–11.

Nelson, J., *The Frankish World, 750–900* (London, 1996).

Oikonomides, N., 'Le serment de l'impératrice Eudocie', *REB* 21 (1963), pp. 101–28.

—— 'St George, Maria Skleraina and the "Malyj Sion" of Novgorod', *DOP* 34–35 (1980–81), pp. 239–45.

Papadimitriou, N., 'Les femmes de rang impérial et la vie monastique à Byzance', in Perreault, *Le monachisme byzantin* (Athens, 1991), pp. 67–85.

Patlagean, E., 'L'histoire de la femme déguisée au moine et l'évolution de la sainteté féminine à Byzance', *Studi Medievali* 17.2 (Spoleto, 1976), pp. 597–624.

Power, E., *Medieval Women* (Cambridge, 1975).

Runciman, S., 'The end of Anna Dalassena', *Melanges H. Gregoire: Annuaire de l'institute de philologie et d'histoire orientale et slave*, 9 (1949), pp. 517–24.

—— 'Some notes on the role of the empress', *Eastern Churches Review* 4.2 (1972), pp. 119–24.

—— 'The empress Irene the Athenian', in D. Baker (ed.), *Medieval Women* (Oxford, 1978), pp. 101–18.

—— 'Women in Byzantine aristocratic society', in Angold, *The Byzantine Aristocracy*, pp. 10–22.

Saradi-Mendelovici, H., ' "L'infirmitas sexus" présumée de la moniale byzantine: doctrine ascétique et pratique juridique', in Perreault, *Le monachisme byzantin*, pp. 87–97.

Talbot, A-M., 'Blue-stocking nuns: intellectual life in the convents of late Byzantium', *Okeanos: Essays presented to Ihor Sevcenko* (Cambridge, Mass., 1984), pp. 604–18.

—— 'A comparison of the monastic experience of Byzantine men and women', *Greek Orthodox Theological Review* 30 (1985), pp. 1–20.

Talbot, A-M., 'Empress Theodora Palaiologina, wife of Michael VIII', *DOP* 46 (1992), pp. 295–304.

Topping, E.C., *Holy Mothers of Orthodoxy* (Minneapolis, 1987).

Treadgold, W., 'The brideshows of Byzantine emperors', *B* 49 (1979), pp. 395–413.

Tsatsos, J., *Empress Athenais-Eudocia* (Brookline, 1977).

Webb, R. 'Salome's sisters: the rhetoric and realities of dance in late antiquity and Byzantium', in L. James, ed., *Women, Men and Eunuchs* (London, 1997), pp. 119–48.

Feminist theory

Alcoff, L., 'Cultural feminism versus post-structuralism: the identity crisis in feminist theory', *Signs* 13 (1988), pp. 405–36.

Anderson, B. and Zinsser, J., *A History of Their Own* (Harmondsworth, 1988).

Ardener, E., 'The problem of dominance', in Dube, Leacock and Ardener, *Visibility and Power*, pp. 98–104.

Ardener, S. (ed.), *Defining Females* (London, 1978).

Ashley, K. and Sheingorn, P. (eds), *Interpreting Cultural Symbols* (Athens and London, 1990).

Barrett, M., *Women's Oppression Today: Problems in Marxist Feminist Analysis* (London, 1980).

de Beauvoir, S., *The Second Sex* (New York, 1953).

Bennett, Judith, ' "History that stands still": women's work in the European past', *Feminist Studies* 14 (1987).

—— 'Feminism and history', *Gender and History* 1 (1989).

—— 'Women's history: a study in continuity and change', *Women's History Review* 2 (1993).

Bensabib, S. and Cornell, D. (eds), *Feminism as Critique* (Oxford, 1987).

Bordo, S., 'Feminism postmodernism and gender-scepticism', in L. Nicholson (ed.), *Feminism/Postmodernism* (New York, 1990), pp. 133–56.

Boswell, J., 'Revolutions, universals and sexual categories', in M. Daberman, M. Vicinus, and G. Chauvney Jr. (eds), *Hidden From History* (New York, 1991), pp. 17–36.

du Boulay, J., 'Women – images of their nature and destiny in rural Greece', in Dubisch, *Gender and Power*, pp. 139–68.

Butler, J., 'Imperfect reflections of reality: de Beauvoir, Wittig and Foucault', in Bensabib and Cornell, *Feminism as Critique*, pp. 128–42.

Cameron, A., 'Redrawing the map: early Christian territory after Foucault', *JRS* 76 (1980), pp. 266–71.

Campbell, K. (ed.), *Critical Feminism: Argument in the Disciplines* (Oxford, 1992).

Chodorow, N., 'Family structure and feminine personality', in Rosaldo and Lamphere, *Women, Culture and Society*, pp. 43–66.

Coates, J., *Women, Men and Language* (London, 1986).

Collier, J., 'Women in politics', in Rosaldo and Lamphere, *Women, Culture and Society*, pp. 89–96.

Collier, J. and Rosaldo, M., 'Politics and gender in simple societies', in Ortner and Whitehead, *Sexual Meanings*, pp. 275–329.

Connell, R.W., *Gender and Power: Society, the Person and Sexual Politics* (Oxford, 1987).

Delmar, R., 'What is feminism?', in A. Oakley and J. Mitchell (eds), *What is Feminism?* (Oxford, 1980), pp. 8–33.

Denich, B., 'Sex and power in the Balkans', in Rosaldo and Lamphere, *Women, Culture and Society*, pp. 89–96.

Dimen, M., 'Servants and sentries: women, power and social reproduction in Kriovrisi', in Dubisch, *Gender and Power*, pp. 53–67.

Dube, L., Leacock, E. and Ardener, S. (eds), *Visibility and Power* (Oxford, 1986).

Dubisch, J. (ed.), *Gender and Power in Rural Greece* (Princeton, 1986).

—— 'Culture enters through the kitchen: women, food and social boundaries in rural Greece', in Dubisch, *Gender and Power*, pp. 195–214.

Eagleton, T., *Literary Theory* (Minneapolis, 1983).

Edwards, J., *Language, Society and Identity* (London and Oxford, 1985).

Epstein, C.F. and Coser, R.L., *Access to Power: Cross-National Studies of Women and Elites* (London, 1981).

Erler, M. and Kowaleski, M. (eds), *Women and Power in the Middle Ages* (Athens and London, 1988).

Faludi, S., *Backlash: The Undeclared War Against Women* (London, 1992).

Farge, A., 'Methods and effects of women's history', in Perrot, *Writing Women's History*, pp. 10–24.

Ferrante, J., 'Male fantasy and female reality in courtly literature', *Women's Studies* 11 (1984), pp. 67–97.

Fine, A., 'A consideration of the trousseau: a feminine culture?', in Perrot, *Writing Women's History*, pp. 118–45.

Firestone, S., *The Dialectic of Sex: The Case for Feminist Revolution* (New York, 1970).

Flax, J., 'The family in contemporary feminist thought: a critical review', in J.B. Elshtain (ed.), *The Family in Political Thought* (Amherst, 1982), pp. 232–39.

—— 'Postmodernism and gender relations in feminist theory', *Signs* 12 (1987), pp. 621–43.

Foucault, M., *The Use of Pleasure* (Harmondsworth, 1985).

Fox-Genovese, E., 'Placing women's history in history', *New Left Review* 133 (1982), pp. 5–29.

Fraser, A., *The Weaker Vessel* (London, 1984).

French, M., *Beyond Power, Men, Women and Morals* (London, 1985).

Frieden, B., *The Feminine Mystique* (New York, 1963).

Friedl, E., 'The position of women: appearance and reality', *Anthropological Quarterly* 40.3 (1967), pp. 97–108; reprinted in Dubisch, *Gender and Power*, pp. 42–52.

Gatons, M., 'A critique of the sex/gender distinction', in J. Allen and P. Patton (eds), *Beyond Marxism: Interventions after Marx* (Leichhardt, 1983), pp. 143–62.

Goldberg, S., *The Inevitability of Patriarchy* (New York, 1973).

Greene, G. and Kahn, C., 'Feminist scholarship and the social construction of women', in G. Greene and C. Kahn (eds), *Making a Difference: Feminist Literary Criticism* (London, 1985), pp. 1–36.

Hastrup, K., 'The semantics of biology: virginity', in Ardener, *Defining Females.*

Herzfeld, M., 'Within and without: the category of "female" in the ethnography of modern Greece', in Dubisch, *Gender and Power*, pp. 215–33.

Humm, M., *A Dictionary of Feminist Theory* (London, 1989).

Illich, I., *Gender* (London, 1983).

Johansson, S.R., ' "Herstory" as history: a new field or another fad?', in B. Carroll (ed.), *Liberating Women's History* (Urbana, 1976), pp. 400–30.

Kandiyoti, D., 'Bargaining with patriarchy', in J. Lorber and S. Farrell (eds), *The Social Construction of Gender* (London, 1991), pp. 104–18.

Kaplan, E.A., 'Is the gaze male?', in A. Snitow, Stansell, and S. Thompson (eds), *Powers of Desire: the Politics of Sexuality* (New York, 1983).

Kelly, J., 'The social relation of the sexes: methodological implications of women's history', *Signs* 1.4 (1976), pp. 809–23.

Kelly-Gadol, J., 'Did women have a renaissance?', in R. Bridenthal and C. Koonz (eds), *Becoming Visible: Women in European History* (London, 1977), pp. 137–64.

Kennedy, R., 'Women's friendships on Crete: a psychological perspective', in Dubisch, *Gender and Power*, pp. 121–38.

Kleinberg, J. (ed.), *Retrieving Women's History* (Oxford, 1992).

Kramarie, C. and Treichler, P. (eds), *A Feminist Dictionary* (London, 1985).

Lamphere, L., 'Strategies, co-operation and conflict among women in domestic groups', in Rosaldo and Lamphere, *Women, Culture and Society*, pp. 97–112.

Laqueur, T., *Making Sex* (London, 1990).

Leacock, E., 'Women, power and authority', in Dube, Leacock and Ardener, *Visibility and Power*, pp. 107–35.

Lerner, G., 'Black women in the United States: a problem in historiography and interpretation', in G. Lerner, *The Majority Finds its Past: Placing Women in History* (London, 1979).

—— 'Politics and culture in women's history', *Feminist Studies* 6 (1980), pp. 49–54.

McConnell-Ginet, S. (ed.), *Women and Language in Literature and Society* (New York, 1980).

Mead, M., *Sex and Temperament in Three Primitive Societies* (New York, 1935).

Miles, R., *The Rites of Man: Love, Sex and Death in the Making of the Male* (London, 1991).

Millar, C. and Swift, K., *Words and Women* (New York, 1977).

Millett, K., *Sexual Politics* (New York, 1970).

Mitchell, J., *Psychoanalysis and Feminism* (Harmondsworth, 1974).

—— *Women: The Longest Revolution* (London, 1984).

Oakley, A., *Sex, Gender and Society* (London, 1972).

Ortner, S., 'Is female to male as nature is to culture?', in Rosaldo and Lamphere, *Women, Culture and Society*, pp. 67–88.

Ortner, S. and Whitehead, H. (eds), *Sexual Meanings: The Cultural Construction of Gender and Sexuality* (Cambridge, 1981).

Perrot, M. (ed.), *Writing Women's History* (French ed. 1984, tr. F. Pleasant, Oxford, 1992).

—— 'Women, power and history', in Perrot, *Writing Women's History* (Oxford, 1992), pp. 160–74.

Perry, R., 'Review of Chodorow, Flax and Yeager', *Signs* 16.3 (1991), pp. 600–603.

Poovey, M., 'Feminism and deconstruction', *Feminist Studies* 14.1 (1988), pp. 51–65.

Rendel, M., *Women, Power and Political Systems* (London, 1981).

Revel, J., 'Masculine and feminine: the historiographical use of sexual roles', in Perrot, *Writing Women's History*, pp. 90–105.

Rich, A., 'Compulsory heterosexuality and lesbian existence', *Signs* 5.4 (1980), pp. 631–60.

Rosaldo, M., 'Women, culture and society: a theoretical overview', in Rosaldo and Lamphere, *Women, Culture and Society*, pp. 17–42.

Bibliography

235

—— 'The use and abuse of anthropology: reflections on feminism and cross-cultural understanding', *Signs* 5 (1980), pp. 389–417.

Rosaldo, M. and Lamphere, L. (eds), *Women, Culture and Society* (Stanford, 1974).

Rowbotham, S., 'The trouble with "patriarchy"', in R. Samuel (ed.), *People's History and Socialist Theory* (London, 1981), pp. 363–9.

—— *Dreams and Dilemmas* (London, 1983).

Rubin, G., 'The traffic in women: notes on the "political economy" of sex', in R. Reiter (ed.), *Toward an Anthropology of Women* (New York, 1975), pp. 157–210.

Russ, J., *How to Suppress Women's Writing* (Austin, 1983).

Sacks, K., *Sisters and Wives: The Future and Past of Sexual Equality* (Westport, 1979).

—— 'Engels revisited: women, the organisation of production and private property', in Rosaldo and Lamphere, *Women, Culture and Society*, pp. 207–22.

Salamone, S. and Stanton, J.B., 'Introducing the *nikokyra*: ideality and reality in social process', in Dubisch, *Gender and Power*, pp. 97–120.

Scott, J., 'Gender: a useful category of historical analysis', *AHR* 91 (1986), pp. 1053–75.

—— 'Deconstructing equality-versus-difference: or the uses of poststructuralist theory for feminism', *Feminist Studies* 14.1 (1988), pp. 33–50.

Shilling, C., *The Body in Social Theory* (London, 1993).

Spender, D., *Man-made Language* (London, 1980).

—— *The Invisible Women: The Schooling Scandal* (London, 1982).

—— *Women of Ideas* (London, 1982).

Steinem, G., 'If men could menstruate', in G. Steinem, *Outrageous Acts and Everyday Rebellions* (London, 1984), pp. 337–40.

Walkowitz, J., *et al.* (eds), 'Politics and culture in women's history: a symposium', *Feminist Studies* 6 (1980).

Weber, M., *The Theory of Social and Economic Organisation* (New York, 1947).

Weiner, A., *Women of Value, Men of Renown* (Austin, 1976).

The eleventh century

Ahrweiler, H., 'Recherches sur la société byzantine au XIe siècle: nouvelles hiérarchies et nouvelles solidarités', *TM* 6 (1976), pp. 99–124.

Arbagi, M., 'The celibacy of Basil II', *BS/EB* 2.1 (1975), pp. 41–5.

Hussey, J., 'The Byzantine empire in the eleventh century: some different interpretations', *TRHS* 32 (1950), pp. 71–85.

Johnson, G., 'Constantine VIII and Michael Psellos: rhetoric, reality and the decline of Byzantium, AD 1025–28', *BS/EB* 9 (1982), pp. 220–32.

Kyrakis, M., 'Medieval European society as seen in two eleventh-century texts of Michael Psellos', *BS/EB* 4.2 (1977), pp. 157–88.

Laiou, A., *Mariage, amour et parenté à Byzance aux XIe–XIIIe siècles* (Paris, 1992).

—— 'Imperial marriages and their critics in the eleventh century: the case of Skylitzes', *DOP* 46 (1992), pp. 165–76.

Leib, B., 'Un basileus ignoré – Constantin Doucas (1074–1094)', *BS* 17 (1956), pp. 341–59.

Lemerle, P., *Cinq études sur le XIe siècle byzantin* (Paris, 1977).

Mullett, M.E. and Smythe, D.C. (eds), *Alexios I Komnenos*, vol. 2, forthcoming.

Oikonomides, N., 'L'évolution de l'organisation administrative de l'empire byzantin au XIe siècle (1025–1118)', *TM* 6 (1976), pp. 125–52.

Skoulatos, B., 'Les premières réactions hostiles à Alexis I Comnène', *B* 49 (1979), pp. 385–94.

Vryonis, S., 'Byzantine imperial authority: theory and practice in the eleventh century', in G. Makdisi, D. Sourdel, and J. Sourdel-Thomine (eds), *Islam, Byzantium, Occident* (Paris, 1982), pp. 141–61.

—— 'Byzantine *demokratia* and the guilds in the eleventh century', *DOP* 17 (1963), pp. 289–314; reprinted *Byzantium: Its Internal History and Relations with the Muslim World*, III (London, 1973).

Titles for imperial women

Bensammar, E., 'La titulature de l'impératrice et sa signification', *B* 46 (1976), pp. 243–91.

Brehier, L., 'L'origine des titres imperiaux à Byzance, βασιλεὺς ετ δεσπότης', *BZ* 15 (1906), pp. 161–78.

Brightman, F.E., 'Byzantine imperial coronations', *JThS* 2 (1901), pp. 359–92.

Cameron, A., 'The book of ceremonies', in D. Cannadine and S. Price (eds), *Rituals of Royalty* (Cambridge, 1987), pp. 106–36.

Carney, E., 'What's in a name? the emergence of a title for royal women in the Hellenistic period', in S. Pomeroy (ed.), *Women's History and Ancient History* (1991), pp. 154–72.

Charanis, P., 'Coronation and its constitutional significance', *B* 15 (1941), pp. 49–66; reprinted in *Social, Economic and Political Life in the Byzantine Empire*, XIII (London, 1973).

Chrysos, E., 'The title *basileus* in early Byzantine international relations', *DOP* 32 (1978), pp. 29–76.

Gautier, P., 'L'obituaire du typikon du Pantocrator', *REB* 27 (1969), pp. 235–62.

Goodacre, H., 'Irene Doukaina', *Numismatic Chronicle* 19 (1939), pp. 105–11.

Grégoire, H., 'Sur les titres imperiaux', *B* 10 (1935), pp. 763–75.

Guilland, R., *Titres et fonctions de l'empire byzantin* (London, 1976).

Laurent, V., 'Une titulature abusive: Anne 1-ère Dalassène', *BSHAR* 27 (1946), pp. 34–41.

—— 'Arétè Doukaina, la kralina', *BZ* 65 (1972), pp. 35–39.

McCormick, M., 'Analysing imperial ceremonies', *JÖB* 35 (1985), pp. 1–20.

—— *Eternal Victory. Triumphal Rulership in Late Antiqiuty, Byzantium and the Early Medieval West* (Cambridge, 1986).

Patlagean, E., 'Les débuts d'une aristocratie byzantine et la témoignage de l'historiographie: système des noms et liens de parenté sux IXe–Xe siècle', in Angold, *The Byzantine Aristocracy*, pp. 23–43.

Sayre, P., 'The Mistress of the Robes – who was she?', *BS/EB* 13.2 (1986), pp. 229–40.

Seibt, W., *Die Skleroi* (Vienna, 1976).

Shahid, I., 'On the titulature of Heraclius', *B* 51 (1981), pp. 288–96.

Stiernon, L., 'Notes de titulature et de prosopographie byzantines: Constantin Angelos (pan)sébastohypertate', *REB* 19 (1961), pp. 273–83.

—— 'Notes de titulature et de prosopographie byzantines: Adrien (Jean) et Constantin Comnène, sébastes', *REB* 21 (1963), pp. 179–98.

—— 'Notes de titulature et de prosopographie byzantines: a propos de trois membres de la famille Rogerios (XIIe siècle)', *REB* 22 (1964), pp. 184–98.

—— 'Notes de titulature et de prosopographie byzantines: sébaste et gambros', *REB* 23 (1965), pp. 222–43.

238   *Imperial women in Byzantium 1025–1204*

Stiernon, L., 'Notes de titulature et de prospographie byzantines.' Theodora Comnène et Andronic Lapardas, sébastes', *REB* 24 (1966), pp. 89–96.

Kinship

Adontz, N., 'Les Dalassènes', *B* 10 (1935), pp. 171–85.
—— 'Les Taronites à Byzance', *B* 11 (1936), pp. 21–42.
Duby, G., *Medieval Marriage: Two Models from Twelfth-Century France* (Baltimore, 1978).
Goody, J., *Comparative Studies in Kinship* (London, 1969).
—— *The Development of the Family and Marriage in Europe* (Cambridge, 1983).
Harris, C.C., *Kinship* (Minneapolis, 1990).
Hughes, D.O., 'From brideprice to dowry in Mediterranean Europe', *Journal of Family History* 3.3 (1978), pp. 262–96.
de Josselin de Jong, J., *Levi-Strauss's Theory on Kinship and Marriage* (Leiden, 1970).
Karlin-Hayter, P., 'Further notes on Byzantine marriage: raptus – ἁρπαγή or μνηστεῖαι?', *DOP* 46 (1992), pp. 133–54.
Leach, E., *Levi-Strauss* (London, 1974).
Levi-Strauss, C., *The Elementary Structures of Kinship* (Oxford, 1969).
Macrides, R., 'The Byzantine godfather', *BMGS* 11 (1987), pp. 139–62.
—— 'Kinship by arrangement', *DOP* 44 (1990), pp. 109–18.
—— 'Dowry and inheritance in the late period: some cases from the patriarchal register', in P. Simon (ed.), *Ein Fleisch, ein Gut?* (Munich, 1990), pp. 89–98.
—— 'Dynastic marriages and political kinship', in J. Shepard and S. Franklin (eds), *Byzantine Diplomacy* (Aldershot, 1992), pp. 263–80.
Magdalino, P., 'The Byzantine aristocratic *oikos*', in Angold, *The Byzantine Aristocracy*, pp. 92–111; reprinted in *Tradition and Transformation in Medieval Byzantium*, II (Aldershot, 1991).
—— 'Isaac Sebastokrator (III), John Axouch and a case of mistaken identity', *BMGS* 11 (1987), pp. 207–14; reprinted in *Tradition and Transformation in Medieval Byzantium*, XII (Aldershot, 1991).
Meyendorff, J., 'Christian marriage in Byzantium: the canonical and liturigical tradition', *DOP* 44 (1990), pp. 99–197.
Mullett, M.E., 'Alexios I Komnenos and the rhythm of imperial renewal', in Magdalino, *New Constantines*.

Needham, R., *Rethinking Kinship and Marriage* (London, 1971).

Polemis, D., *The Doukai: A Contribution to Byzantine Prosopography* (London, 1968).

Shaw, B., 'The family in late antiquity: the experience of Augustine', *P and P* 115 (1987), pp. 3–57.

Shaw, B. and Saller, R., 'Close-kin marriage in Roman society', *Man* 19 (1984), pp. 432–44.

Skoulatos, B., *Les personnages byzantins dans l'Alexiade: analyse prosopographique et synthèse* (Louvain, 1980).

Vannier, J.-F., *Familles byzantines. Les Argyroi (IXe–XIIe siècles)* (Paris, 1975).

Verdery, K., 'A comment on Goody's *The Development of the Family and Marriage in Europe*', *Journal of Family History* 13.3 (1988), pp. 265–70.

Patronage

Beaton, R., 'The rhetoric of poverty: the lives and opinions of Theodore Prodromos', *BMGS* 11 (1987), pp. 1–28.

—— '"De Vulgari Eloquentia" in twelfth-century Byzantium', in J.D. Howard-Johnston (ed.), *Byzantium and the West c.800–1200* (Amsterdam, 1988) *BF* 13 (1988), pp. 261–68.

Boissevain, J., 'Patronage in Sicily', *Man* n.s. 1 (1966), pp. 18–33.

Campbell, J.K., *Honour, Family and Patronage* (Oxford, 1964).

Cormack, R., 'Aristocratic patronage of the arts in eleventh- and twelfth-century Byzantium', in Angold, *The Byzantine Aristocracy*, pp. 158–72.

Davis, J., *People of the Mediterranean* (London, 1977).

—— *Exchange* (Buckingham, 1992).

Drummond, A., 'Early Roman clientes', in Wallace-Hadrill, *Patronage in Ancient Society*, pp. 89–115.

Eisenstadt, S.N. and Roniger, L., *Patrons, Clients and Friends: Interpersonal Relations and the Structure of Trust* (Cambridge, 1984).

Gautier, P., 'Le dossier d'un haut fonctionnaire d'Alexis Ier Comnène, Manuel Straboromanos', *REB* 23 (1965), pp. 168–204.

Gellner, E., 'Patrons and Clients', in E. Gellner and J. Waterbury (eds), *Patrons and Clients in Mediterranean Societies* (London, 1977).

Gilsenan, M., 'Against patron–client relations', in E. Gellner and J. Waterbury (eds), *Patrons and Clients in Mediterranean Societies* (London, 1977), pp. 167–83.

Gold, B. (ed.), *Literary and Artistic Patronage in Ancient Rome* (Austin, 1982).

Jeffreys, E., 'The Comnenian background to the *romans d'antiquité*', *B* 50 (1980), pp. 455–86.

—— 'The *sebastokratorissa* Eirene as a literary patroness: the monk Iakovos', *JÖB* 32/3 (1982), pp. 63–71.

Jeffreys, M., 'The vernacular *eisiterioi* for Agnes of France', in M. and E. Jeffreys and A. Moffatt (eds), *Byzantine Studies* (Canberra, 1981), pp. 101–15.

—— 'The nature and origins of political verse', *DOP* 28 (1974), pp. 142–95; reprinted in E.M. Jeffreys and M.J. Jeffreys, *Popular Literature in Byzantium*, IV (London, 1983).

Johnson, T. and Dandeker, C., 'Patronage: relation and system', in Wallace-Hadrill, *Patronage in Ancient Society*, pp. 219–41.

Morris, R., 'The Byzantine aristocracy and the monasteries', in Angold, *The Byzantine Aristocracy*, pp. 112–37.

—— 'Monasteries and their patrons in the tenth and eleventh centuries', *BF* 10 (1985), pp. 185–232.

Mullett, M.E., 'Aristocracy and patronage in the literary circles of Comnenian Constantinople', in Angold, *The Byzantine Aristocracy*, pp. 173–201.

—— 'Byzantium: a friendly society?', *P and P* 118 (1987), pp. 3–24.

—— 'Patronage in action: the problems of an eleventh-century bishop', in R. Morris (ed.), *Church and People in Byzantium* (Birmingham, 1990), pp. 125–47.

—— 'Writing in early medieval Byzantium', in R. McKitterick (ed.), *Uses of Literacy in Early Medieval Europe* (Cambridge, 1990), pp. 156–85.

Parker, R. and G. Pollock, *Old Mistressess. Women, Art and Ideology* (London, 1981).

Saller, R., *Personal Patronage under the Early Empire* (Cambridge, 1982).

Tannery, P., 'Théodore Prodrome sur le grand et le petit (à Italikos)', *Annuaire de l'association pour l'encouragement des études grecques en France* 21 (1887), pp. 104–19.

Wallace-Hadrill, A. (ed.), *Patronage in Ancient Society* (London, 1989).

Wallman, S., 'Kinship, a-kinship and anti-kinship: variations on the logic of kinship situations', in E. Leyton (ed.), *The Compact: Selected Dimensions of Friendship*, pp. 105–16.

Waterbury, J., 'An attempt to put patrons and clients in their place', in Gellner and Waterbury, *Patrons and Clients*, pp. 329–42.

Weingrod, A., 'Patronage and power', in Gellner and Waterbury, *Patrons and Clients*, pp. 41–52.

Zetzel, J.E.G., 'The poetics of patronage', in Gold, *Literary and Artistic Patronage*, pp. 87–102.

Ideology

Ardener, E., 'Belief and the problem of women', in S. Ardener (ed.), *Perceiving Women* (London, 1975).

Duby, G., 'Ideologies in social history', in J. le Goff and P. Nora (eds), *Constructing the Past: Essays in Historical Methodology* (Cambridge, 1985), pp. 151–65.

Geertz, C., *The Interpretation of Cultures* (London, 1975).

Janeway, E., *Man's World, Women's Place* (Harmondsworth, 1977).

Langer, S., 'The growing centre of knowledge', in S. Langer, *Philosophical Sketches* (Oxford, 1962).

Larrain, J., *The Concept of Ideology* (London, 1979).

Leis, N.B., 'Women in groups: Ijaw women's associations', in Rosaldo and Lamphere, *Women, Culture and Society*, pp. 223–42.

Mann, M., *The Sources of Social Power*, 2 vols (Cambridge, 1986).

Parsons, T., 'The superego and the theory of social processes', in T. Parsons, R.F. Bales and E. Shils (eds), *Working Papers in the Theory of Action* (New York, 1953).

Sicherman, B., 'American history: review essay', *Signs* 1.2 (1975), pp. 461–85.

Index